SAGE was founded in 1965 by Sara Miller McCune to support the dissemination of usable knowledge by publishing innovative and high-quality research and teaching content. Today, we publish more than 750 journals, including those of more than 300 learned societies, more than 800 new books per year, and a growing range of library products including archives, data, case studies, reports, conference highlights, and video. SAGE remains majority-owned by our founder, and on her passing will become owned by a charitable trust that secures our continued independence.

Los Angeles | London | Washington DC | New Delhi | Singapore

interrogating
Women's
leadership and empowerment

interrogating
Women's
leadership and empowerment

Edited by
Omita Goyal

India International Centre

www.sagepublications.com
Los Angeles • London • New Delhi • Singapore • Washington DC

First published in 2015 by

 SAGE Publications India Pvt Ltd
B1/I-1 Mohan Cooperative Industrial Area
Mathura Road, New Delhi 110 044, India
www.sagepub.in

SAGE Publications Inc
2455 Teller Road
Thousand Oaks, California 91320, USA

SAGE Publications Ltd
1 Oliver's Yard, 55 City Road
London EC1Y 1SP, United Kingdom

SAGE Publications Asia-Pacific Pte Ltd
3 Church Street
#10-04 Samsung Hub
Singapore 049483

Published by Vivek Mehra for SAGE Publications India Pvt Ltd, Phototypeset in 10.5/12 Berkeley by RECTO Graphics, Delhi and printed at Saurabh Printers Pvt Ltd, New Delhi.

Library of Congress Cataloging-in-Publication Data Available

ISBN: 978-93-515-0079-7 (HB)

The SAGE Team: Supriya Das, Alekha Chandra Jena, Anju Saxena and Rajinder Kaur

CONTENTS

Karan Singh
FOREWORD

Omita Goyal
PREFACE

Malavika Karlekar
INTRODUCTION

CHAPTERS

FOREWORD

The concept of women's empowerment is deeply embedded in our cultural heritage. In fact, I write this during the *Navratras*, the nine days which occur twice a year, in which the Goddess is widely worshipped by Hindus around the world, not as a spouse but in her own right. It is also interesting to recall that all the Hindu deities are invariably bracketed with a feminine figure whose name precedes them—Gauri-Shankar, Sita-Ram, Radha-Krishna and so on. Therefore, as far as the cultural aspect is concerned, the bulk of people in India should not have any difficulty with the concept of women's empowerment.

However, the social reality is entirely different. With a few exceptions, the woman has been relegated to a secondary and inferior position within most of the religions of India. Records of ill-treatment of women, the growing incidents of rape, and the general attitude of male domination continue to prevail. It is in this context that the contemporary movement of women's empowerment has to be viewed.

There are several dimensions of empowerment. There is a much-needed change in social attitudes which should respect women and the girl child, and which is dramatically illustrated by the growing gender imbalance even in the more affluent states. Then there is economic empowerment, and for this many of the new schemes that the government has launched in the last few years have been especially aimed at the women of India. They are encouraged to open their own bank accounts into which government grants can flow. Thirdly, there is educational empowerment. Although the percentage of girl students has considerably increased over the last decade, there is still a substantial imbalance, and the dropout rate of girl students is much higher than that of boys. One of the factors which is now being tackled is the absence of separate toilets for girls in village schools, which are essential in order to retain girl students beyond the primary standard. Fourthly, medical facilities for safe delivery, widespread availability of contraceptive technology and nutritional inputs for pregnant and nursing mothers have also to be substantially increased.

These are just some of the aspects of women's empowerment, which this book seeks to address. The title, *Interrogating Women's Leadership and Empowerment*, shows an interesting spectrum of views. Politically, women played a major role in the freedom movement under Gandhiji and have also adorned the highest positions in the land from time to time. This fact has to be appreciated because it proves that our Constitution and electoral system give ample scope for women to rise to the top at the Centre and in the states.

The authors in this volume present an impressive array of intellectual insights into the various aspects of women's empowerment. Taken together, they bring clearly before us the whole array of challenges that confront India today. I need to stress that women's empowerment cannot be achieved without the full cooperation of men and, therefore, we must all work in unison to achieve the desired goals. It is interesting to note that on the issue of one-third reservation of women in Parliament, both the ruling party and the opposition party are, for once, in agreement.

KARAN SINGH

◆

PREFACE

When we began thinking about putting together a volume on the theme of women's leadership and empowerment, we realised we didn't have enough space within these pages to do it justice. This is not a definitive collection on women's empowerment and leadership, but it does encompass a wide range of views, often divergent, that look at the situation of women in, and their contribution to, politics, business, education, social and economic development, the women's movement, health, law, insurgency, art, music, dance, cinema, literature and craft. Governmental efforts through constitutional guarantees, capacity-building programmes and *poorna shakti*, or holistic empowerment as defined by the National Mission for Empowerment of Women, have worked alongside non-governmental and individual initiatives to set the empowerment process in motion. The women's movement, both by way of the expanding centres of women's studies and grassroots activism, has played a significant role in women's empowerment. But we cannot be complacent.

What constitutes empowerment and leadership? Is it equal access to education, employment and health? Political participation and decision making? Is it ownership of one's body and freedom of choice? Does empowerment also address marginalisation of women by caste, class and religion? A common strand that runs across the chapters in this volume is the very notion of empowerment (also its converse, 'disempowerment'), and its (re)definition.

It is hard to fathom why, in the 21st century, we still talk about the need to empower half the population of this country. India is a paradox. On the one hand, some of the earliest initiatives to educate women date back to the late 1800s. Some historical texts see the origins of the women's movements in India in the social reforms of the 19th century when the first women's organisations were set up by both women and male social reformers. The Indian Constitution is not stagnant and unlike in many parts of the world, has seen several amendments, including within it laws relating to women's rights. On the other hand, we are still battling an adverse sex ratio, a high dropout rate and an inherently patriarchal society.

The chapters in this volume reflect this dichotomy, at the same time demonstrating how far we have come in our efforts towards empowering women. For instance, while women panchayat leaders are seen to play a more development-oriented, 'soft power' role than a political one, it is important to note that they are no longer powerless proxies for the men. While the number of women in the corporate sector is still less than desirable, women are entering non-traditional fields like banking and bio-technology. Examples of women and communities who have battled great odds to leave behind the constraints of tradition, either through the political route or through the arts, are many. An interesting fact comes from Ashish Khokar—in 1977, the then prime minister, Morarji Desai's nomination for the highest post of President of India was Rukmini Devi Arundale. Another concern that comes out in more than one chapter is the notion of the woman's body. It is unfortunate and shameful that sexual abuse and violence against women in situations of conflict are endemic. At the same time, we have illiterate Dalit labouring women who have attempted to transcend pain by developing an intellectual space of their own through painting.

This book is an unusual collection that expands the definition of empowerment to encompass several aspects of women's lives and professions. As the contributors illustrate, there is change—but there is still a long way to go.

OMITA GOYAL

◆

INTRODUCTION

I

Though a popular buzzword since the 1980s, there has been little informed discussion on the term 'empowerment'. As the eminent sociologist Andre Beteille wrote, most analyses around the term so far have been more context-driven than theory-driven. It is important then to look at the context in which discussions over empowerment and indeed women's empowerment have arisen. On the whole, the context is one where there is a contradiction between 'a hierarchical social order and a democratic political system' (Beteille, 1999: 589), where the rights of citizenship and a democratic constitution founder against entrenched tradition and prejudice. The process of empowerment—which can be understood in many ways—aims at overcoming these disabilities through a range of strategies. The chapters in this unique volume encourage the reader to view the concept in the very many ways in which Indian women have become empowered. Some point to what remains unfinished if not ignored.

While empowerment 'may be invoked in virtually any context', be it human rights, basic needs, capacity-building, skill formation or overall economic security' (Beteille, 1999: 590), the meaning of this holdall term has nonetheless to be narrowed down. At a macro-political level, it can mean political participation and sharing in power. If one limits the discussion to the work space, it means a process of participation, awareness of rights and obligations as well as the growth of a sense of self-confidence and self-worth (Sreelakshmamma, 2008). Intra-familial dynamics point to yet other configurations of entitlements, negotiation and power sharing—Amartya Sen's impressive work over the past three decades being a case in point. Now, his classic theory of entitlements has ensured that the South Asian family can never be viewed as a democratic space, but one of cooperative conflict, bargaining and stress (Sen, 1981, 1990).

Historically, in India, ideas about the empowerment of women gained credence after 1975, known as the International Year of Women; more specifically, this year had a particular salience in India as it coincided with the publication of the path-breaking *Towards Equality*, the Report of the Committee on the Status of Women in India. This report not only highlighted women's position in a range of fields but also quite pointedly asserted the need to strengthen their political, social and economic bases. In other words, it was essential to empower them and provide them with the means of gaining control over their lives. It meant a shift away from the welfarist model of growth that treated women as objects of munificence, doled out by the family, society and indeed government. Women needed to take charge of their lives, and this meant challenging the development from the above approach. Naila Kabeer has argued that empowerment questions the notions of selfhood into which girls and women are socialised; by bringing about a change in the 'distribution in material and symbolic resources and opportunities between women and men in the development process', it is possible to give women agency and the power to question accepted notions of selfhood (Kabeer, 1999). This can often mean something as quotidian as asserting the right to come out of the home, into mixed company. It becomes particularly relevant in the context of the 73rd Amendment to the Constitution that brought thousands of women into the political process through Panchayati Raj (Baviskar and Mathew, 2009). Women who had not known the outside world have overnight become the repositories of power and authority.

Thus, the empowerment of women entails their visibility and ability to make choices; such choices may challenge the established power hierarchy not only within the home, but in society as well (Kabeer, 2010). This means the agency of a positive kind that can be transformative. Given women's overall subordinate position, they can also have what Kabeer calls 'passive agency', where they take action in a situation where there is little choice. An example of this would be organising a daughter's marriage when the decision of who the bridegroom should be is taken by the men in family. It is, however, the positive aspects of agency that constitute empowerment. This necessarily means self-awareness, commitment to change and to involve oneself in participatory endeavours through building on one's latent talents as well as developing new skills, both in the sphere of personality and in the areas of work and employment.

Based on his extensive field work in rural West Bengal, Banerjee (1997) argued that this capacity-building places a heavy dependence on the self. In some senses, it is this meaning of empowerment which is the most relevant in the present context. The notion of capacity-building stresses individual growth as much, if not more than, as an external adjustment in the sharing of power and authority. Nonetheless, as enhancing individual capacity involves new skills as well as new ways of viewing oneself, the process may cause a woman to reflect on her situation, including a sense of autonomy or lack of it; it may also help her to work towards a better adjustment to domestic power relations as well as her attitude to a wider environment.

At the same time, at the interpersonal level, the empowerment of some may lead to the disempowerment of others or at any rate, a perception that they are being disempowered. This is particularly true of men within families who often feel threatened when women organise. Empowerment clearly leads to a better sense of self-worth, often through collective action that aims at, among other things, economic betterment. For empowerment is largely about 'ordinary, common people, rather than politicians, experts and other socially or culturally advantaged persons', an improvement in the quality of life is integral to an understanding of the term (Beteille, 1999: 590). Banerjee argues that there are indications that 'women exposed to some amount of mobilisation show great potentialities, receptiveness and defining capacities once the direction is appropriately conveyed' (Banerjee, 1993: 7). Often, the so-called illiterate women who are exposed to some amount of mobilisation show great potential and capacity for leadership. Women's organisations, Panchayati Raj institutions and even the State have facilitated the empowerment of women; various case studies in this volume bear testimony to this overarching fact.

There is enough evidence to show that the role of the Indian State has not been insignificant in the evolution of women's organisations and their differing goals. The relationship between the two, however, tends to be ambivalent, and the government has often been challenged by women's organisations. Contentious issues range from policy to specific situations where the State is held responsible, for example, for not protecting women from crime or violence. While the Indian government cannot be characterised as a monolithic entity, which always speaks in a single voice on every issue concerning women, nonetheless, its efforts at addressing women's questions have had a long history. There are numerous and notable instances of the government's receptivity to voices, not only from the contemporary women's movement, but also from the 'welfare' agendas of the older women's organisations. On occasion, the State has been instrumental in raising women's issues and accordingly creating policies and programmes and setting up special organs within its administration for their implementation. All of these can be construed as measures taken by the State for the benefit of women's empowerment.

Issues such as the relationship between organisations and the State acquire a particular salience in the age of global economies. The State and its apparatus are in the process of being 'discursively transformed through neoliberal rhetoric and strategies and through grassroots praxis'. In this situation of flux, women's empowerment results in 'reconfiguring the relationships between the state and local actors, transforming development, and reshaping citizenship and popular politics...' (Sharma, 2010: xvi–vii). Sharma reiterated the well-known view that the neoliberal Indian State has little to offer to those at the margins of society; the middle classes and elites have been the gainers in a world where consumerism has grown exponentially.

It is against this backdrop of growing inequalities where fallacious arguments on how much is needed for a poor family to keep the wolf from the door sound particularly hollow that issues of empowerment become increasingly significant. As Satish Agnihotri points out in the present volume, there is a need for gender-sensitive versus gender-blind governance. It is not enough to carry out multitudinous surveys without disaggregating the data. Known for his work on the declining female sex ratio, Agnihotri regrets that those in charge of collecting and analysing statistics whether it be for the Integrated Child Development Scheme or on the health of young children often do not keep in mind the need to determine differences based on gender in nutritional status or in access to services. Official myopia often works against attempts to facilitate the empowerment of women and girls. And in situations of ethnic conflict such as in Nagaland, women and children are often innocent victims; on the basis of a study in the Dhemaji district of Assam, Sanjoy Hazarika found that combatants were not security forces or organised militant groups but ethnic groups which 'saw threats from "the other" to their identity and control of land'; in such contexts, where survival is at stake, the empowerment of women becomes but a remote chimera. In fact, it becomes all the more necessary to look not only at conflict-management processes but also at legal reform as essential for an atmosphere where women will feel secure. Feminist lawyer Kirti Singh points out that while it was the gang rape of December 2013 'which forced a reluctant government to bring about change', the women's movement, various organisations and individuals have been agitating for gender-sensitive laws from the 1980s onwards. However, as her brief history of sexual assault laws shows, there is still a long way to go. While the notion of struggle is not absent in many accounts of women's quest for empowerment, a number of essays in this volume are success stories often moving out of the usual paradigm of power-sharing to other fields where women have become icons of success in a difficult environment.

II

The philosophical concept of women's empowerment and its practical implications has matured and developed considerably over the years; while political participation, economic self-reliance and social awareness would be the obvious parameters to judge 'levels' of empowerment, going back occasionally in time, this collection introduces us to women as craftspersons, dancers, singers, actors, litterateurs, businesswomen and doctors. These are, to use a cliché, symbols of emancipated Indian womanhood. But there are others too, those recently empowered by grassroots' organisations and State intervention. Some contributions paint with broad strokes, providing a macro-picture, while others introduce us to individual women and their genius or to institutions that became path-breakers. Familiar and somewhat conventional terms are used by most authors while a few introduce us to the world of gender budgeting and gender mainstreaming. From the 1980s onwards, discussions around women's status in the South have relied on the well-known Women in Development (WID) theories. These have gradually been superseded by the more inclusive Gender and Development (GAD) approach that tackles the question of inequalities in power and looks to empowerment in all fields (Kabeer, 1995; Razavi and Miller, 1995). No matter which approach is adopted and by whom, the volume introduces us to empowered women in many fields, ranging from the political sphere where sharing in leadership remains a major issue to the delicate tracery of the Madhubani artist, imbued with a sense of inequality and the consequent search for self-expression.

The changing parameters of women's leadership are skilfully etched by Devaki Jain and Padmini Swaminathan, both significant actors in the theory and practice of the Indian women's movement. Jain (assisted by Deepshika Batheja) points out that the nature of women's leadership challenges existing notions of power and 'the concept of representation and leadership'. Women's study centres ('powerhouses and catalysts') and the recently anointed Internet age have expanded the parameters of debate and discourse while, as Swaminathan argues, certain organisations (in this case, the MV Foundation in Andhra Pradesh) have introduced gender mainstreaming where 'economic transformation [comes] with social emancipation'. Renana Jhabvala's insider account of the functioning of Self-employed Women's Organisation (SEWA) and case studies of individual women only goes to strengthen the belief that power-sharing is not alien to women. The 73rd Amendment to the Constitution of India which reserves a third of seats for women in all elected local government bodies has been a historic step, bringing over a million women into the political sphere. It has interrogated the private–public dichotomy and forced discussion on issues such as women's traditional roles, familial expectations and changing responsibilities. J. Devika's study of women Panchayat members in Kerala gives a lie to the notion that it is governance by proxy. In fact, a new model of authority, that of 'gentle power', has emerged, one that has the full approval of men. Women get their way at the micro-political level by subtle, non-threatening strategies in keeping with established and acceptable notions of feminine behaviour. However, as Sudha Pai points out, when at the top, women politicians are as adept as men in the language and methods of negotiation and power-brokering. At the margins, the problems are different and there are not many Mayawatis on the political stage. When it comes to participation in the public sphere, Dalit women, writes Gopal Guru in an insightful essay, have very specific problems: the stigma of caste has to contend with the patriarchal worldview of their men which attempts to keep them at the margins. Self-expression in the form of *Godna* paintings from the Madhubani district of Bihar and their distinct form of poetry such as the *ovie* of Maharashtra are powerful release mechanisms. The collective nature of labour is carried over to the field of creativity. There are exceptions though, such as the dictated biography of Viramma or Kumud Pawade's 1981 memoir. Feminist historian Uma Chakravarti discusses both, underlining the inherent violence of such lives described so well by Bama in *Karukku*.

Unlike most other collections on women's empowerment, contributions to *Interrogating Women's Leadership and Empowerment* go well beyond conventional understandings of enhancing women's strength and self-confidence through socio-political and economic means: a quick look at the history of a couple of centuries brings into focus early doctors, singers, dancers, actors and, of course, craftspersons. Paid and unpaid labour in agriculture and agriculture-related activities accounts for the time and energy of the largest number of Indian women. A close second is the crafts sector. It is only in recent years that there has been an awareness of the need to hone existing skills of craftspersons as well as train them in new designs and techniques. Though as early as 1919, Rabindranath Tagore introduced crafts into the curriculum at Kala Bhawana, it is only less than a decade ago that Kala Raksha Vidyalaya in Kutch and the Handloom Weaving School in Maheshwar were set up to teach traditional artisans the use of alternate dyes, innovative weaving techniques and so on (Sethi in this volume). If middle-class imaginations have rarely stretched to the benefits of training craftspeople, there was no lack of interest and indeed initiatives in training girls of their own background. In 1886, Kadambini Basu and Anandibai Joshi became the first women doctors of the British Indian Empire only because their husbands took advantage of the facilities available to young women (Karlekar in this volume). Such facilities had taken firm root by the end of the 19th century, first in the three Presidencies and then in other parts of the country.

As well-known historian of education Aparna Basu writes, 'in the late 19th and early 20th centuries, north India was one of the most backward areas in the country in terms of women's education'. Deep-rooted prejudices, fears of challenges from educated girls as well as fewer institutions than in other parts of the country meant fewer literate girls. Aware of the need to change things, a handful of elite Delhites set up the Indraprastha Putri Pathshala in 1904. Twenty years later, the school was to become Indraprastha College, and in 1916, Lady Hardinge Medical College was established. Young women in Delhi could now hope to become doctors—albeit several decades after Kadambini from the Bengal Presidency and Anandibai in faraway Philadelphia had qualified to practise.

To be a doctor, teacher or even a lawyer were the most popular career options available to young middle-class Indian women in pre-Independence India. It was only the exceptions who became pilots like Sarla Thukral or photographers as did Annapurna Datta and later Homi Vyarawalla, or joined the Telengana movement and learnt to wield rifles long before the Maoists started raising cadres of young revolutionary women. For those a bit older, the All-India Women's Conference, various *mahila mandals,* women's groups and organisations were respectable fora—and many introduced members to issues of power-sharing and decision-making within the organisation. Today, often generating programmes for government and implementing others of their own, women's groups also perform the role of vigilantes and assist in counselling and arbitrating in cases such as marital discord, domestic violence and sexual harassment (Karlekar et al., 1995). Some organisations are successful in training women for managerial positions in a non-business context, SEWA being a case in point.

That managerial positions for women in higher education needed special attention was recognised by the National Educational Policy of 1986 and a programme under the auspices of the University Grants Commission was started in 1994. As one involved in this process of capacity-building, Karuna Chanana was able to put her years of university teaching in a department of education to good use. At the end of Sensitization, Awareness and Motivation or SAM workshops, she found that a number of participants became 'aware of the larger role that they can play within their institutions'. If moving into management positions may be new for college and university teachers, it is the raison d'être for those in business and corporate houses. Yet, as Pushpa Sunder shows, while almost 50 per cent of those who graduate from Indian Institutes of Management are women, only 10–15 per cent are swiftly absorbed in jobs. In the fast-growing hospitality and IT sectors, 'the gender ratio is heavily skewed in favour of men'. And for those who become managers, many get sidelined into non-strategic positions. The overweening presence of the glass ceiling means that a mere 6 per cent make it to corporate boards. Aggressive masculine values are valorised—even though as Sunder argues that in banking, financial and HR services, the so-called feminine traits of empathy and patience could well be equally valuable.

If the reader feels a slight despondency at the persistent inequalities in areas of high visibility such as the corporate and business worlds, Rita Sethi's detailed historical sweep of the development of crafts in post-independent India by Kamaladevi Chattopadhyay, Rukmini Devi Arundale, Pupul Jayakar and, much later, Laila Tyabji and Jaya Jaitley reaffirms the belief that Indian women's empowerment in certain areas has been well on its way for several decades. Nor would it be judicious to brush aside such achievements as being those in 'soft' areas: a major employer of both men and women, the indigenous craft sector is not one where leadership is a cakewalk. Like any other sphere of collective activity, it has meant a long and difficult meander to not only convince and carry along one's cohorts, but also to be taken seriously. Admittedly, these women at the helm have been privileged not only by birth, but also by their proximity to the existing power elite. Though Jayakar was close to Indira Gandhi (the elegant Prime Minister gave the handloom sari a place in the sun), she too had surely to contend with gender biases and prejudices against the sector.

When one moves away from institutions and entrenched power elites to the area of individual genius, it is to the likes of Mahasweta Devi's *Dopdi* that one turns. Her mesmerizing prose and searing word images, writes Radha Chakravarty, bring tribal women who have been silenced for centuries, into the discourse of power. The naked raped and humiliated Dopdi becomes 'a terrifying figure of vengeful female wrath' while her tormentors, the hated men in uniform, quail at the sight of her violated body. A few decades before Mahasweta Devi, another woman had made history by bringing the métier of a different group of disprivileged and oppressed women into focus. In Madras, Rukmini Devi Arundale took *sadir,* the dance of the *devadasi*s, on to the public stage. She not only successfully transgressed the boundaries set for a Brahmin woman but also made Bharatanatyam, as she renamed it, acceptable for generations of young women. Documenter of dance, Ashish Mohan Khokar, traces the life of this amazing young woman who not only defied conservative society by marrying the 42-year-old Theosophist, George Arundale, but also went on to be an institution-builder (Kalakshetra), a brilliant innovator, a teacher of dance and an animal rights' activist.

At about this time, the 1930s, women in India had started entering the film industry, the earliest being of Anglo-Indian, Eurasian and Jewish origin. Sarah Rahman Niazi points out that though actresses 'enjoyed freedoms unknown to women from other socially sanctioned respectable professions', they elicited deep-seated moral indignation and anxiety from an essentially conservative society. However, there were few like Devika Rani from the Tagore family who not only acted but also ran her own studio company. Some years later, Durga Khote from a not dissimilar Maharashtrian background became a well-respected actor. For those who have seen *Bhoomika*, the angst of the early woman film actor (Hamsa Wadkar) so poignantly portrayed by Smita Patil, comes as no surprise. On the other hand, for those from families where performance was not a taboo, it was an easier social transition. Jaddan Bai came from a family of *tawaif*s and soon created a niche for herself in the Talkies. At different levels of expertise and performing often for a disparate clientele, women Hindustani classical singers such as Kesarbai Kerkar, Girija Devi, Kishori Amonkar and others brought a new dimension to an understanding of the feminine presence in an art form. Kumud Diwan Jha, an exponent of the Banaras *Gharana* writes about them as being the Alpha song birds—vibrant, powerful and brilliant. As creative activities, dance, music and singing have had women exponents for well over a century—though it may only have been since the 1930s that there was a grudging public acknowledgement of their right to do so. Women have been writing fiction since the late 19th century, but interestingly enough, while folk artists have perhaps painted the mud walls of their homes for centuries, the middle-class woman artist emerged, again in the 1930s. Kala Bhawan and the Bengal School of Art were among the first to encourage young women not only to paint but also to make wood blocks and elaborate works using batik. At the individual level, there was the genius of Amrita Sher-Gil and some decades later Anjolie Ela Menon. Many contemporary women artists have a deep feminist sensibility, acutely aware of their role as women. Thus, Deeptha Achar discusses the work of contemporary artist Nilima Sheikh who has commented on the close approximation of her work to the women's movement.

That in 2014, it is still necessary to devote a volume to women's leadership and empowerment indicates that many questions remain unanswered. Among other things, it is never too late to interrogate the increasingly minimalist role of the State in vital areas such as education and health. By implication, some contributors have looked at the negative role of the State; others have acknowledged its role in initiating pro-woman laws. At the same time, individual initiatives and collective ventures outside the purview of the State have worked, often more for women. Whether they be activists, performers, lawyers, administrators, journalists or academics, the contributors to this collection have brought into focus once again the need to keep stretching the parameters of women's empowerment. These are not a given—and if individual life stories are inspiring, there are many more that remain untold if not forgotten. Through its emphasis on areas not usually regarded as 'empowering' or areas of work and interest as those befitting 'empowered women', *Interrogating Women's Leadership and Empowerment* has brought into focus many lives and their varied stories. Some have been shrouded in silence; others were known by only a select few. Yet others have been acknowledged but not regarded as germane to discussions on women's leadership and empowerment. And of course, as must be expected with well-established scholars, activists and performers, each author has her or his own take on people, institutions and situations. Points of view will differ and some acknowledged experts in particular fields may not appear in the dramatis personae; these should not be viewed as omissions—but as challenges to readers to make space for different readings of well-known contexts and trends. After all, the aim of this volume is to enlarge the discourse, questioning notions of what can and should be included in ideas of empowerment. Borrowing from Andre Beteille, it questions the authority of a gender-based hierarchical order within an ostensibly democratic system. Some contributions provide answers to this questioning; others discerningly point to the road that yet lies ahead.

◆

REFERENCES

Banerjee, Narayan. 1993. *Grassroots Empowerment (1975–1990)* (Occasional Paper No. 22). New Delhi: CWDS.

Baviskar, B. S. and G. Mathew. 2009. *Inclusion and Exclusion in Local Governance Field Studies from Rural India.* New Delhi: SAGE Publications.

Beteille, Andre. 1999. 'Empowerment', *Economic and Political Weekly*, Vol. xxxiv (10 and 11) March 6–13: 589–597.

Kabeer, Naila. 1995. *Reversed Realities: Gender Hierarchies in Development.* New Delhi: Kali for Women.

———. 1999. 'From Feminist Insights to an Analytical Framework'. In Kabeer, Naila and Ramya Subramanian (eds). *Institutions, Relations, Outcomes.* New Delhi: Kali for Women, pp. 30–48.

———. 2010. 'Gender and Women's Empowerment: A Critical Analysis of the Third Millennium Development Goal', *Gender and Development*, Vol. 12, No. 1 March 2005, pp. 13–24.

Karlekar, M., Maithili Ganjoo and Anuja Agrawal. 1995. *No Safe Spaces... Report of the Workshop on Women and Violence.* New Delhi: CWDS.

Razavi, S. and C. Miller. 1995. *From WID to GAD: Conceptual Shifts in the Women and Development Discourse* (Occasional Paper). Geneva: UN Research Institute for Social Development.

Sen, A. 1981. *Poverty and Famines: An Essay on Entitlement and Deprivation.* Oxford: Clarendon Press.

———. 1990. 'Gender and Cooperative Conflicts'. In I. Tinker (ed.), *Persistent Inequalities: Women and World Development.* New York: Oxford University Press.

Sharma, Aradhana. 2010. *Paradoxes of Empowerment—Gender, Development and Governance in Neoliberal India.* New Delhi: Zubaan.

Sreelakshmamma. 2008. *Empowerment of Women in India.* New Delhi: Serials Publications.

◆◆

UNDERSTANDING LEADERSHIP
Lessons from the Women's Movement*

DEVAKI JAIN#

DEFINING LEADERSHIP

Locating the idea or concept of leadership in a narration on the women's movement in India has been a challenge for many reasons. One of the most notable, but not sufficiently recognised, aspects of feminist/women's movements is the questioning spirit or the interrogating mode of understanding and explicating ideas, concepts and language.

The feminist philosopher, Helen Longino, frames this issue well, when she says:

> The feminist agenda raises questions on what constitutes knowledge and how the disciplinary divisions are created. This questioning creates a 'politics of disturbance'. It unsettles the given and starts to plough up inherited turfs without planting the same old seeds in the field. (Sylvester, 1998: 44–66)

In another place, at another time, I called it the *nethi nethi* syndrome, taking off from the Upanishads, defining by negation (Jain, 2005). Hence, the questioning and redefining of the idea or concept of leadership is crucial.

Most definitions, or explanations, of leadership do have a touch of what can be called 'inclusiveness'. For example: 'Leadership is the art of mobilising others to want to struggle for shared aspirations,' according to J.M. Kouzes and B.Z. Posner (1995). This does resonate with feminist thought on leadership—whether one looks at the past or the present, what seems to come through as leadership or expressions of leadership in the women's movements, then and now, is providing voice and negotiating justice but, most of all, changing perceptions, ideas, methods ... but always a collective effort.

However, a haunting question for feminists is: towards what is the leader, single or collective, leading?

During the heyday of the international women's movement and world conferences (Jain, 2005), there was a demand for women to be included in councils of power and political forums to give space to women's leadership. But we asked, '... do we want to sit at the table with generals?' This was in the context of the fact that many nations had military governments. Do we want to eat part of the poisoned cake? was another, when it came to extremely unjust economic policies. 'Let us set our own table ...', was the reply. Hence, the notion of leadership as a value needs interrogation and has to be underpinned by an ethical attribute towards justice, towards affirmation of human rights and towards freedom.

Leadership is also linked to power; feminist claims on the political arena are not just to share power, but to change the nature of power; not just to govern, but to change the nature of governance. Women have many ways of enhancing, transforming and expanding the notion of power and politics, and giving full meaning to the concept of representation and leadership.

RECALLING THE PAST EXPERIENCES OF LEADERSHIP BY THE INDIAN WOMEN'S MOVEMENT

There are so many versions, or characterisations, of the history, or histories, of the women's movement in India. One of the standard ones is to divide the periods: move from reformist efforts to post-freedom ethos and then to the so-called *new* women's movement, which, it is suggested, is more radical and which also came into being with the 1975 landmark—the first UN world conference on women. Here, Ritu Menon's introduction to the volume of essays, *Making a Difference: Memoirs from the Women's Movement in India* (2011), captures this narration with precision, as does another narrative by Samita Sen, *Toward a Feminist Politics? The Indian Women's Movement in Historical Perspective* (2000).

Says Ritu Menon: 'It is difficult now, in this new century, to recapture or imagine the enormous optimism of those early years of what is called *the second wave* of the women's movement in India.' Second, here, implies that the first wave was prior to this more radical phase.

> For one, it is autonomous and, like the international women's movement, it has no formal structures, no hierarchies, no 'party line', no high priestesses. For another, it is polyphonic; it speaks in many voices, using many tongues. It is often, but not always and not uniformly, feminist, and it may or may not be always uniformly secular. It is urban and rural, and though 'political' in the fundamental sense of the word it has not, so far, been part of party politics....

Samita Sen says:

> The women's movement in India took off in the 1920s, building on the 19th-century social reform movement. The women's movement progressed during the period of high nationalism and the freedom struggle, both of which shaped its contours....

> The turning point came in the 1970s, when several events—some within and some outside India—gave a radical turn to the women's movement.... In the 1970s, the New Women's movement attempted to revive the Uniform Civil Code within the framework of gender politics. But women's rights became articulated within a State-led reform agenda, re-inscribing the concerns of national integrity, modernity, and progress. (Sen: 2000)

Of particular importance to the women's movement were agitations like the Shahada agitation and the subsequent formation of the Shramik Sangatana in the 1970s of the Bhil (tribal) landless labourers against exploitative landlords, which was triggered off by the rape of two Bhil women. Radha Kumar describes the militant role played by women in this agitation:

> They led the demonstrations, invented and shouted militant slogans, sang revolutionary songs and mobilised the masses. They went from hut to hut to agitate the men and persuade them of the necessity to join the Shramik Sangatana. (Kumar, 1993)

DIFFERENCES IN ASSESSMENT

This categorisation of time or space would, however, be challenged not only by historians but also by those who are not in national and international spaces of time and activities, but in an even earlier period of transformation; and, also, whether effectiveness should be seen in terms of what impact it has on women, or on other spaces, on ideas, on the general landscape of mind and body.

Romila Thapar, writing in the first edition of *Indian Women*, makes the point that participation of women in the Independence movement led to greater participation of women in the post-Independence era than their Western counterparts (Thapar, 1975). She says, 'Participation in the politics of the national movement was an act of patriotism and political life became a respectable vocation for a woman.'

This is an important base as it helps to understand the role and contribution of several women leaders from the political firmament who made a difference to women's lives in the 1950s and 1960s. While women who picketed shops, marched in processions, or went to jail or threw bombs, did not question male leadership or patriarchal values, it did generate in them a sense of self-confidence and a realisation of their own strength. Many returned to their homes, but others continued their activities in the public arena. An example is the story of Chameli Devi Jain, who left a traditional Jain home with nothing but a pair of sandals and the sari she wore to picket shops that were selling imported textiles, and was arrested and jailed in Lahore.[1] On her return '… she resumed the role that she always played—as the centre of the family *angan*—she remained close to the extended kinship group and inculcated in one and all, the philosophy of simplicity and of wearing home spun' (Jain, 2012).

However, these 'political' women did shake the ground under other women, especially in the areas of economic and social support. For example, a challenge to the characterisation of old as conservatives, and new (1970s) as radicals, came from a committee that was set up by the Congress Party in 1939 named 'Woman's Role in Planned Economy (WRPE)', comprising women political leaders of those times, that gave a report that would match the informed recommendations in the current times.[2] The Report covered seven areas: civic rights, economic rights, property rights, education, marriage, family and miscellaneous issues such as widowhood, caste, prostitution, etc.

Says Nirmala Banerjee:

> The Report of the WRPE is worth our notice, if only because of its historical relevance: it shows that, even then, Indian women were by no means the icons awaiting male handouts, as has been visualised by many scholars. In the final report, they did demonstrate a clear understanding of the issues at stake and an ability to put them in the framework of contemporary national and international thinking. They could also set up a network of working groups in different parts of the country in order to get region-wise inputs.

The sub-committee insisted that the traditional vision of the man in front carving out new paths, and the woman trailing behind with the child in her arms, must be changed to 'man and woman, comrades of the road, going forward together, the child joyously shared by both'.

Perhaps the most radical recommendation of the WRPE, looking back, concerned women's unpaid labour, both in the family's economic activities and in the household. About the former, the WRPE recommended that the economic value of the work must be recognised and, in lieu of payment, 'she should have the right to claim all facilities given by the State to other workers (e.g., medical help, crèches, training, etc.' (p. 103).

The 1950–65 period had one more aspect which was enabling, which is missing in the current scenario—namely, women leaders with political clout, but who had an interest in women's rights. The role of these persons and their organisations is often seen as less radical, and more heavyweight than the peasant and worker movements that were part of the New, as outlined by some of the records of the history of women's movements.

However, they made significant and enduring changes to the political economy. Some of them led all-India women's organisations, but many were individual political persona who, however, had a sense of identity with women's concerns. Aruna Asaf Ali, an important freedom fighter as well as a voice of the Left, led the National Federation of Indian Women, an organisation that took up issues of women workers, amongst other things. Other significant women who were in Parliament or in the cabinet were Renuka Chakravarty and Lakshmi Menon, and each brought with her, agendas for women's emancipation. Dr Phulrenu Guha, for example, who was the Chairperson of the Committee on the Status of Women, encouraged and put forward an outstanding report on this issue in 1975.

Another such powerful leader was Kamaladevi Chattopadhyay, who had emerged from the freedom struggle from the socialist wing of the Congress Party and was a prominent figure of the times (Chattopadhyay, 1983). Kamaladevi Chattopadhyay was instrumental in setting up the All India Handicrafts Board and, as its first chairperson, championed the idea of the 'use' and relevance of craft as a means of livelihood as well as a consumer good, not only as an art object (Nanda, 2002). Another such initiative was the Central Social Welfare Board (CSWB),[3] which was set up in 1953 by Dr Durgabai Deshmukh. It undertook setting up socio-economic units, taking care of abandoned women, giving livelihood and educational options to those who are excluded from the mainstream, and continues to provide sustenance (Jain, 2011). Another known figure, Suchitra Kripalani, set up the Lok Kalyan Samiti in 1952 to extend a health cover to the deprived, with the objective of implementing welfare programmes for women and children through voluntary organisations.[4]

There are some other breaking-out histories from sub-national spaces which, rooted in mythology, deal with empowerment of women. Akka Mahadevi, the famous mystic belonging to the Virashaiva Bhakti movement in 12th-century Karnataka, challenged a seminary to look at spirituality not as body defined, by presenting herself in the nude to the seminary.[5] Avvaiyar, saint-poetess of the Tamil country in the 13th century, created oral literacy as she was denied education, propagating the fragrance of Tamil literature, and also speaking about morality and spirituality. She acted as a messenger between warring Tamil kings and brought peace among them (Srinivasan, 2002). While these were of earlier centuries, they were radical initiatives and challenged the idea that 'the new' was born in the 1970s.

Hence, the argument on which phase was radical, and which conservative, needs to be seen within a broader historical frame as well as with a lens which also includes hard-core economic support.

A SIGNIFICANT STREAM OF THE MOVEMENT—WOMEN'S STUDIES

An actor in the movement which played, and still plays, a leadership role is the Women's Studies movement. Madhuribehn Shah, coming in as the Chairperson of the UGC, introduced the programme on Women's Studies in the UGC in 1985: a unique, enabling and lasting contribution to the women's movement. There are currently 67 Women's Studies Centres (WSCs) established in various universities and colleges in the country.[6] Establishing the women's studies centres showed brave leadership, of charting new terrain (which was discredited as not really a 'discipline'), and which also broke the dichotomy between the classroom and the movement.

It is the typical offspring of a movement for justice, recognition and emancipation from subordination. It embraces within itself, academia and action, theory and practice, voices and scripts. It has been a powerful tool for calling attention to the intellectual and ideational skills of women across the world, and to the importance of role distinction between men and women in society at large. This difference was uncovered by women's studies at both material and intellectual planes.

Scholars in women's studies challenge the philosophical underpinnings of human knowledge and critique-existing paradigms in all intellectual disciplines (Rajput and Jain, 2003).

With women's studies being recognised as a politically significant activity in the quest for equality, some of the pioneers got together to organise the first National Conference on Women's Studies in 1981 at SNDT University, Mumbai. This historic conference viewed women's studies as a 'critical perspective' that needed to be integrated into all disciplines and recognised the need for universities to focus on the women's question through research, teaching and engagement in activities. To further these aims, the conference resolved to set up the Indian Association for Women's Studies (IAWS), which was registered as a membership-based organisation in 1982. IAWS foregrounds the collective voice to central issues at its regular national conferences and in its publications.

Women's studies domains created new knowledge— challenging theories as well as giving voice to women's ideas and proposals in all domains—as well as drew attention to the value of women's collective efforts at self-strength (Jain, 1980). But while these efforts led to the healing of some wounds and broadening of the space of women's collective efforts, no real change took place, or has taken place, in accommodating women as intellectual leaders, as people with game-changing powers or attributes (Jain, 2007).

ENTER THE INTERNET AND THE NEW FEMINISTS

Apart from the women's studies centres serving as the powerhouse and catalysts of the 'feminist consciousness', what has emerged as a new force has been the World Wide Web, or the Internet. The Internet has enabled many networks—categorised according to age, topic of interest, etc. These groups galvanise opinions and offer collective voices on public issues. Social media has given a voice to those who were previously denied. The Internet and debates in specific have given individuals a chance to express their opinions, assert their intelligence, and potentially reach out to other feminists, even those who have yet to be identified as one. In other words, it has made 'leadership' more diffused. At the same time, the energy and visions generated by mass movements have been gradually percolating to the society and polity outside the consumer world of the middle class.

It is relevant to recall here that the nature, form and content of the movements that give expression to the discontent have also undergone radical change. They have been providing peoples' suffering an expression of vibrant dissent and resistance, and mobilised a section of the media. There are civil-society network campaigns; legal and judicial activism; civil disobedience; non-party political processes; carnivals; humour, laughter and performance; demonstrations, etc., to harness the creativity of marginalised people and has brought them to the 'front line'. Modes of questioning, protest and dissent have been changing to open up places and spaces for debates, discussions and political mobilisations. Most significant is that the intentions of the State, and its claim that it is an embodiment of popular aspirations, are being questioned.

Into this ocean of waves, or rising above them, appeared the response to the gang rape in a moving bus, of a 23-year-old student. In the dark night of the Delhi gang rape, the rising of the young has been an inspiration. Every corner of conventional power has been shaken into acknowledging this uprising. The majority of those who are engaged in it are the young, largely women students, and almost an equal number of young men. Many of us the so-called elders merged with them.

While this mobilisation is across the board, not bound by leaders or strategies or pre-determined demands, it is definitely a moment for negotiating the feminist agenda. There is recognition of the power of the challenge, as it has led every conventional power place to bend its head in order not to be brought down. This is an opportunity; it has given the spokespersons for women the biggest-ever presence in the overpowering system of governance from heads of political parties, including the prime minister, and other levels of political persona, through to the leaders of opinion across different domains. Across the board, they bent.

A space has opened up for negotiations by women in areas other than the law or reservation in politics. This space also offers an opportunity for women's movements to grab or enter this ether with the other demands that people's movements have been voicing: jungle, zameen, work—recognised and unrecognised—and other areas of protecting other forms of brutality that women, especially among the masses, are facing.

This lively sharing, not only of information but of ideas for action, the coming together across networks, locations and even political differences/platforms in response to the brutal rape of the young student in Delhi, reminds one of earlier times—the 1970s. In the 1970s, and even perhaps in the early 1980s, women's organisations, apart from individual women leaders, came together in solidarity and hammered out a unified set of proposals and responses to acts of injustice. It covered, of course, not only rape and other acts of violence against women, but also examined economic injustices. While there was no Internet then, the advantage was that there were many all-India membership-based women's organisations and, of course, there was the telephone.

Seven all-India women's organisations, separated by political ideologies, mostly associates of principal political parties, came together and called themselves the Seven Sisters. These were the National Federation of Indian Women (NFIW); All India Democratic Women's Association (AIDWA); All India Women's Conference (AIWC); Young Women's Christian Association (YWCA); Mahila Dakshita Samiti (MDS); Joint Women's Programme (JWP) and Centre for Women's Development Studies (CWDS). Other centres, such as the Institute of Social Studies Trust (ISST), were in solidarity, even though they did not have an all-India presence. Mobile Crèches, an organisation which was working with children on construction sites, was one of the most brilliant, forward-looking organisations in Delhi at that time, touching the rest of the women's movements, but looking also at economic injustice.

While these organisations were sometimes even at 'war' with each other due to their political ideologies, when there were issues such as the Mathura rape case, all of the Seven Sisters, along with women's studies centres such as the ISST and others, took out processions with deep solidarity. It was not limited only to the Mathura rape case, but extended to issues such as the setting up of the National Commission on Women, and other policy structures and issues.

However, despite all these extraordinary initiatives and networking in the past, real negotiating of feminist understanding of justice, of human rights, of economic reasoning, had not lifted the blinds of the 'other' (Jain, 2013)—what is often derided as the *male stream* instead of main stream, until the shock of the 16 December 2012 event.

But the rising after 16 December has changed the terms of trade. This *rising* provides an important illustration of a movement, which is spearheaded by women, but drawing together a wide range of categories of people towards what can be called one purpose or one voice. The gathering and protests were unique for their inclusion of diversity, for their persistence, width and impact on the public domain.

This collective voice drew attention to an issue that is not new, but one that had remained in cloistered spaces. This was the issue of the sanctity of women's bodies. For the first time, the attention that was called to women's bodies has not been trivialised or used in questionable terminology, but seen as a deep and undesirable scar on India's body. It has roused the conscience of an assortment of India's citizens, who are usually divided by caste, location, religion, class and age. The movement, which can be called the Jantar Mantar movement of December 2012, superseded and overpowered this fracture.

It could be suggested that the movement led, or has revealed how a movement can *lead*, a broad range of citizens across India to speak in one voice on violence against women, or what is now broadened as sexual violence.

SOME EXPLORATIONS FOR THE FUTURE

There is a role for feminists to illuminate the special qualities and ethics of women, and to politicise the national and world wide women's movements around it. There is also a role for development agencies and personnel to reorganise their understanding and there is also need to upturn economic reasoning to accommodate the urgency of women's condition.

The issue of violence, especially against women; the issue of women's rights as human rights, which are linked to the struggle against violence, and the political restructuring of a kind that also restructures the economy need to come onto the agendas of the various streams of the women's movements ... The time is now!

◆

* Assisted by Deepshika Batheja.
# This chapter was first published in 2013 in the *IIC Quarterly*, Vol. 39, Nos. 3 and 4.

NOTES

1. Aparna Basu, 'Indian Women's Movement', from Department of History, Delhi University, Human Rights, Gender and Environment. http://www.du.ac.in/fileadmin/DU/Academics/course_material/hrge_15.pdf (accessed on 3 February 2013). The Chameli Devi Jain Award was instituted in 1982 to honour women journalists.

2. The Sub-Committee to discuss women's role in the planned economy was formed on 16 June 1939 to 'deal with the place of woman in the planned economy ...' ranging from family life, employment, education and social customs that prevent women's participation in the economy. Reference to K.T. Shah's 'Introduction' (p. 27) of 'Woman's Role in Planned Economy'. Report of the Sub-Committee, National Planning Committee Series. Bombay: Vora & Co., Publishers, 1947. The chairperson of the Committee was Rani Lakshmibai Rajwade and the Committee included prominent women of that time: Sarla Devi, Vijaylakshmi Pandit, Begum Zarina Currimbhoy, Sarojini Naidu, Durgabai Joshi and Dr (Smt) Muthulakshmi Reddy.

3. Official website of *Central Social Welfare Board* (CSWB) http://wcd.nic.in/cswb1.htm (accessed on 31 January 2013).

4. Official website of http://www.lokkalyansamiti.in/About.aspx (accessed on 2 February 2013).

5. Dr Vijaya Guttal of Gulbarga University's presentation on 'Women Saints in Indian History', 14 February 2003, at the Katha Literary Festival, 2003.

6. University Grants Commission. '*Guidelines for Development of Women's Studies in Indian Universities and Colleges During Eleventh Plan (2007–2012)*' http://www.ugc.ac.in/oldpdf/xiplanpdf/womenstudies.pdf (accessed on 31 January 2013).

REFERENCES

Chattopadhyay, Kamaladevi. 1983. *Indian Women's Battle for Freedom*. New Delhi: Abhinav Publications.

Jain, Devaki. 2013. 'Full Frontal Feminism', *The Asian Age* http://www.e-paper.asianage.com/columnists/full-frontal-feminism-452 (accessed on 28 January 2013).

Jain, Devaki. 2012. 'Chameli Devi Jain', in Latika Padgaonkar and Shubha Singh (eds.), *Making News, Breaking News, Her Own Way*. New Delhi: Tranquebar Press.

Jain, Devaki. 2011. 'What is wrong with Economics? Can the *aam aurat* Redefine Economic Reasoning?' Council for Social Development and India International Centre.

Jain, Devaki. 2007. 'To be or not to be: location of women in public policy' in 'Women weave peace into globalization: Some contributions to the theme'. *Economic and Political Weekly* http://www.epw.in/governance-and-development-karnataka/be-or-not-be.html.

Jain, Devaki. 2005. 'Women Development and the UN: A Sixty-Year Quest for Equality and Justice.' UNIHP. Bloomington and Indianapolis: Indiana University Press.

Jain, Devaki. 1981. 'Journey of a Freedom Fighter', *Mainstream*, 22 August.

Jain, Devaki. 1980. 'Women's Quest for Power'. Institute of Social Studies.

Kouzes, J.M. and B.Z. Posner. 1995. *The Leadership Challenge*. San Francisco: Jossey-Bass.

Kumar, Radha. 1993. *History of Doing: An Illustrated Account of Movements for Women's Rights and Feminism in India, 1800–1990*. Delhi: Zubaan.

Menon, Ritu (ed.). 2011. *Making a Difference: Memoirs from the Women's Movement in India*. Delhi: Women Unlimited.

Nanda, Reena. 2002. *Kamaladevi Chattopadhyay: A Biography*. Delhi: Oxford University Press.

Rajput, Pam and Devaki Jain. 2003. *Narratives from the Women's Studies Family: Recreating Knowledge*. Delhi: SAGE Publications.

Sen, Samita. 2000. *Toward a Feminist Politics? The Indian Women's Movement in Historical Perspective*. Policy research report on gender and development working paper series. World Bank. Development Research Group/Poverty Reduction and Economic Management Network.

Srinivasan, T.R. 2002. 'Study on Avvaiyar', *The Hindu*, 8 October. Available at http://www.hindu.com/thehindu/br/2002/10/08/stories/2002100800060300.htm [Online] (Accessed: January 2013)

Sylvester, Christine.1998. 'Homeless in International Relations? Women's Place in Canonical Texts and in Feminist Reimaginings', in Anne Phillips (ed.), *Feminism and Politics*. Oxford: Oxford University Press.

Thapar, Romila. 1975. 'Looking back in History', in Devaki Jain (ed.), *Indian Women*. Publications Division, Ministry of Information and Broadcasting, Government of India.

◆◆

2
REVISITING THE THEME OF WOMEN'S 'EMPOWERMENT'
How Leadership Matters

PADMINI
SWAMINATHAN#

THE CONTEXT

The idea and agenda of 'empowering' women by governments, funding agencies and other non-state actors has a long and chequered history within and across countries. Till date it is not clear at what point one can emphatically assert that the programme of 'empowering' women has been successfully achieved or is on the verge of being achieved; countries across the world, in particular developing countries, whose women are generally deemed to be the most 'disempowered' have in place a whole array of 'women-empowerment' programmes designed to address one or several aspects of the functioning of [formal or informal] institutions/societies that contribute to 'disempowering' women. Following Kabeer (1999), we conceptualise power as the

> ability to make choices: to be disempowered, therefore, implies to be denied choice ... the notion of empowerment is that it is inescapably bound up with the condition of disempowerment and refers to the processes by which those who have been denied the ability to make choices acquire such an ability. In other words, empowerment entails a *process of change*. (ibid.: 436–437, emphasis as in original)

Against the backdrop of the above notion of 'empowerment', this chapter discusses two different kinds of attempts and approaches to 'empower' women that the author has studied in some depth (Swaminathan and Jeyaranjan, 2008: 77–86; Swaminathan, 2008:

48–56). These approaches, among other things, reveal how the leadership instrumental in conceptualising and implementing these programmes had completely opposing views of what constitutes women's empowerment, thereby leading to divergent results. The relevance of revisiting these studies lies in underscoring the point that the State's agenda of 'empowering' women continues to be charity/welfare-based, such that the 'process of change' mentioned above results in dependency rather than empowerment.

CASE 1: CREATING SYNERGY ACROSS GOVERNMENT PROGRAMMES AND ENSURING OFFICIAL DELIVERY OF SERVICES

This case study explores the manner in which a non-governmental organisation (NGO) has, through its programme aimed at 'Empowering Women through Collective Action', operationalised to a substantive extent the notion of *gender mainstreaming*[1] by combining economic transformation with social emancipation. It also highlights the processes that are required and those that need to be put in place to expand the substantive freedoms of people (Sen, 1999), both as the 'principal means' and as the 'primary end' of development.

This case study is a programme of the M.V. Foundation (henceforth MVF), namely, 'Empowering Women through Collective Action and Environment Programme', operational in the Ranga Reddy district of Andhra Pradesh, a rural hinterland, whose economy is inextricably linked with the expanding urban economy of Hyderabad. Like many rural hinterlands, Ranga Reddy district provides the much needed unskilled labour force for the city, among other things. Most of these workers are small peasants and are generally from the lower caste and class. The land that they owned in the hinterland was uncultivable and they had no resources, either in kind or money, to convert this land into productive assets and/or use the land productively. Most of their land was 'assigned' land. Assigned lands are the redistributed surplus lands to the landless by the State under some land reforms programme. Under these circumstances, when the city of Hyderabad provided some regular employment, most of the peasants either migrated or began commuting daily to the city. The living conditions in the city were deplorable but in a situation where they had no productive employment in their villages, the peasants chose to work in the urban economy. They were discriminated in the urban labour market as well. They managed to fetch only poorly paid and irregular employment when compared to other migrant workers.

NATURE OF MVF LEADERSHIP

M.V. Foundation entered the arena (towards the end of the 1990s, early 2000) at a time when the situation had considerably worsened. It set out to regenerate the environment and livelihoods of these marginalised peasants in the hope that if it could demonstrate that the land at the disposal of the peasants, however degraded, could be converted into a dependable livelihood source and if, in addition, it could establish the viability of land-based activities, including agriculture, the distress migration of peasants to the city in search of some source of livelihood could be arrested. To achieve this objective, MVF devised a unique strategy. It firmly believed that the State had, over a period, conceived, announced, but half-heartedly implemented several land- and rural-based programmes that could be profitably sourced; more importantly, MVF also realised that most of these programmes were backed by sufficient budgetary allocations. It leveraged such programmes to achieve its objective. Towards this, it worked with the targeted marginalised communities on the one hand, and the State bureaucracy on the other. A more crucial aspect of the model that we will elaborate concretely as we go along is that a catalyst is needed to create the much-needed synergy and sequential interlinkage between conception, resource dedication and implementation of the programmes on the ground. M.V. Foundation played this crucial catalytic role.

The core competence of MVF is the strategic alliance that it establishes constantly with key actors. On one side is the State. The State is referred to here in a very broad sense. The State, with its developmental and social sector agenda, has periodically announced several programmes that directly impinge on the lives and the livelihoods of the people. However, it is quite well understood by now that only a fraction of the intended benefits have reached the people for whom the programmes have been conceived and for which programmes enormous scarce resources are being earmarked, year after year. The problem is not just in the realm of implementation. The Foundation has correctly diagnosed the problem as one that, of necessity, requires multiple and simultaneous action on several fronts to actualise the benefits of the programmes. Where MVF stands out is that it has ventured to work along with the State and through this collaboration make the State accountable to the people for whom the latter has designed the programmes. In contrast, many NGOs intervene by mobilising resources from various sources and in the process project themselves as a substitute for the State. Can any organisation substitute for the State? The philosophy of working through the State, or rather make the State programmes work, has been the guiding principle for MVF, not only in this relatively little-known programme of 'Empowering Women through Collective Action', but also in its universally well-known programme of education and child labour.

GROUP VERSUS INDIVIDUAL BENEFICIARIES: PROCESS OF EMPOWERING

The beneficiaries of MVF programmes are clearly differentiated on the basis of caste and gender. While Dalits and tribals in general, and women among them, in particular, are the main focus, in some areas, other backward classes (OBCs) are also included, as many of the programmes are implemented for a group as a whole; hardly any programme is individual-based. The Foundation facilitates and ensures full and continuous participation by beneficiaries in all of its programmes. For instance, under the wasteland development programme, the State earmarks a fixed sum but often such sums are grossly inadequate to complete the task. Under such circumstances, the beneficiaries are required to put in considerable resources in terms of both time and money to complete the work and realise the benefits. As a policy, MVF does not mobilise money from any other source to supplement State-funding, and hence, the beneficiaries have to put in their own resources. However, and as a consequence of this strategy, beneficiaries own the programme. Further, the continued functioning and viability of a programme depends not just in being able to access funds from the government for that particular programme, but in being able to source other related programmes involving different departments of the government. Sourcing resources and technical help from several departments of the government in itself is a huge task apart from being time-consuming. Beyond initial facilitation by MVF, beneficiaries are themselves required to follow up with the various government departments to access related programmes to bring about the much-needed synergy that the simultaneous functioning of these programmes create.

For example, the ability of beneficiaries to procure heads of cattle distributed under a particular programme is directly linked to their ability to procure fodder, which, in turn, needs land as well as initial technical inputs in terms of the kind of fodder that can be profitably grown on degraded land. Such interlinked factors need inputs of all kinds—technical, monetary, personnel and physical. Above all, the most crucial input that it requires is coordinated effort on a sustained basis so that beneficiaries do not lose the initial momentum because of delays in any one link or effort. The M.V. Foundation ensures that its intervention helps in facilitating the creation of synergy between programmes, in enabling beneficiaries to make their presence felt in various government departments, in overseeing the operationalisation of these efforts on the ground, and in ensuring that, at all times, beneficiaries adhere to the basic principles that made them a beneficiary in the first place.

Even if MVF's programme intervention is largely biased in favour of the marginalised, ultimately who benefits or gets defined as a beneficiary depends to a large extent on the nature and type of the programme. While some programmes can be clearly targeted, other programmes are not amenable to such targeting. For instance, the wasteland development programme clearly targets Dalits and Adivasi landholders towards land improvement so as to ensure a stable and sustainable livelihood for them. In contrast, the watershed development programme cannot be as clearly targeted, since, in this case, it is the common property resource of the social system that is accessed. And, therefore, the benefits of such an improvement cannot be confined to the intended beneficiaries alone. In fact, the benefit to non-intended beneficiaries because of the watershed development could be much larger as compared to the intended beneficiaries. A series of check dams are constructed in a village and the rain water is stored. This, in turn, results in the rise of the groundwater table of the village. Anybody who has a tube well can benefit from this rise in the groundwater level. Given our social structure, one can easily expect the better-endowed farmers to benefit disproportionately because they possess more tube wells, as well as land for cultivation when compared to the peasants at the margin. But, wherever possible, MVF has clearly targeted its beneficiaries.

MAKING GOVERNMENT GENDER-SENSITIVE: STRUGGLING AGAINST GENDER DISCRIMINATION

Despite the visible presence of women in the forefront of activities related to land and natural resource management in general, and despite the knowledge that MVF was facilitating the operationalisation of the programme under its larger agenda of empowering women, different government departments dealing with land-based development programmes actively discriminated against women. The most visible form of discrimination was in the fixing of wages for the different tasks of a land-development programme. As soon as MVF provided relevant information to women on official guidelines regarding payment of wages, women questioned the rationale of payment of unequal wages and made it an issue for discussion and resolution at their meetings with all concerned departments. Apart from ensuring that government departments pay equal wages, MVF ensures through the women's *sanghams* that equal wages are the norm in all of its activities. While the institution of payment of equal wages is no mean achievement, the challenge for women remains to continually demonstrate their ability and capacity to carry out all tasks hitherto solely performed by males, namely, construction of check dams, measurement works, etc.

ADDRESSING RURAL ENERGY PROBLEMS AS DEVELOPMENT, NOT AS A WOMEN'S ISSUE

Availability of fuel and sources of energy for domestic and agricultural work is a major, but scarcely addressed, theme in the rural areas and among the marginalised sections of the population. M.V. Foundation set out to confront this issue head-on. To begin with, MVF staff was given an orientation on local sources of energy for agriculture as well as for domestic use, climate change and its possible link with recurrent drought. Thereafter, this information was imparted to women's groups in the 35 villages that showed interest in exploring different sources of energy. One aspect of the energy programme was the demonstration of the use of solar energy for lanterns, driers (that would facilitate drying, pounding and preservation of excess agricultural products, thereby adding value) and street lights. Initially, 105 solar lanterns and three solar driers were procured by 16 women's groups on credit. The women's groups had to decide the logistics of operating the solar lanterns and driers, which included the logistics of product manufacturing, sales, book-keeping and accounting, and, sharing of profits among the women who had come together to operate a drier and/or commercially hire out the solar lanterns. The number and intensity of use of solar driers and lanterns started increasing as women gained confidence in the technical and financial aspects of their use and operation. Besides, the process of solar drying ensured hygienic preservation, the reduction of wastage of products due to non-availability of such facility earlier and, more important, it has led to value addition to local products. The demand for these dried and powdered products from urban areas has also increased due to the credibility that they have earned as being unadulterated. The success of solar lanterns has a lot to do with availability of trained technicians (including among women) to maintain these facilities at the village itself. Households using these lanterns spoke of reduction in their electricity bills over time. The challenge, however, is the need to address the procurement of spares that are expensive, leading to heavy recurring cost.

Another aspect of the energy programme consisted in exploring the possibility of using biomass and biofuels for the generation of electricity. For this, women's groups were given training on: the kind of plants that needed to be cultivated (such as jathropa and pongamia) for the eventual production of biofuels; the technicalities of installation and the functioning of oil-expellers that extracted the oil from the seeds of these plants. The women were also sent on exposure visits to other places in Andhra Pradesh and to neighbouring Tamil Nadu where biofuel was being produced through such plantations and oil-expellers. It was also demonstrated to the women that trees from whose seeds biofuel could be extracted could be intercropped along with vegetables, minor millets and other nurseries. Quite a few women in several villages opted for such cultivation. The Government of Andhra Pradesh has recognised the beneficial impact of the kind of efforts taken towards new energy sources and has allocated resources for nurseries and bio-plantations. This recognition and allocation has created a ripple effect, such that farmers who were initially not enthusiastic about the programme have now come forward to experiment with the same. These initiatives are as yet nascent and have already thrown up several challenges. Apart from the fact that they require constant upgrading of technical skills, the fact that the country as yet has a long way to go in terms of research and field experience with large-scale cultivation, production and use of biofuels, means that the village community has very little to fall back upon when, and if, it wants to upgrade its knowledge and/or technology.

We have discussed only a few of the several activities that MVF has facilitated in the villages where it has intervened through its programme aimed at empowering women through collective action simply to highlight the process and conditions of intervention that underlie all MVF activities. These processes and conditions are, at one level, making governments accountable to people by 'delivering development' through the various schemes that have been and are periodically announced for the welfare of the people and for the improvement of sources of livelihood of the most marginalised. At another level, MVF believes in investing time and effort (but very little money) in mobilising stakeholders and working *along with them* rather than *for them* despite this process being time-consuming and difficult, only so that the stakeholders develop an abiding interest in the programme and sustain it once they are convinced of its beneficial impact on their lives and livelihood.

PERCEPTION OF STAKEHOLDERS ABOUT MVF

The marginalised sections, women among them in particular, are the prime stakeholders of this programme of MVF. They have a very high regard for the manner in which MVF has conducted the programme. Specifically, in areas where MVF has been working for quite some time, and which we had occasion to visit, we not only witnessed but also heard and conversed with women who had benefited from being part of the programme. They clearly articulated how initially they had reacted sceptically to MVF's plan of action; it took them a while to realise that:

(a) MVF was not after their land; on the contrary, MVF wanted to reclaim assigned lands and hand it over to the rightful owners.

(b) MVF's priority was food security; MVF also targeted women rather than men since it realised that years of neglect of land and/or unavailability of work in agriculture had led to seasonal migration of men. Women's opportunities to migrate being less than men, the demonstration of viability of working on land and creating opportunities for livelihood in the village itself could be better achieved through women.

(c) MVF's emphasis on making livelihoods sustainable and its willingness to struggle along with the villagers to make the government and bureaucracy operationalise the various programmes earmarked for land development, among others, has contributed immensely to the real empowerment of women and their households.

(d) On being asked whether they still needed MVF support in their struggles, the women were able to express very clearly that, while they would now be able to manage a number of tasks on their own, including knocking at the doors of the government for their legitimate demands, they needed MVF support to tackle larger issues such as urban encroachment, environmental changes because of indiscriminate construction, pollution of groundwater, among others.

UNDERSTANDING EMPOWERMENT THROUGH THE MAINSTREAMING OF GENDER IN DEVELOPMENT

How does this account of the process of operationalising the programme of 'empowering women through collective action' by MVF cohere with our understanding of the notions of gender-mainstreaming and engendering development? It would be useful to recapitulate the nature of shifts in gendered relations and operations that have taken place consequent to the intervention by MVF. The most significant aspect of the intervention has been the attempt to address the issue of erosion of livelihoods leading to permanent or seasonal male out-migration and which left women to shoulder the full responsibility of the farming household. What needs to be underlined here is the fact that MVF did not resort to the conventional set of activities that normally make up programmes aimed at women's empowerment, namely, pumping money to train women to take up income-generating activities in the name of introducing women to non-conventional activities. The several adverse fallouts of such modes of intervention are too well known, not least among them being the inability of intervening NGOs to monetarily sustain these trainings and activities beyond a period as well as the tremendous difficulties faced in marketing products produced from these activities. The unreasonable emphasis that many funding agencies place on achieving and making results visible in the shortest possible time prevents any sort of intervention that is aimed at investing time and effort in mobilising the affected/marginalised community of people, such that the very mode of intervention convinces the community of the long-term benefits and sustainability of the programme. The Foundation has gone several steps further. It has not only mobilised and worked along with the most marginalised among the affected community, but it has, through this mobilisation, enabled the community to approach the governments in power and make the latter operationalise and release funds for several land development programmes to which the community and area is entitled. The catalyst's role played by MVF has not only facilitated the development of synergy among the different land-based programmes, thereby strengthening association among the community of beneficiaries and in enhancing the effectiveness of the programmes, but in also placing the most marginalised women, in particular, at the centre of all of its intervention.

A significant gender-mainstreaming shift that has ensued is the incorporation of a gender perspective to the manner in which the mainstream economic agenda of the land-based development programme was operationalised on the ground. As already mentioned, the area in which MVF chose to intervene was marked by considerable distress migration on the part of the male members of a number of households. Hence, to that extent, MVF had to perforce begin work with the women members of these households. Nevertheless, MVF and the women whom MVF had identified as beneficiaries of its programme had to explicitly deal with patriarchy and the caste bias that began to unfold when women knocked on government doors to demand (of government institutions and bureaucracy) information regarding the different development programmes, including rules that governed release of funds allocated to these programmes. Since many of these programmes were not the usual 'women-only' 'empowerment' programmes, and since the unwritten rule of not recognising women as farmers continues, MVF and the women beneficiaries had to expend considerable time and effort in convincing the bureaucracy of the rights of women as citizens, and of the capability and seriousness of women to source and make use of land-based programmes of the government.

Another development, an important shift towards gender-mainstreaming, is not only that equal representation of women and the marginalised is ensured in all programmes, be it natural resource management, watershed development programmes, etc., but considerable effort also goes into ensuring that members of these committees acquire the necessary gender expertise to be able to become conscious of the mechanisms that cause and reproduce gender equality. Thus, for example, MVF beneficiaries were able to prevail over the forest department and their own menfolk in resisting monoculture in the forestry programme, which would have otherwise curtailed the area or even destroyed the sources of minor forest produce items gathered by women in particular, and which contributes to household income and food security. The knowledge that the extension of monoculture, though financially beneficial in the short run, plays havoc with the forest environment over time leading to entire villages/households dependent on forests for their livelihoods to be adversely affected is well understood. In MVF villages, through a process of education, negotiation and struggle, the beneficiaries have managed to take along with them the forest department and officials in not only conserving green cover, but in productively using forest resources to enhance their incomes. Further, women have been at the forefront of changes in watershed practices in forest areas and this has visibly resulted in the regeneration of water bodies within the forests as well as in the adjoining villages and also in enhancing the quantum and regularity of the supply of biomass to the village.

We have not explored in any detail what shift has taken place within the households of the beneficiaries. However, the fact that an MVF beneficiary household has to adhere to certain non-negotiable norms, such as ensuring that all children are in school and not made to labour at the expense of schooling, that violence against women in any form is not tolerated, etc., combined with the emphasis by

MVF on payment of equal wages, has considerably enhanced the value and status of women, and of girl children, in all areas where MVF has a presence. These shifts have not come overnight, neither are they complete for us to certify that a social transformation from a gender perspective has already taken place. But, given the fact that MVF's intervention consists largely in targeting people along with activities with almost nil transfer of money from MVF to its beneficiaries, and given that all interventions are premised on an adherence to certain norms that inform the broad philosophy of the Foundation, it would not be off the mark to state that the programme of women's empowerment through collective action is not just aimed at gender-mainstreaming but its actual operationalisation on the ground is visibly resulting in centre-staging and addressing development programmes from a gender perspective. To that extent, by incorporating a gender-mainstreaming perspective into its intervention MVF has, in our opinion, succeeded in at least engendering delivery of development services.

◆◆◆

CASE 2: DELIVERING WELFARE BUT NOT NECESSARILY EMPOWERING PEOPLE

The economic surveys presented to Parliament, year after year, just before the annual budget do not evaluate the effects of economic development and growth on the more material aspects of the well-being of people, such as, for example, the quantum and nature of employment generated by economic growth. In an interesting exercise, Dev and Mooij (2002) have analysed the budget speeches of finance ministers starting from 1988–89. Among other things, they find that all the 12 budget speeches analysed by them were generally silent about employment-creation in the regular economy. While they found separate sections devoted to agriculture and industry, there was hardly any mention of employment and labour-market policies, except of specific anti-poverty employment programmes. It is ironical that the first time that the labour market is specifically discussed in a budget, it is to make the point that lay-offs, retrenchments and closures should be made easier... 'It would be no exaggeration to state that, as far as one can judge from these budget speeches, India in the 1990s had no employment policy.... *A new term brought into the budget speeches in 1999 is empowerment....*

This empowerment has nothing to do with changing power relations or a redistribution of productive assets' (ibid.: 52, emphasis added). Further, according to the authors, the post-1998 budgets reveal the implicit interpretation of poverty by the government. 'It [poverty] is a residual interpretation—in contrast to a relational one. Poverty is seen as something that can disappear with a capital injection. A relational interpretation, on the other hand, would hold that poverty is the result of social and economic relations: the poor are poor as a result of their position within the social and economic structure' (ibid.).

What this discussion reveals is that the disjunction between development and employment generation is built into the basic conceptualisation of economic growth in the annual budgets of the government.

The conventional notion that growth powered by the secondary and tertiary sectors would generate sufficient employment so as to absorb surplus labour from the primary sector has not taken place; on the contrary, the primary sector continues to maintain its rank as the largest employer of the rural people even as income from the primary sector has declined over time. In an attempt to understand the nature of risks faced by the poorest among the poor and also their coping mechanisms, we undertook a 'livelihood assessment survey' in several villages across Tamil Nadu between July and October 2004. The relevance of reproducing here the observations from the survey lie in the remarkable manner in which people on the ground, women in particular, in their own words, linked their inability to make a transition to a better life because of the disjuncture they perceived between the macro-economic issues of employment and growth on the one hand, and on the other, the low scale and poor quality of the otherwise 'functioning' welfare institutions in their villages.

The field visits provided crucial insights into how the vulnerability of the rural agricultural households had increased over time. At the outset, it needs to be recorded that across the villages, and among almost all sections of the agricultural labouring population, the risk and, therefore, vulnerability due to declining agricultural activities (the most important source of livelihood for those with and without land) had increased considerably. The villagers, women included, traced the decline in agricultural activities to a combination of factors: continuous failure of monsoons, depletion of groundwater, change in cropping patterns, changes in institutional patterns that govern agrarian relations, among others, all of which had combined to erode their livelihood base. A direct economic consequence of this combination of factors was the decline in the number of days of employment, hitting landless agricultural labouring population the hardest. Most villages had no other major activity that could provide alternate employment to agriculture. Landless households among the agriculture-based employment groups were the most vulnerable. They were forced to cope by cutting down the number of meals they took in a day, discontinuing schooling of their children, delays in seeking medical attention for their ailments, defaulting on repayment schedules on their loans and/or become more indebted, thereby further increasing their vulnerability. The gender question that emerged here was the differential impact that this vulnerability held for men and women: while to some extent men ventured out in search of coolie work, at times even staying out of the village for days together, such options were not available to women. They had neither the resources nor the support system to enable them to make these search trips. At the same time, we realised that a resolution to this gender problem did not lie only (or not even) in enabling women to go out in search of coolie work, but in addressing the larger question of the erosion of the main source of their livelihood.

A drop in and/or lack of income had other adverse fallouts. For example, women in one village pointed out that all children were not in school and further that there was considerable dropout at the middle and higher levels for one or several of the following reasons: deteriorating income standards meant that they were forced to pull out their children from classes that did not serve noon-meals and also because they could not meet other school-related expenditure, such as travel to the secondary school outside the village and schoolbooks. In some cases, older children had to discontinue schooling in order to share household responsibilities while their parents went out in search of work. In quite a few villages, girls' education was especially constrained by the combination of limited income as well as poor transport. While parents expressed their willingness and desire to educate their daughters further, they could not translate this desire into practice. Hence, beyond the eighth standard, the gender gap in educational levels becomes stark.

Another dimension of the gendered nature of the problem was the following: in almost all villages women clearly expressed the point that, while they were happy that some among their village children, girls as well as boys, had managed to study up to the 12th standard, they were very aware of the futility of being 'educated' only up to the 12th standard. It was pointed out that pursuing education beyond this was expensive, even in government higher educational institutions, and also at times non-accessible (because of non-fulfilment of eligibility criteria by these children). Not everyone could afford to educate all their children; forced to make a choice, parents opted to spend on higher education and hostel accommodation for their sons rather than for daughters. The parents had a reason for this gendered choice: opportunities for employment outside of the ones available in the village, namely, agriculture, were nil, unless the educated chose to go to large metros and towns. While in fact a few boys from these villages had found some service jobs in metros like Chennai (such as lorry-booking, cleaner jobs with transport companies, etc.), educated girls were handicapped by the lack of social support and economic opportunities, and were therefore confined to their households. Villages close to metros such as Chennai were sourced for adolescent girl labour to work in garment units, particularly in the EPZ; the latter organised pick-up and drop services for such labour, but most villagers were reluctant to send their daughters.

All sections of the population were extremely anxious about the uncertainty facing their children, educated or otherwise. Their hopes were shattered because of the realisation that their children had no future either in the 'traditional' occupation of agriculture or in 'modern' occupations, the latter requiring the kinds of qualifications that the village population could, as of now, ill afford. Women were frustrated that their work and earnings were not sufficient to enable their children to rise above a certain level of education and/or acquire some professional skill. This, in turn, implied that they could not get into better paying jobs—a necessary condition for reducing the insecurity of their lives. The institution of self-help groups (SHGs)—a much-touted women's empowerment intervention policy of the government—had a pervasive presence in almost all the villages that we visited. However, what came out quite clearly was that the nature of activities and the ability of SHGs to sustain these activities had a lot to do with the general level of economic activity in the village, the cohesiveness of the village population, plus the institutional support provided by the panchayats. The women in almost all the villages were also aware of the limits of SHG-sponsored activities and realised that while their SHGs could tackle short-term contingencies and support them in times of crises, the SHGs were no alternative to large-scale employment, good infrastructure and functioning public institutions—in all of which the State has a primary role to play. During the discussions on the quantum, nature and adequacy of the government's welfare policies aimed at different categories of people such as the poor, women, disabled, widows, destitutes, girl children, pregnant women, among others, the women were very emphatic that, while through their local bodies and/or SHGs, they did source the different programmes and very often also ensured that the targeted population benefited from the welfare schemes, these ad hoc 'schemes' did not address the two hard questions that they posed: one, restoration of their livelihoods, and two, what would enable their children to make a transition to a better life since their present levels of education had failed to do so. These questions made us re-examine the rationale of our 'social sector/welfare policies' and its relationship to 'economic development'.

REFLECTIONS

For governments in this country, the picture of gender gaps in achievement/outcomes that analyses of secondary data relating to employment and education indicate, the solution consists in instituting 'welfare' measures ostensibly aimed at eliminating such discrimination and in also 'empowering' the discriminated. For political leaders the persistence of poverty and vulnerability despite the 'social sector' has contributed very little to the way they perceive discrimination; there is, in fact, at the policy or macro-economic level, very little use for nuanced analysis (of the type provided in the case study from Tamil Nadu) of the underlying causes contributing to gaps/discrimination, vulnerability and disempowerment. On the other hand, there are, across the country, individuals and organisations like MVF, who are involved in operationalising schemes that are making a difference to the lives of people on the ground, including women. The insights from some of these efforts at engendering development clearly point towards the range of measures that need to be taken *simultaneously* when addressing the intertwined issues of poverty, caste, class and gender. By the same token, such initiatives also reveal the risks, dangers and sacrifices that are inherent when the effort is not merely towards redistribution, but also towards restructuring social, political and bureaucratic institutions and ways of functioning. Therein lies the rub. Scaling up such interventions to cover larger geographical areas and numbers of the marginalised would immediately attract political, bureaucratic and social opposition since entrenched, unjust privileges will need to be parted with. Therefore, while pockets of inclusive development models exist wherever organisations like MVF function, the models themselves cannot be replicated through political or administrative fiat. Neither will a programme of political mobilisation and action alone suffice, since their sustainability needs to be premised on access to and protection of sources of livelihoods. In other words, what the MVF leadership model has demonstrated is not only that the State needs to be brought in, but, more important, the State needs to be held accountable to its citizens and to its promises.

◆

This chapter was first published in 2013 in the *IIC Quarterly*, Vol. 39, Nos. 3 and 4.

NOTE

1. We have applied the notion of gender mainstreaming provided by Emanuela Lombardo and Petra Meier (2006), according to whom, at least five shifts in the policy-making process must be found to be able to say that a feminist reading of gender mainstreaming has been put into practice. These include: a shift towards a broader concept of gender equality that necessarily implies changes also in men's lifestyles; evidence of incorporation of a gender perspective into the mainstream political agenda; an equal political representation of wo/men as a way to ensure that women will, at least numerically, be part of the mainstream; shift in the institutional and organisational cultures of political decision-making; and a shift that requires both 'displacement' and 'empowerment' for mainstreaming to be a transformative feminist concept.

REFERENCES

Dev, Mahindra S. and J. Mooij. 2002. *Social Sector Expenditures and Budgeting: An Analysis of Patterns and Budget-Making Process in India in the 1990s.* Working Paper 43. Hyderabad: Centre for Economic and Social Studies.

Kabeer, N. 1999. 'Resources, Agency, Achievements: Reflections on the Measurement of Women's Empowerment', *Development and Change,* Vol. 30 [3], July, pp. 435–64.

Lombardo, E. and P. Meier. 2006. 'Gender Mainstreaming in the EU: Incorporating a Feminist Reading', *European Journal of Women's Studies,* Vol. 13[2], pp. 151–66.

Sen, A. 1999. *Development as Freedom.* New Delhi: Oxford University Press.

Swaminathan, P. and J. Jeyaranjan. 2008. 'Mainstreaming Gender, Engendering Development: Reflections on a Case Study', *Economic and Political Weekly,* Vol. XLIII, No. 17, 26 April, pp. 77–86.

Swaminathan, P. 2008. 'Exclusions From and Inclusions in Development: Implications for Engendering Development', *Economic and Political Weekly,* Vol. XLIII, No. 43, 25 October, pp. 48–56.

◆◆

3
WOMEN LEADERS IN EVERY *MOHALLA,* EVERY VILLAGE

RENANA
JHABVALA[#]

Though are natural leaders everywhere and, given the right conditions, these leaders will emerge and inspire others to action. I have been part of the SEWA movement for 35 years and have seen many women leaders at all levels rise within the movement and bring thousands of other women with them, leading to positive change in their villages, in their *mohallas,* and in the country. The Self-Employed Women's Association (SEWA) completes 40 years and its membership is over 17 lakh. These 40 years of the SEWA movement embody centuries of experiences in the lives of poor women, as numerous women have been part of the growth of SEWA.

The growth of a positive, inspiring leadership requires the correct soil and the correct nurturing. SEWA founder, Elaben Bhatt, believed that values formed the core of any movement and that SEWA would grow and be successful only if these values were part of every member's actions. As she described it, it is these values that link us all together like beads on a necklace. These values emerged from the tradition from which Elaben came, that is, for want of a better word, the 'Gandhian' tradition. Through SEWA, Elaben was able to translate Gandhian values into actions. One of the most important legacies of Gandhiji has been the leadership role he ascribed to women. Since non-violence and *satyagraha* were the weapons of choice, it was women who would take leadership. As he said,

> My contribution to the great problem lies in my presenting for acceptance truth and *ahimsa* in every walk of life, whether for

individuals or nations. I have hugged the hope that in this woman
will be the unquestioned leader and, having thus found her
place in human evolution, she will shed her inferiority complex.
(Gandhi, 1940: 13)

These values are the guiding principles for every emerging leader
within SEWA. It helps her to take decisions and to give direction to
her actions.

WORK, VALUES AND EMPOWERMENT

SEWA's members are poor women working in the informal
economy. For them and their families, work is the centre of their
lives. Work is not the only way that people sustain themselves, but
it is also the source of their identity and their dignity. So for SEWA,
most actions centre on a woman's work and her identity as a worker.

Ahimsa is a central theme in the lives of women, especially
poor women, who face many different forms of oppression. To
them, a life free of violence, physical and emotional, is often all they
aim for. However, as women become more empowered and as they
join together to change their lives, ahimsa becomes a way of acting, a
way to ensure that the struggle remains positive and works towards
bringing people together, rather than dividing them.

Satyagraha is the recognition of truth and the resolve to act
on it, despite all odds. It requires clear sight and great courage and
it is a very rare individual who is able to wage satyagraha alone.
However, SEWA is a 'Sangathan'—a means for women to come
together to identify with each other, to craft a common need, a
common message, and to give each other strength and courage to
change their lives through satyagraha. Sangathan ensures that she is
not alone.

Empowerment is a term often used nowadays. It is the desire
of people who feel powerless to have more control over their lives.
Women feel powerless in many ways. They feel that their lives
are ruled by forces over which they have no control, which are too
powerful for them. Powerlessness causes fear that their lives might be
crushed, or destroyed, or reduced any time. It kills the human spirit.

This feeling of powerlessness is very strong in poor women.
Because of their daily struggle for survival against strong economic
and social forces, poor women constantly feel disempowered not

only outside, but also within the household. Empowerment is the process by which disempowered, or powerless, people can change their circumstances and begin to have control over their lives. Empowerment results in a change in the balance of power, in living conditions and in relationships. Perhaps the most important effect of empowerment is when the person says, 'Now I do not feel afraid.'

That is where leadership comes in. At every level people need leaders who show them, by example, that empowerment is possible. The leaders strengthen resolve, build hope and a direction for all. Leaders give the disempowered confidence and make them feel worthy.

WOMEN'S LEADERSHIP IN THE FOUNDATION: ANASUYABEN AND ELABEN

SEWA has grown through its women leaders. Its first leader was Anasuyaben, a colleague and a co-worker of Gandhiji. Anasuyaben belonged to a family of mill-owners but, as was the custom, she was married off at a young age, although she had wanted to study. Her husband did not like her studying, and finally, she left him and came back to her parents' home where, after the death of her father, she was supported in her wishes by her brother, Ambalal Sarabhai. She went to England and came back as a socialist and a feminist. She began working with families of mill-workers and, after some years, the mill-workers came to trust her and asked her how they could be rid of exploitation by mill-owners. Anasuyaben led the first workers' strike in Ahmedabad. However, a few years later, she turned to Gandhiji who was living in Sabarmati Ashram. After undertaking complete research to understand the truth of the situation, Gandhiji and Anasuyaben led a strike of textile workers in 1917. This was perhaps Gandhiji's earliest experiment with satyagraha in India and, after the successful completion of the strike, he inspired Anasuyaben and other leaders to start a Trade Union. The Textile Labour Association (TLA) was founded in 1920 with Anasuyaben as the President.

Against this background of active involvement in industrial relations, social work, and local, state and national politics, the ideological base, provided by Mahatma Gandhi, and the feminist seeds, planted by Anasuya Sarabhai, led to the creation by the TLA of their Women's Wing in 1954. Its original purpose was to assist women belonging to households of mill-workers and its work was focused largely on training and welfare activities. By the 1950s, classes in sewing, knitting, embroidery, spinning, press composition, typing and stenography were established in centres throughout the city for the wives and daughters of mill-workers.

Ela Bhatt joined the TLA after qualifying as a lawyer in 1956 and, a decade later, was the head of the Women's Wing. She expanded the scope of its activities in the early 1970s when a survey was conducted to probe complaints by women tailors of exploitation by contractors. The survey brought out other instances of exploitation of women workers and revealed the large numbers untouched by unionisation, legislation and government policies.

In 1971, a small group of migrant women working as cart-pullers in Ahmedabad's cloth market came to the TLA with their labour contractor. He had heard of a transport workers' union organised by the TLA and thought they might be able to help the women find some housing. At the time, the women were living on the streets without shelter. After talking with the women in her office, Elaben went with them to the areas where they were living and to the market where they were working. While there, she met another group of women who were working as head-loaders, carrying loads of clothes between wholesale and retail markets. As she sat with them on the steps of the warehouses where they waited for work, they discussed their jobs and their low and erratic wages.

Following the meeting, Ela Bhatt wrote an article for the local newspaper and detailed the problems of head-loaders. The cloth merchants countered the charges against them with a news article of their own, denying the allegations and testifying to their fair treatment of head-loaders. The Women's Wing turned the release of this story to their own advantage by reprinting the merchants' claims on the cards and distributing them to use as leverage with the merchants.

Soon, word of this effective ploy spread and a group of used-garment dealers approached the Women's Wing with their own grievances. A public meeting of used-garment dealers was called and over a hundred women attended it. During the meeting in a public park, a woman from the crowd suggested they form an association of their own. Thus, on an appeal from the women and at the initiative of the leader of the Women's Wing, Ela Bhatt and the President of the TLA, Arvind Buch, the Self-Employed Women's

Association (SEWA) was born in December 1971, with women readily paying membership dues to join.

The women felt that as a workers' association, SEWA should establish itself as a Trade Union. This was a fairly novel idea, because the self-employed have no real history of organising. The first struggle SEWA undertook was to obtain official recognition as a Trade Union. The Labour Department refused to register SEWA because it felt that since there was no recognised employer, the workers would have no one to struggle against. It was argued that a Union was not necessarily against an employer, but was for the unity of the workers. Finally, SEWA was registered as a Trade Union in April 1972.

Today, SEWA has over 17 lakh members in 10 states of India; it has expanded to include over 112 cooperatives, some companies and associations, and thousands of self-help groups. SEWA is like a forest of banyan trees, with many trees joined together, and yet each separate and sustainable on its own.

WOMEN'S LEADERSHIP IN STRUGGLE: KARIMABIBI, INDIRABEN, RAJMANI

When I first joined SEWA, we were in the midst of a struggle by Muslim women who stitched quilts from small cloth scraps called *chindi*. They were given the raw materials by shopkeepers and they stitched in their homes and were paid by the dozen. Their homes were their work places. It was around Diwali time and there was a sudden rise in inflation, but the women were paid the same piece-rates for many years; they were not able to make ends meet. These women approached their employers and asked for a revision in rates, but it was refused. The women were very distressed; they met in Karimabibi's house and discussed what to do next. Karimabibi's house was a small one-room apartment in the inner-city area of Dariapur. She was a widow and also the sister of one of the employers but, whereas her brother was doing well in life, Karimabibi was poor and made ends meet by stitching quilts; but she was a natural leader. 'There is one organisation in the city which cares about wages and that is the Textile Labour Association', she told her co-workers, 'we should approach them.'

So the seamstresses approached Shekhubhai, the local TLA representative. Shekhubhai said, 'Since you are not textile-mill workers, the TLA cannot take up your case. But SEWA has just been formed and I will take you to Elaben, to see if she can help.' Many of the women were scared. 'We have never been out of our mohallas', they said, 'How can we go so far and meet these strange people? Will our husbands and fathers allow us to go?' they asked. Karimabibi rallied them all. She told them that if these rates continued they would all sink into poverty, and their children would have no future. 'We must fight', she said, 'we face injustice and ours is a just cause as we work so hard.'

Karimabibi was the spokesperson of the little group of women who finally went to meet Elaben. To verify the reality of the situation, Elaben came to Dariapur and conducted a small study of wages and working conditions, and found that they were indeed paid extremely low rates, much below minimum wage. Elaben and Karimabibi approached the Labour Commissioner with the results of the study. However, the Labour Commissioner said, 'These women work in their own homes, they are not workers, they do not work in a factory under control of the employer, they are housewives.' Karimabibi had been silent so far, intimidated by the big office. But these words incensed her. 'Of course we are workers, we work ten hours a day, we are paid money for our work, you must protect us,' she said.

Somehow, we were able to convince the Labour Commissioner that there was an employer–employee relation, and that he could intervene in the dispute. The Labour Commissioner invited the women and their employers to his office for a meeting. For the women it was a new moment in their lives, a moment of empowerment, when they sat across the table from their employers and were able to talk to them as equals. As Karimabibi said, 'We felt we had thrown away the *char diwari* and a new world had opened.'

A settlement on rates was reached. And, although the employers did not pay the full amount there was still an increase of rates. However, the unfortunate part was that the women who had been most active in the struggle were victimised and not given work. Many women turned against Karimabibi and said, 'You led us into an even more difficult situation.' But Karimabibi did not give up. She said, 'If these traders will not give us work, let us try to get some work on our own.' So SEWA approached the textile mills for chindi, and sold the quilts in the market. As this was successful we were able to get a small shop in the same market as the employers, and so SEWA's first cooperative was born. 'Let us call this cooperative "Sabina",' Karimabibi said, '*Yeh sabi ka hai, na!*'

♦♦♦

In spite of the ban on smoking, the bidi industry is one of the largest employers in India and is showing few signs of shrinking. The workers in this industry are employed in the sectors of tobacco-growing and processing, tendu collection and bidi-rolling. All three groups of workers are SEWA members and many women leaders have risen from the tobacco heaps!

Kheda district in Gujarat grows most of the bidi-tobacco in the country; tobacco farmers and processors are mainly the well-off higher castes, whereas the workers are poor local Dalits, or backward castes, or migrant tribals. The workers were not only paid very low wages, but had to work in extremely hard conditions, breathing in tobacco. Women often faced sexual harassment from contractors and employers.

Indiraben was born in a village in Kheda and she as well as all her relatives worked in tobacco fields and factories. After her marriage, Indiraben moved to Ahmedabad and worked in a recycling factory where all workers were on contract. However, her natural instincts as a leader soon ensured that she began organising the workers in the factory and brought them to SEWA. Soon, she was organising contract workers all over Ahmedabad and joined SEWA as a full-time organiser. 'My heart was always in Kheda', Indiraben said, 'there is the worst exploitation there.' She took the lead and tried to get her relatives and other workers in the tobacco fields and factories to join SEWA, but they were too afraid. Earlier, too, some people had tried to start a trade union and had been attacked.

However, Indiraben did not give up. She talked to the women workers and found that they were most worried because they took their children to the fields where tobacco was processed, and the children were playing inside tobacco heaps. Indiraben started simple child-care centres with contributions from the women, and she even managed to get some contributions from farmers and employers. The workers strated to trust SEWA and slowly began to listen to her when she talked about this sangathan.

It came to a point when one large farmer closed down his factory and moved it far away. The workers began a non-violent struggle; they faced many threats but did not back down and finally they were able to receive compensation for unemployment. Another incident flared up when some tribal workers also joined SEWA and the employers/farmers in whose compound they were living burnt down their houses. Lalitaben, a young tribal woman, took the lead and saved the houses by getting many SEWA members to help, and by getting police protection. Over time, employers came to accept SEWA as a responsible and peaceful force that had no other agenda except the well-being of the workers. They were even inspired to form their own Tobacco Farmers' and Processors' Association (TFPA), to enable them to bargain with SEWA. Today, Lalitaben is an influential leader of SEWA in the district and also goes to other parts of the country to organise other women like herself.

Meanwhile, the workers in Kheda began to form self-help groups and their own federation. They were extremely enthusiastic about forming these groups and saving their money, and the groups just grew by word of mouth. Finally, the women formed a Federation and carried out savings and credit for themselves. In this way, they were further able to liberate themselves from this dependence on the large farmers.

However, tobacco farming and processing is hard work and harmful, so women wanted themselves, and especially their children, to find better work. Through the savings and credit federation many women were able to release small plots of land which they had mortgaged many years ago, and thus had an alternative source of income. Some families had been weavers, but had to put away their looms because of a lack of capital and markets. SEWA helped them to get training and some capital, and now these families are producing popular saris, towels and many products for the local markets.

The SEWA movement spread in Kheda and today there are over 136,000 members in Kheda alone. The president of SEWA, Ramilaben, is a tobacco-worker from Kheda. At the same time, the second generation of women has taken the lead and SEWA's general secretary, Jyotiben Macwan, is also from Kheda and, in fact, is Indiraben's daughter.

Ten years later, in a different locale, in the districts of Madhya Pradesh, SEWA was organising tendu-leaf collectors, some of the poorest tribals in Madhya Pradesh. The villages were far and scattered and there was no easy connectivity by road. The villagers survived on forest products and could also harvest one crop a year. But, after the winter months, they all migrated out of the villages in search of labour. For these villagers, the forest department was supreme and they had to face many hardships at the hands of forest personnel. They had to pay bribes, give away their chickens and goats to them; they were often beaten, and even shot to death; and the women faced rape and sexual harassment.

Rajmani's family emigrated from a village in Tamil Nadu and settled in the tribal areas of Madhya Pradesh, where her father worked as a carpenter. When she heard about SEWA she said that she wanted to join the organisation and work to remove exploitation. When she first went with the SEWA organisers to these areas, the people ran away and hid themselves. 'Let us go to the village *haats*', she suggested, 'That is where all the villagers come every week.' Rajmani took the lead in the haats to meet the villagers and note complaints about the harassment and non-payment of dues, and forwarded them to the forest department. At first, the forest department officials took no notice; then they reprimanded Rajmani and the SEWA organisers but, finally, after a big demonstration in Bhopal, they realised the gravity and sincerity of the demands; they began to recognise the complaints and take action.

Rajmani says:

> We had to face both dacoits and Naxalites. Once, a SEWA jeep was ambushed by dacoits. We were going to meet the tendu-leaf pickers in a village. The road was very bad and we were going very slowly. Suddenly, all these men dressed in black with their faces covered, jumped down from the trees. Some had guns and they made us stop the jeep and come out. We were scared, but I began to talk to them.... I told them about SEWA and our work organising tendu-leaf pickers. I said we were trying to bring justice and dignity and better incomes to the tribal villagers. It seems the dacoits were from the village where we were going, so they accompanied us, gathered all the villagers and made them our members.

MANAGING MONEY: CHANDABEN, GEETABEN

Leadership involves many different skills, and dealing with money is one of them. For poor working women, money is often a means to empowerment, and leaders can show them how to best preserve and manage their money. Chandaben, Sumanben and Anandiben were three friends, all street vendors, who joined SEWA in its early years. They ran their businesses by taking loans from private money lenders or from their wholesale suppliers and, in either case, had to pay high interest rates of anywhere between 10 per cent a month to 10 per cent a day! They were keen to get loans at lower interest rates. At the same time, they needed a safe place to put their money. Although they earned cash every day, they had no place to put it and were at the mercy of petty thieves or even members of their own families. Finally, in spite of a regular income, they had little financial security for traumas such as illnesses or disasters, and no financial security for their old age. Their savings were only in the form of gold or silver, which they wore on their person. For all these reasons, the vendor-trio asked Elaben to approach nationalised banks and open accounts for them.

However, these banks were not interested in such a clientele. The attempts were frustrating, while the women's expectations were high. Chandaben came up with a solution. 'We are poor but we are so many', she said, 'let us pool our small amounts together and start our own bank.' And so, the SEWA Bank was started. Chandaben, Sumanben and Anandiben, and many like them, persuaded the women to put their hard-earned savings in this newly formed bank. Because of the high level of credibility that these women leaders commanded, thousands of women invested in shares and opened accounts in the bank. Today, the SEWA Bank has more than four lakh account holders and a capital of nearly ₹200 crore, all of it only from the savings and shares of these women.

Geetaben and Leelaben are street vendors from Delhi. They joined SEWA, Delhi, and were taken to Ahmedabad to see the working of the SEWA Bank. 'We want such a bank of our own', they said. And, indeed, they quickly collected shares and started a similar organisation in Delhi.[1] This cooperative grew fast and Geetaben's great achievement was that she persuaded the chief minister of Delhi to enter into partnership with the cooperative!

INTO THE FUTURE

Movements grow through their leaders and leaders are shaped by the movement. Existing leaders serve as role models for emerging new ones; they show the way and shape directions through their lives and their actions. I have observed that every 10 years a new batch of leaders emerges, as younger women join SEWA. New leaders emerge in new trades and in new states; it takes time for them to understand what leadership means in the SEWA or Gandhian sense. For most people the only leaders who come to them are the political leaders, and so they associate leadership with politics. Even the word 'leader' or 'neta' is associated with politics. That is why it has been necessary to find a different word for leaders, and we have chosen *agevan*, that is, one who is ahead. This form of leadership has been nurtured, developed and taught for 40 years, and we can see it flowering into the future.

◆

This chapter was first published in 2013 in the *IIC Quarterly*, Vol. 39, Nos. 3 and 4.

NOTE

1. They started with a Savings and Credit Society, which has been now registered and working in Delhi since the last five years. When it acquires the requisite capital, it can become a bank.

REFERENCE

Gandhi, M. K. 1940. *Harijan*. 24 February.
http://www.mkgandhi.org/momgandhi/chap60.htm

◆◆

4
ROCKETS WITH FIRE IN THEIR TAILS?
Women Leaders in Kerala's Panchayats

HOPE AND DESPAIR

I learned the hard way that rising above narrow considerations, bringing in the ideas of more and more people into the everyday business of governing, is utterly dangerous. But I do not regret what I did, for today, even though not in power, I am treated by the people of the panchayat as a 'public leader' [*pothunetaavu*] though I am not really a powerful politician...

... I became aware of politics and of things beyond the panchayat and how the world is changing. This changed the way I think. I began to speak my mind and fearlessly point to things going wrong, though it was not easy at all. But that was the only way I'd value myself. The more fearlessly I speak, the more I value myself.

... The most valuable thing that I learned in this is the pleasure of public life. Mummy and others [referring to her mother-in-law and relatives] in this house tell me often, enough of this, give it up, this is wearing you out. I tell her, Mummy, the pleasure of this must be experienced to be known. So many people salute you with affection when you step out of the house! Truly, it is only when we come out of the narrowness of our homes that we learn to love ourselves. We learn to value ourselves. This can happen only in the public. No matter how much love we receive in our homes, this cannot happen.

ecent research on the reservation of 33 per cent seats in
Panchayati Raj institutions in India in the mid-1990s has
revealed that the measure had indeed permitted the entry of
an unprecedented number of women into local governance in most
parts of the subcontinent. On the other hand, there is research which
reminds us that many of the initial hopes which this move aroused
in feminists—for example, the idea that a 'critical mass' of women in
local bodies will help to change priorities and raise collective issues
of relevance to them—are unfounded.

In some fairly recent research on gender, governance and
politics in Kerala, I spoke with 'successful' women presidents—
'success' defined as presence in local governance, in any one of
the tiers, in the three successive terms—trying to understand their
ability to stay in the system. They were clearly a diverse set, but
overwhelmingly from the Malayali 'new elite'—of those communities
which had reaped the greatest gains from the intense social reform in
20th-century Kerala, the Syrian Christian, the Nair, leading groups
of the Muslim community, and the Ezhava.

Posing this question from this research, one is left with a
mixed picture: more than anything else, it seems to have ignited a
struggle or the possibility of one. Consider, for instance, the voice
quoted above: that of a woman ex-president of a village panchayat
in one of Kerala's south-eastern districts in the last term (2006–11).
However, it holds out a message of hope and throbs with the
potential that the women's quota in decentralisation holds out
for the women of the state, for it belongs to a young woman who
had faced many stiff challenges, but managed to get past them.
Her efforts to make decision-processes more inclusive brought her
considerable recognition. But her rising popularity threatened the
local male politicians of her own party. Her party shared power
with another in her panchayat; they devised a way to get her to
'voluntarily' step down before her term was over.

Clearly, there is reason to be hopeful. At least one 'macro-
myth' about women in local government—that they are merely
'proxies' completely controlled by family members and local
politicians—seems to have been rendered largely invalid, at least
for Kerala. And judging from the fact that in the present term,
more than half of all the local bodies in Kerala are led by women,
it may appear that their success is widely acknowledged and

welcomed—it may even appear that their struggle for acceptance is over.

That, however, would be too hasty a conclusion. This voice is a relatively lone one. And the 'success' of women leaders in local governance is ambivalent; it does not necessarily mean the loosening of patriarchal ties. There is no neat pattern of sinking below and rising above patriarchy evident. What may indeed be charted is an on-going struggle, experienced with deep ambivalence by women who have been catapulted into its very heart.

'GENTLE POWER' AND 'KNOWING THE RULES'

The need to exercise caution in judgement becomes all the more evident when we consider the fact that these opportunities have largely opened up to 'development femininity' in Kerala, which is implicated in forms of power that are undeniably patriarchal. In other words, successful women leaders are often the bearers of a specific form of 'gentle power' linked to the deployment of sentiment and affect associated with ideal femininity since the late 19th and early 20th centuries. 'Gentle power' has been projected as characteristically 'feminine'—relying upon persuasion, moral admonishment, caring and rarely assuming a strident posture. Indeed, it is power that does not claim to be power at all. That successful women leaders of local governance have chosen to deploy such power is perhaps only to be expected in a society in which women are most often directed towards the modern domestic realm as the true domain of femininity, which they may legitimately claim, from which they may derive resources to make sense of and deal with the world in general.

The contours of 'development femininity' were apparent to us from the biographies of the successful women leaders we interviewed. First, we found that their previous public exposure was not of political agitation but of developmental activism. Second, they pointed to certain conditions that may be largely accessible only to new elite women, such as the presence of the husband/male member as escort and guide, and interestingly, access to cash. Both these are linked to the women's need to maintain respectability in the local community. And even when they proclaimed to be political, these women rarely identify themselves as politicians in the sense of handling or desiring political power. Rather, they projected themselves as altruistic agents of welfare disbursal who 'give' welfare to the poor, and manage their disappointments and anger through the deployment of the 'gentle power of persuasion' which, of course, is historically perceived as typical of the ideal feminine. No wonder, then, that many women argued that their work was 'social work', and in an exceptional case, a president serving her third term in a village panchayat remarked that this was her way of performing charitable deeds:

> My father had given us some property when he died which he wanted us to devote to charitable purposes. I'd planted rubber in that plot and it yielded well. It is that money which I use to fund my work in the panchayat. The honorarium is a pittance, you know, and as president, you have to attend to everybody ... marriages, sicknesses, all kinds of collections.... I had donated the income from that plot to the poor much earlier, now I use it for this. Now the rubber's being replanted, and I'm a bit exhausted!

Such power allows the woman president a certain closeness— an intimacy—with welfare seekers, especially women. Our interviewees, across party lines, very frequently identified this as the defining quality of women's presence in panchayats. Interviewee after interviewee claimed that women are blessed with 'natural talent' that makes people open up to them and reveal their most intimate issues, while with men, there will always be aloofness. As another woman panchayat president who vouched very strongly for the efficacy of 'gentle power'—a form of power women could hold with full male approval—observed:

> When women presidents give their word on something, there is an advantage. Because people do feel we are more sincere, we are more forthcoming. Maybe that's because of our style. When it is a woman leader, she takes care to ask the person approaching her to take a seat. She speaks gently and sympathetically, reassuringly. She gives detailed reasons and assurances about the speediest disposal of the issue. Male politicians aren't like that. They will examine the issue and give a view, and the person usually has to withdraw and wait for further action. When it is a woman, they can approach us at home and there too, we will offer a seat and kind words.

'Gentle power', we found, was efficacious in many diverse situations. For example, it worked well in panchayats where the traces of earlier militant working-class mobilisations of the Left were still active. Kerala has had a fairly long history, stretching from about the 1940s to the late 1980s, of militant popular mobilisations often led by the Left parties, demanding welfare, in which State welfare was understood to be 'people's right', as above bureaucratic wrangling and, therefore, permissive of 'ethical illegality'. While this political culture has suffered seriously in and after the 1990s, it does persist, and sometimes strongly, in some villages. In these panchayats, welfare beneficiaries were impatient with the bureaucratic norms through which welfare handouts were administered and resorted more frequently to the older political language of welfare as 'people's right', the rules of which ought to be eminently bendable in the interests of the poor. Here, the women leaders, especially of the Left, had to mediate between the altered regime of welfare in the state and the militant poor. 'Gentle power' was found not only useful, but absolutely indispensable in such instances. Another instance where it worked was when the staff of the panchayat was difficult. Women leaders are extremely aware of the fact that precisely because local governance involves considerable bureaucratic tangle, the cooperation of staff— especially the secretary—is an absolute must for even the routine functioning of the panchayat. Here, they felt, there was entrenched patriarchy which could be 'softened' only through the exercise of 'gentle power'. This seemed peculiar to women—as one of them commented,

> Male panchayat presidents can be closer to the officers. After all they are men, they can all go off and have a drink or smoke together. But we can't do that.

Thus the exercise of 'gentle power' involves careful strategic moves, such as not ringing the bell for the peon, and instead picking up the files, walking to the concerned clerk's desk, sitting down beside the clerk, and getting the matter settled. The thin dividing line between subservience and gentility was sometimes blurred; the challenge was to keep it sharp and clear and this is where 'knowledge of the rules' mattered. Almost every woman leader we interviewed stressed that while docile behaviour can indeed be turned strategically into a useful tool, ignorance can only disempower. 'Gentle power', they say, comes naturally, but not 'knowledge of the rules'. Historically, the project of domestic-oriented 'female education' was rejected in Malayali society in the 1930s in the wake of the Great Depression, which forced many women of the emergent new elite into the labour market, especially into teaching and other professions deemed 'genteel'. More and more women sought to enter higher education in the 1930s and after, hoping to find such work. The history of women's education in Kerala is of course much celebrated: unlike elsewhere in India, high literacy rates have been characteristic of the Malayalam-speaking areas since the early 20th century and these achievements have continued to flourish later. Early access to modern schooling also meant that a considerable number of women entered higher education earlier and became familiar with modern governmental and disciplinary institutions. No doubt, it is this historical trajectory of education that works to women's tremendous advantage in local governance, which calls for handling a great amount of official paper work and decision-making according to the ever-changing rule and procedure. Some of the most interesting anecdotes we heard, retold by women leaders with a great deal of pride and pleasure, were about how they dealt with harassment from hostile bureaucrats and local politicians who were either envious or irritated by their uncorrupt and independent stance. For example, a Muslim woman president, serving a third term in local governance, told us about how a politically well-connected minor official had tried to bully her into approving a list of *anganwadi* workers:

These people think we do not know the rules. They are mistaken. We know procedure much better than them. This man [the auditor] was quite taken aback to see that I had kept the rules perfectly. He returned without a word. You can get a bill, a record here anytime, I told him. The four per cent commission is appropriated not by an individual but a semi-government institution.... They think that these women from Malappuram [a northern Muslim majority district of Kerala, thought to be relatively 'backward' in social development] will pee in their sarees out of fear if they quote us a few rules. Well, he learned a good lesson—that women here are like rockets with fire in their tails!

This woman leader nevertheless insisted that she did not want to be known as a politician or even as a developmental worker, but as someone 'capable of wiping the tears from the eyes of another'. Clearly, the combination of 'gentle power' and 'knowledge of the rules' worked well for her. However, we also found that where women have tried to combine the latter with political power—the political authority conferred upon the head of the panchayat as a Constitutional body—they have faced greater hostility. And a major limitation of women who prefer to stick to 'gentle power' is that while many of them have achieved considerable respect in their local community, very few have been able to significantly influence local developmental priorities. Some significant instances seemed to show that the support of senior leaders in high politics is necessary for women leaders to intervene effectively in local developmental priorities, which are otherwise laid down by the male-dominated party local committee according to the entirely non-local priorities set by the State leadership of the party. Only when the woman leader exercised 'gentle power', knew the rules, and also became influential within her political party did significant synergies grow between her achievements, which made her appear indispensable to local development.

And there were other limitations that the combination imposed: 'gentle power' tends to trap women leaders in the role of welfare distributors and limit their ability to influence local developmental agendas. Indeed, one gets a distinct sense of a frustration at confinement in many interviews. A woman leader who had just waxed eloquent about how she was loved by welfare beneficiaries in her panchayat for being accessible, suddenly mentioned her fear that this did not really empower *her*:

> The panchayat is always full of people. They are very free with me—they come right up to where I sit and speak to me, *mole*, *makkale* [daughter, child], I need this, I must have that ... even if they see quite well that I'm hard at other work. I wonder, isn't all this a bit too much? If it were a man sitting in that chair, this kind of behaviour wouldn't happen ... nobody would walk into the room without permission ... men are identified mostly with the party, but we are identified with the panchayat and so people take this extra freedom with us.

Moreover, despite their espousal of 'gentle power' as the best way to deal with officials, many women were painfully aware of their sheer dependence upon them, especially when support from the local party was shaky. Also, some pointed out that if they knew the rules, male leaders and panchayat officials had 'knowledge of bending the rules'! Women leaders are also painfully aware of the fact that for all their knowledge of the rules, they can hardly change any, as a woman leader pointed out humorously:

> See, it is all a husband–wife affair, even now. The Department [of Local Self-Government] is like the husband. He hands over a certain sum for various expenses to the wife, the Panchayat, in this story. The wife must spend that money according to certain established ways. She isn't free to change that way—even if things at home demand a change. She has to wait for his permission first. And that is hard to get! There is no consideration of whether the woman is capable, or is healthy, or has enough support. Uhuuh! At the end of the month the money must be spent in the right way. If not, she will be shouted at! We haven't even got past the husband–wife system over here, and we are expected to behave like empowered women!

DALIT WOMEN LEADERS AND THE DILEMMAS OF EMPOWERMENT

Interestingly, if expectedly, we found that the above combination was largely available to educated, middle-class women of Kerala's powerful new elite communities, Ezhava, Nair and Syrian Christian. Dalit women leaders, who had less access to it, were clearly faced with an uphill climb decidedly steeper. Historically, they have been confined to the margins of political mobilisations until recent times and so the present opportunities are perceived as doubly valuable. However, they present a series of tough challenges as well. The design of decentralised governance structures is such that group interests are acknowledged in welfare distribution, but leadership positions, such as that of the panchayat president, are supposed to be 'neutral', representing 'general' interest. Since the claims and interests of different social groups are acknowledged in the norms of welfare distribution fixed by the state government, 'neutrality' means the proper adherence to these norms. However, as many of our interviewees, both Dalit and non-Dalit, pointed out, the norms are often too rigid and following them too strictly would result in losses to the deserving poor. Thus, Dalit women presidents have to adhere to the neutrality mentioned earlier, but also try their best to ensure that their communities benefit most by bending (not breaking) the rules as far as possible—that is, by subverting the disciplinary apparatus to the greatest extent possible.

This leads to two kinds of dilemmas. Firstly, Dalit women have to both protect the interests of their communities *and* represent the panchayat generally. Secondly, the norms of welfare distribution have to be respected—indeed, defended as absolutely necessary—but stretched to the utmost so that the communities are served the maximum. Of these, the second dilemma is more pervasive. All interviewees agreed that, very often, welfare distribution did require them to bend the rules, especially when it came to spending funds earmarked for Scheduled Castes and Tribes. Here, however, there was frequent conflict between the president and the officials. In the case of a young Dalit woman president, a very assertive person, her office staff complained bitterly about how she had harassed them because they had refused to bend the rules for her regarding the distribution of funds to Dalit families for toilets. 'She locked the ladies toilet and walked away,' said one of the female staff. 'When we asked her for the keys, she refused to give them and said, "why don't you try the bushes outside?" Is she a woman at all?' The speaker of these words obviously did not see the point that the president was trying to make; all she could see was that the president lacked 'proper gender qualities' and hence the latter was presented to us as a 'rapacious, power-hungry, mannish woman'.

Interestingly, Dalit women perceived 'gentle power' quite differently: for them it was neither 'feminine' nor empowering but a strategic position to assume when the odds were stacked against you heavily. Secondly, they had to often openly state that welfare entitlements and reservations for the SC/ST groups were no favour done to them by the rest of society but an entitlement guaranteed by the State. In other words, they could hardly depend on love, sentiment, or affective techniques to secure these entitlements—they had to quote the rule straight. These women hardly evoke 'femininity'; they evoke more frequently their education. Another young Dalit president, of the Congress, told us that her education gave her the confidence to take on the vice-president of her panchayat, her senior in the party:

Don't try to control me because I am an SC woman, I said. He threatened to remove my whip. Ok, I said, please do. But there's an MA degree that the university has conferred upon me. You can't remove that, however you try!.... Senior leaders know that I'm putting up a constant fight with this man. They of course value me as an educated Dalit woman.

Dalit women also have to directly confront those who may try to harass them; they often do not have powerful supporters in the party who may try to mediate and resolve issues. This, as one Dalit woman president put it, makes them 'not nice all the time'. An anecdote related to us by a young and rather inexperienced Dalit woman president carried an important insight: if new elite women can afford not to highlight the power conferred upon them as the head of the panchayat, it appears that Dalit women can scarcely do so:

There was a Secretary here, a very vulgar man. He knew that I was inexperienced, my husband was not powerful in the party, we are poor, and I had become president only by chance. So he thought he could [sexually] harass me as much as he pleased. I had felt uneasy right from the beginning—his behaviour was quite sickening. He would try to touch me, poke me here and there. Initially I tried to keep quiet; it was such a disgusting thing to reveal! But one day he came in as if to give me a piece of paper—and crossed the limit. He tried to grab my hand, even as people were watching. That REALLY was the limit. I became president for the first time! I slapped him hard on his cheek. The man was stunned. He fell into the chair for a second, holding his cheek. 'Tcchii! How dare you sit down without my permission, you scoundrel!' I shouted. 'I am the president in this panchayat! Get up right now!' The man jumped up and left. He went on leave immediately and got himself a transfer. After that the members have been quite respectful, and some old sharks who had their eyes on me became quite disciplined.

'ROCKETS WITH FIRE IN THEIR TAILS'

The ideological roots of 'gentle power' are indeed very much in 20th-century social reform, which legitimated the social dominance of the communities that drew advantage from the massive social upheavals from the late 19th to the early 20th centuries. But, even if one were to imagine that it grew beyond its new elite moorings, it would still limit women leaders. It may make them more accessible to welfare beneficiaries, but this may not translate into greater acceptance of their rightful place in the political public. The 'peaceful' atmosphere that they seem to precipitate in the panchayat may look like a positive gain, but it may also help to entrench the idea that women are non-political, and thus help perpetuate their confinement in domestic norms and values. But it is clear that women leaders of local governance, even those who claimed that they were uninterested in politics, do recognise themselves as located within fields of political power, albeit reluctantly, and even as they proclaim themselves to be disinterested in political power. Part of their disaffection with 'politics' was precisely their perception that the public–political realm had deteriorated to the extent to which it was no longer shaped by political communities, but by various predatory interests. But many who voiced such views also perceived their entry into local governance as offering a degree of relief from confinement in the private, even as they pointed to its narrow focus and its distance from the political public. It is fascinating to note how the hope of entering a truly political community continues to glimmer, despite many negative experiences, in many of these narratives.

But also, it is no wonder that women leaders, even of the new elite, find 'empowerment' an ambiguous deal, something that enables and confines simultaneously. When asked about the notion of *shaakteekaranam* (empowerment), a dynamic Muslim woman president of the Muslim League from northern Kerala responded with a 'story':

> One day, a rocket and an airplane met in the skies high above. The plane was impressed by the rocket's fantastic speed, and told her, 'How fast you fly! What is your secret?' The rocket threw her a glance and said, 'Didn't you notice, my tail is on fire! You too would fly like me if your tail were on fire!' And then she continued, 'Well, I'm flying very fast, but I have no clue where I am going and whether I will come back home safe! You are flying slow, yes, but aren't you relieved that you know where you are going, and will get home in time, too?' Well, I think 'empowerment' is what the rocket is experiencing!

In putting it thus, she was expressing a wariness explicitly voiced by many Muslim League women leaders (who often remark how they are indispensable now, after the reservations, but are still denied formal full presence in their party), and implicitly, by a great many others. Yet, interestingly enough, the same woman who had vowed that she would never fight an election again, contested the panchayat elections of 2010 and is presently an elected member of the district panchayat! Empowerment—not to mention liberation—can never be linear. Kerala's women leaders of local governance live that complexity in their everyday lives.

◆

This chapter was first published in 2013 in the *IIC Quarterly*, Vol. 39, Nos. 3 and 4.

◆◆

Pardhan Gond Painting: Collecting Mahua
Artist: Saroj Venkat Shyam
All paintings exhibited during the IIC Festival of the Arts, 2010.

5
LABOURING INTELLECTUALS
The Conceptual World of Dalit Women

GOPAL GURU[#]

More than a decade ago, I was present at a conference that was held in one of the villages in the district of Karnal in Haryana. This particular conference, which was held to discuss the social problem of Dalit women in India, was attended by many Dalits, the majority of whom were Dalit women labourers. What was even more interesting about this conference was the hierarchical organisation of the occupied space along the gender and class line. This hierarchy was evident in the spaces that were occupied by three different sets of participants. Thus, those who occupied space inside the tent were Dalit women labourers who were not only constantly present in the tent, but were also actively engaged in listening to all the speakers on the occasion. The second set of participants included Dalit males together with non-labouring, English-educated female mentors for those women who were inside the tent. Members of this set were to be found either gossiping outside the tent, in the first case, or monitoring/mentoring the women labourers, in the case of the second. Mentoring and monitoring perhaps was required to attend to Dalit women's needs such as translation and interpretation of conference deliberations into their own tongue. Finally, on the stage were those who belonged to a different class in as much as they were educated and urbanised Dalit women and men who had come to make speeches for the benefit of Dalits.

This fragmentation of space, in effect, also provides Dalit males an opportunity to enjoy more autonomy in terms of participation in the deliberations of the conference. Most of them did not appear to be interested and were found outside the tent (*bahara*), thus leaving the women inside the tent. Such patriarchal attitudes did reproduce inner/outer dimensions in the Dalit public sphere. This ambition to control the outer indicates the paradox within Dalit imagination. At one level, they would like to fight their own marginalisation, as produced by the upper-caste public sphere, but, at the same time, they are also required to reduce Dalit women to the margins so that they occupy their own 'centre'. They require Dalit women labourers to create this margin so that they can enjoy their centrality within the space. This fragmentation of space might lead one to draw rather mutually exclusive conclusions that those who showed complete commitment to the cause for which they had gathered were serious about it. And, hence, they were driven by the ethic of conviction which, as a moral resource, can help those in question to enrich their understanding with much more transformative potential. Secondly, those who chose to remain outside the tent were conditioned more by compulsion rather than conviction.

Before I begin to argue in the rest of the essay that labouring Dalit women acquired a distinct subjectivity to themselves through their intellectual response to their existential condition, it is necessary to delimit the focus of the essay to the illustrations from Haryana, Bihar, West Bengal, Madhya Pradesh, Gujarat and Maharashtra. The case of Madhya Pradesh is interesting in as much as it is not Dalit women but tribal women who have represented *Modern Ambedkar in her Gond Painting* (Natrajan and Anand, 2011).

The central concern of this essay revolves around the claim that it is a particular kind of labour that provides an intellectual context for the feminist articulation in various forms such as tattooing, paintings and folk poetry by Dalit women labourers. Secondly, while these women enjoy autonomy in developing a distinct language for their articulation, they do draw on the intellectual resource that is available in Ambedkar. Dalit women, who do not have the privilege of a formal education, cannot access Ambedkar through discursive practices. They establish the connection with Ambedkar only through posing trust in his thought. To put it differently, they seem to have carried the force of conviction with them.

Let me explain in some detail why I privilege the labouring body as a crucial background condition, which has provided an intellectual basis for both creation as well as articulation of labouring

Dalit women's *self-perception of emancipation*. Labouring Dalit women do perceive the class and caste structures of domination, and they also take intellectual and political initiative to first interrogate these structures and then suggest its transcendence. Of course, the dominant perception is also active to attach a morally objectionable meaning to these women's bodies. The upper-caste landlord always constructs the labouring Dalit woman's body as an object of lust.

In the present context, I would like to define Dalit women's empowerment not in temporal, material terms that can be done through certain government policies. On the contrary, I define their empowerment in terms of their intellectual/spiritual stamina to produce the language of resistance, as formalised through their oral poetry. In my understanding, an oral capacity rather than textual skill becomes the epistemological basis for the creation of their conceptual language. Dalit intellectual empowerment could be defined in terms of the self-critique as well as the critiques of the dominating system. As a part of this empowerment, Dalit labouring women do produce a certain local language that is full of loaded meaning that has a bearing on their subordinated, suppressed life. For example, look at the following dictum in Marathi: '*Sarai Pakhal Kahi Nahi Sapala*' (Every attempt of mine to reform my husband and mother-in-law has failed). The following statement would show that the Dalit labouring women's critique is outwardly directed against the exploitative system. Dalit women, while working in the fields, would share with other women the following, '*Dhau! Dhau pishi pan datale nahi mishri*' (Whatever hard labour I put in is not enough for my meaningful survival). It is also possible to offer another dictum for further substantiation of the point under consideration. A Dalit woman labourer says, '*Bamanachya pori karoo noko tu guman! Tule pajin me pani dila asara Bhima na*' (Hey, Brahmin girl! Do not possess an oversized ego. I will flatten your ego as I am empowered by the enlightened way as shown by Bhimarao Ambedkar). These very expressions, when shared publicly, are made by Dalit women fighting a mute subject from within.

Let me begin with a claim that labour involves a bodily activity and bodily activity, in turn, generates power. Power generated through bodily activity removes the distinction between animal labour and human. To put it simply, both animals and humans generate power through physical exertion like ploughing the field. Bodily labour, thus, necessarily seeks to metamorphose human beings into tame animals. However, labour is not considered a preferred resource for producing knowledge. In fact, since Aristotle's time, bodily labour has been considered a source of contempt and disgrace (Arendt, 1958: 81–82). Aristotle considers labour as the meanest because it deteriorates the body (ibid.). In India, among labouring women, Dalits and Tribals form the most vulnerable sections. The bodily conditions of labouring Dalit and Tribal women indicate an alarming state of deterioration. Their malnourished bodies give us the feeling that many of them are dragging their bodies as if they are carrying their bones and mostly sick babies along with them while they walk (ibid.). It could be argued that such bodies, in Aristotelian reading, are worthy of contempt.

If labour is the source of contempt, then is it available for knowledge generation? For these Dalit women, what provides the basis for intellectual (reflection) activism—labour as a source of joyful experience or a painful experience? I believe that for them, labour is less of a joyful experience and more of a painful experience. It is painful simply because, for most Dalit women, it is physically exhausting as it tends to exceed limits of time and space. They work almost round the clock. Their work, like rag-picking and scavenging, is also morally demeaning, resulting in drudgery and wretchedness. They cannot escape this work simply because, among other things, their existential need to reproduce themselves individually (survival) forces them into such physically and morally tormenting labour. It is this experience, which is inherent in labouring activity, that triggers off the intellectual imagination, involving a search for an emancipatory alternative. For these women, alternative views of decent life find an echo in normative thought, as provided by Babasaheb Ambedkar. These women find Ambedkar's thoughts on self-respect and dignity most fascinating. It is also interesting to note that their access to this thought is cognitive in nature. Their literary sensibility, taking shape in the context of labouring activity, looks at Ambedkar's alternative as different from other thinkers, most particularly Gandhi. Why is labouring activity a source of intellectual activity?

First, there is a moral significance to Dalit women's labouring activity, in as much as it, due to its tormenting nature and coercive character, provides the necessary intellectually motivating, rather than stimulating, context. This context is morally significant as it forces Dalit women to produce tragic, rather than tantalising, insights into their understanding. Dalit women labourers seem to have adopted their own genre of folk poetry or painting that has definitely helped them to assign poignancy to their insights. It is the specific labouring context—for example, collective harvesting—that has enabled them to produce a particular or distinct form of folk poetry—*ovie*—in Marathi,[1] which belongs to oral tradition. Similarly, Godna painting by Dalit women from the Madhubani district of Bihar is also a distinct form of knowledge, which is an artistic abstraction of everyday labour done by Dalit women (Guru, 1997: 27; Rairkar *et al.*, 2011: 186–87). Put differently, it is clean labour that forms an epistemological basis for the creative imagination. The lack of formal education does not become a hindrance for such women as it may become for working Dalit women. To put it another way, we do not find many working (educated and urbanised) Dalit women producing oral poetry like ovie, as the preferred mode of their intellectual assertion. Conversely, one wonders whether a scavenging Dalit woman or the rag-picking Dalit woman have produced a distinct form of poetry (textual or oral) to represent their pain. I would like to further argue that obnoxious work like scavenging and rag-picking is quite alienating. It is alienating, both from the larger society but also from the self. This self-alienation does not encourage Dalit women to add any worth to their moral personality, neither does it encourage them to reflect on their predicament with intellectual creativity.

It is the collective nature of labour—for example, paddy plantation, or harvesting, or cotton-picking, or grinding the hand-mill in the home—that makes knowledge-generation a participatory activity. In the oral tradition, it becomes easy for Dalit women to make common efforts to add and subtract while translating their experience in an abstracted language of oral poetry or the texture of their paintings. In other words, the collective nature of labour discourages and sets aside individual attempts to conceptualise the experience on the field. Of course, they do not enjoy the leisure that is necessary to produce higher forms of abstraction or assigning a greater degree of elevation to intellectual creation. They remain content with producing elevation to their intellectual activity which is adequate to their own collective understanding. The language of labouring intellectuals is much more straightforward and direct in terms of its expression and also in terms of the power of its communication. As a number of studies show, Dalit women have invented a language of their own.[2] Dalit women from Bihar have also tried to make conceptual sense of their pain and used Godna as an idiom to make an elevated sense of Dalit emancipation, which they explain in terms of annihilation of caste and the restoration of *manuski* (dignity to themselves) (Guru, 1997: 27; Rairkar *et al.*, 2011: 186–87). Third, since Dalit women did compose their poetry spontaneously and shared oral poetry with their co-labourers right on the field, it served, at least in the past, as the site for its articulation and dissemination across several villages.[3] It is the unified labouring context across villages that made circulation of the ideal of dignity through ovie much easier. This site of production and communication is similar to the site of a shoemaker—a labouring intellectual—as perceptively described to us by Hobsbawm in his historical work on the labouring class in England (Hobsbawm, 1998: 53). In India, shoe-making is a collective activity. It involves collective labour rights: from skinning the raw hide to finished labour. Collective labour is distinctly related to the pre-modern form of leather production.

Finally, this mode of presentation has a definite politics, in that it does not require any interpreter. This is because oral poetry, unlike textualised Dalit poetry (Guru, 1997: 27; Rairkar *et al.*, 2011: 186–87) entails the metaphors that are unmediated and taken from the experience of the field activity. This kind of language format serves a cognitive purpose to generate a sharply polarised sense of one's own existential condition and those social forces (both non-Dalit and Dalit patriarchy) which are responsible for producing and reproducing such existential conditions. This language also performs another cognitive function in as much as it radically differentiates itself from other forms of representations. The literary creation of these women has a definite political purpose in as much as it seeks to disambiguate the upper-caste minds that choose to render the concrete caste experience as ambiguous. For example, the metaphysics that the defenders of casteism would put the caste beyond the realm of human social relationship, thereby suggesting that it is god-given and, hence, one has to accept it.

However, it is interesting to note here that labouring Dalit women's activism gets built up around the complex imagery of Ambedkar. Using their cognitive power they import, in their oral poetry, Ambedkar as a figure who intellectually dominates his adversaries.[4] When Dalit women turn their intellectual attention inward, they find in Ambedkar not an intellectual who takes on his upper-caste adversaries, but as a messiah super-intellectual who can help them cope with the pain that is resulting from domestic pain (Rairkar *et al.*, 2011: 186–87).

This kind of labouring intellectualism had the following distinct dimension to its expression. Firstly, arguably, Dalit women labourers enjoyed greater intellectual freedom from Dalit patriarchy. They did not require any intellectual assistance from the Dalit male who was actually in the textual mode of writing poetry (Gaikwad, 1993: 318). Dalit patriarchy did not object to such intellectual activism, partly because its impact was limited to the specific field and had unified gender boundaries, in the sense that these songs travelled from one group of Dalit women of one village to another in the neighbouring village. Secondly, these Dalit women enjoyed greater intellectual autonomy from the Dalit cultural establishment and could avoid depending on the latter for any kind of intellectual patronage. Neither did these women intellectuals lament the lack of recognition or exclusion from the larger intellectual sphere. They did not have to fight for the copyright of their intellectual creation. In another way, the logic of possessive individualism did not overwhelm their intellectual creativity. It is their experience, rather than the written text on Ambedkar, that made their literary creations resonate with Ambedkar's thought. Their commitment to Ambedkar's idea was unconditional. Their imagination was spontaneous; the language unmediated, taken straight from the field of experience.

However, it needs to be mentioned here that this oral tradition, within which labouring intellectuals took shape, is fading away fast, at least in Maharashtra. Growing labouring intellectual activism is also evident from other regions like Uttar Pradesh. There are three main reasons that can help us to understand this decline in labouring intellectuals in Maharashtra. First, TV serials and the discussion involving these serials have begun to impact Dalit women as well. Since most serials, even on

Marathi TV, are about '*Sas, Bahu*' themes, the mental preoccupation with such themes accompanies Dalit women right up to the field of agricultural activities. This changing cultural taste is significant, particularly in the case of Dalit women, because their literary expressions have been very vocal in criticising Dalit patriarchy. This, in effect, replaces the need to generate any purposive poetry depicting their existential conditions. These songs, as mentioned earlier, are the supplementation of the poetry on the field. Secondly, the cultural need to listen to Dalit music is fulfilled by professional Dalit women singers whose number is growing in Maharashtra. The need to comment on the general Dalit condition is supplemented by ever-growing popular music through cassettes and now CDs. Dalit women may not need to generate poetry on their own. Thirdly, there is a structural reason that can explain this decline in intellectual activities that was developed by Dalit women while on the field. Earlier, long hours of work did offer some space for Dalit women to formulate poetry right on the field. Dalit women could take a little time off to formulate their ovies. Unlike earlier times, today Dalit women are much more pragmatically conscious about their individual rights relating to fixed hours of labour and wages. This individualisation of interest has left little time for them to think through the idea of Ambedkar that is necessary to make collective sense of common interest. Finally, the growing migration of labouring Dalit women to urban centres has destroyed this need to create the oral poetry that once expressed both collective pains and the protection of collective interests. The nature of the work of rag-picking and domestic help in urban cities necessarily fragments the social collectivity that is so necessary to produce the collective consciousness that is built around intellectual resources, and that developed through the narrative mode of communication that was used by Dalit intellectuals to disseminate the ideas of Ambedkar. Finally, the handmill-grinding that once formed part of everyday labour in Dalit households, and hence provided the context for literary creation, has been replaced by electricity-driven grinding mills.

Although labouring intellectualism is disappearing from among Dalit women, particularly in Maharashtra, one can see the emergence of critical thinking. As a part of this, many Dalit women singers who, taking their cue from Ambedkar, are now are offering scathing criticism of the failing Dalit leadership from the state (Guru, 1997: 27; Rairkar *et al.*, 2011: 186–87).

For example, a popular song in Marathi by a leading Dalit female singer, Kiran Patankar, reflects on the nuanced character of Dalit cultural imagination.

> *Diksha Bhumi Bole Chaitya Bhumila*
> *(Diksha Bhumi, a place of Buddhist conversion in Nagpur, is requesting Chaitya Bhumi, the cremation ground at Mumbai where Ambedkar was cremated on 6 December 1956)*
> *Paratuni De Ga Bhim Maza Mala*
> *(Please give my Bhim back to me)*
> *Je Ale Bhima pathi, Sarve te swartha sathi*
> *(The post-Ambedkar leadership is self-interested)*
> *Vedana janun Ghei, Asa Nahi Kuni aaj Mitial*
> *(There is no ethical self who can understand the pain of a common Dalit)*
> *Jo to Beiman Hoi Dinicha aaj Mitila*
> *(Today every leader is dishonest to the Dalit cause)*

Similarly, we have Dalit feminist writings that have been asserting expressions—though far more nuanced—of their intellectual intention and intuition. In contemporary times, Dalit feminist intellectual assertion is being articulated on much more complex issues such as the Dalit feminist body through pages of the *Economic and Political Weekly*, and on the theme of sexuality, at least through regional research journals, particularly in Marathi. It will not be out of place to report here a very rich and, perhaps, bold debate that has been taking place on the issue of Dalit feminist sexuality, which has invoked angry responses from Dalit patriarchy. This debate, which took place in Maharashtra in the journal called *Pariwartanacha Watsaru* involves two leading Dalit feminist writers, Urmila Pawar and Pradnya Pawar, who have produced a complex understanding of sexuality. This, in my opinion, is certainly a new moment in the life of the Dalit feminist mind.

Although this requires full-length academic treatment, I am not going to deal with this aspect of intellectualism of working Dalit women. Instead, I would like to continue mapping the trajectory of the labouring intellectual, taking my cue from the Godna paintings of Dalit women from Bihar. The Godna painting, in my

Pardhan Gond Painting: Tree of Life
Artist: Dileep Shyam

Pardhan Gond Painting: Deer at the Water's Edge
Artist: Subhash Vyam

opinion, presents a much more fascinating and inspiring history of intellectual assertion by Dalit women.

Godna (art of tattooing) was adopted by the Imperial power in the provinces, particularly in Bihar and Bengal, to mark the bodies of prisoners, and had an indirect impact on the local configuration of power, signifying the dominance of upper castes (ibid.). In contemporary times, Dalit women have reinvested this historical intellectual resource—Godna—in not only representing the notion of nature and everyday forms of labour around them but also, in some cases—particularly from Gujarat—representing Ambedkar in their paintings (Anderson, 2000: 20). Of course, painting from Gujarat is different from Godna-tattooing. Today, Godna painting is aimed more at indicating the difference between the upper-caste Madhubani painting, rather than challenging the social relationship based on social dominance. In order to mark this difference, it is necessary to offer a certain historical analysis of the Godna as an act of subversion.

Let us begin with the assertion that Godna painting by Dalit women had a purpose to challenge social hierarchies in the society. This has been documented in one of the important studies done by a historian. Clare Anderson perceptively records the Godanewalia (tattooists), most of whom, according to his study, were from the lower caste.[5] Lower-caste, illiterate women (in today's terminology, Dalits) tattooed upper-caste bodies with the letters as drawn for them by the imperial authorities. Dalit women invested their extraordinary skill and transformed this mechanical work with monotonous order into decorative design which they inflicted on the 'pure' bodies of upper-caste prisoners. Thus, Dalit women used their aesthetic insight to make the mechanical arrangement of words look 'beautiful' on upper-caste bodies. Anderson points out that prisoners were not happy with these words, howsoever decorative they might have been (Anderson, 2000: 20). Although this study gives us an important clue to the subversion of social hierarchies through the tattooing of upper-caste bodies, it does not tell us anything about the following: was the tradition of painting natural to Dalit women rather than other women? Why did Dalit women develop Godna painting? Secondly, why did the colonial power choose Dalit women?

In response to the first question, taking a cue from Santosh Varma (ibid.), who has done extensive work on Godna paintings, it could be to affirm that Godna paintings continue to remain popular among Dalit castes. Santosh Varma further argues that for Dalit women, Godna was an attractive alternative which, at a symbolic level, replaced real ornaments with ornaments in decorative designs. Decorative Godna designs around their neck and ankles were made to get the aesthetic pleasure of ornaments.[6] This tradition of tattooing among Dalit women perhaps solved the problem of imperial authority which, as has been mentioned by scholars, found it difficult to locate Indian tattooists who could tattoo the prisoners.[7] This assignment empowered Dalit women to inflict markers on upper-caste bodies that always treated Dalit bodies as repulsive and, hence, unseeable.

Tattooing by Dalit women may be seen as an act of inversion of Manu's codes, which had prescribed demeaning ornaments for Dalit women so that they could be easily identified and avoided whenever they were allowed to enter the public sphere. They were forced to wear ornaments made of iron or raw, inferior metals. Secondly, the legal sanction that sought to legitimise touch through tattooing, in effect, undermined social hierarchy. However, in contemporary times, one can see a qualitative change in the social perception of artists from among Dalit women whose paintings now depict Ambedkar in a three-piece business suit. Modern Dalit women's painting also suggests the shift from the body as the site of cultural imagination, to Ambedkar as the symbol of social revolution, that has been a new development in Bihar. As a consequence, one can trace the trajectory of the intellectualism of Dalit women labourers from Bihar who made their statement with decorative tattooing, then penal tattooing and, finally, shifted their intellectual focus to paintings of Ambedkar on paper. While one welcomes the more institutionalised and visible intellectualism of working Dalit women, at the same time one is worried about the growing threat of elimination of subaltern intellectualism among Dalit women labourers, at least from Maharashtra.

◆

This chapter was first published in 2013 in the *IIC Quarterly*, Vol. 39, Nos. 3 and 4.

NOTES

1. This is my field observation of women from the Nalanda District of Bihar. However, such women could be found in more backward districts of every region of India.
2. This is the collection of Godna Paper Paintings, documented by the Dalit Foundation, Delhi.
3. The work of Santosh Varma was shared with me by Manindra Thakur, who teaches at the Centre for Political Studies, Jawaharlal Nehru University, Delhi.
4. In this category there are several Dalit writers, both male and female. Prominent among them are Daya Pawar, Baburao Bagul, Narayan Survey, Namdeo Dhasal, Hira Bansod, Pradny Pawar, Nalini Somkuwar.
5. Dalit Foundation.
6. Manindra Thakur.
7. Ibid.

REFERENCES

Anderson, Clare. 2000. *Legible Bodies: Race, Criminality and Colonialism in South Asia.* Oxford: OBERG.

Arendt, Hannah. 1958. *The Human Condition.* Chicago/London: University of Chicago.

Gaikwad, R.D. 1993. *Ambedkar Chalwalichya Athwani.* Marathi. Pune: Sugawa Publication.

Guru, Gopal. 1997. *Dalit Cultural Movement and the Dialectics of Dalit Politics in Maharashtra.* Mumbai: Vikas Adhyayan Kendra.

Hobsbawm, Eric. 1998. *Uncommon People: Resistance, Rebellion and Jazz.* London: ABACUS.

Gye, Potovie and Hema Rairkar. 2011. *Dr. Babsaheb Ambedkarnchya Athwaniche Atmabhan.* Pune: Sugawa Publication.

Natrajan, Srividya and S. Anand. 2011. *Bhimayana Art by Durgabai Vyam and Subhash Vyam.* Delhi: Navayana Publishers.

◆◆

6

CZARINAS OR GIRL FRIDAYS?

Women in the Corporate Sector

PUSHPA
SUNDAR[#]

Pictures of smiling, elegantly dressed, Indian women CEOs of large national and international companies can beguile one into thinking that, at least in the corporate sector, women have got their due. However, this is wishful thinking rather than the reality. As the English say, 'one swallow does not a summer make'. Overall, the number of women in the corporate sector is still low and the number of women in senior management even lower. The corporate world has been traditionally dominated by men and continues to be so.

According to the most recent *Human Development Report* of the United Nations Development Programme (2013), the overall participation rate for women in the workforce is itself very low, at only 29 per cent as compared to 80 per cent for men. Partly, this is due to the lower female literacy rate of 62 per cent as against 85 per cent for men. Therefore, it is not surprising that women in the corporate workforce are estimated at only 30 per cent of the total workforce of corporate India.

The distribution of this workforce is very uneven in different sectors of industry. The services sector employs the greatest percentage of women employees; and within this sector, the financial services and insurance, IT industry, professional services, and media and entertainment industries employ the largest number, according to the Gender Gap Reports of the World Economic Forum. The sectors that employ the lowest percentage of women are automobiles, mining and agriculture.

There is also discrimination in wages and opportunities. Gender inequality in the workplace is exhibited in various forms, such as occupational segregation, gender-based wage gap and discrimination. Working women have constantly battled against not only horizontal segregation, but also, the separation of women and men into gender-specific jobs. Although Indian law legislates equal wages for equal work by men and women, in fact, women's remuneration is lower. According to the Global Gender Gap Index, 2009, of the World Economic Forum, women's estimated earned annual income (approximately ₹55,790) is less than a third of men's income (approximately ₹174,102). However, the perceived gap in wages for similar work is a little narrower, with women's incomes perceived to be roughly two-thirds of men's incomes.

Even where they are employed in significant numbers, such as in the IT and the hospitality industries, the gender ratio is skewed heavily in favour of men with the ratio of men to women ranging from 2:1 to 24:1. Most women are employed in junior positions and there is a significant 'pipeline leakage' from junior to middle-management ranks. They are estimated to hold less than one in eight management roles in Indian companies and this falls to one in twenty at executive levels. Advancement of women in management jobs has not kept pace with the corresponding increase in the number of working women. Their presence at senior management levels is negligible.

Multinational corporations operating in India have a better record, with one in five women in management and one in ten in executive roles, but the balance is still rather skewed.

Although the numbers of women graduating is almost 50 per cent of the total number of graduates, only 10 to 15 per cent of students admitted to the Indian Institute of Management (IIM), or the Indian Institute of Technology (IIT), which would guarantee entry to senior management levels right away, are female. Consequently, although many are entering management positions, there is a bottleneck at the middle management level.

Even at the senior management level, women are still fewer when it comes to board-level positions in Indian companies. It is estimated that out of 1,112 directorships of 100 companies listed on the Bombay Stock Exchange, only 59 positions, or 5.3 per cent, are held by women. This compares with 15 per cent in Canada, 14.5 per cent in the US, 12.2 per cent in Britain, 8.9 per cent in Hong Kong and 8.3 per cent in Australia.

In December 2005, the Confederation of Indian Industry (CII) released a study, 'Understanding the Levels of Empowerment of Women in the Workplace in India', covering 149 large- and medium-sized companies across regions. The Report highlights the fact that women comprise 16 per cent at junior management levels, four per cent each at middle and senior levels, and only one per cent in organisational leadership positions, i.e. as CEOs.

On an average, women account for six per cent of seats on corporate boards, and eight per cent on executive committees. That is strikingly low when compared with Europe and the US, where the comparative figures—though still low—are 17 per cent and 10 per cent, and 15 per cent and 14 per cent, respectively. According to the survey conducted by MyHiringClub of more than 1,400 companies in India, women constituted just 6.69 per cent of the total number of board members in 2012.

The negligible presence of women at the board level is also borne out by *Fortune* magazine's annual listings. As of 2006, over 77 per cent of the 200 largest companies in the world, as ranked by *Fortune*, had at least one woman director on their board. It also mentions that only 36 per cent of Indian companies have women holding senior management positions as compared to 91 per cent of companies in China. India ranked 30th in terms of the presence of women directors of companies.

The failure to reach top management positions is for many an indication that a 'glass ceiling' operates to prevent women from advancing in their careers. The glass ceiling comes in many forms: women's under-representation in the corporate hierarchy, gendered wage gap, occupational segregation, discriminative corporate policies, lack of attention to the specific needs women have, sexual harassment at the workplace, exclusion of women from informal networks, among others.

To describe and measure the discrepancies between the job opportunities and wages available to women, and those of men, the global Gender Gap Index was introduced by the World Economic Forum in 2006 as a framework for capturing the magnitude and scope of gender-based disparities and tracking their progress. India's position on this index was 105th of 135 economies surveyed, while China was far ahead at 61st place. The United States (52 per cent), Spain (48 per cent), Canada (46 per cent) and Finland (44 per cent) have the highest percentage of women employees at all levels among the responding companies. India is the country with the lowest percentage of women employees (23 per cent).

Female employees tend to be concentrated in entry or middle level positions and remain scarce in senior management or board positions in most countries and industries—the more senior the position, the lower the percentage of women. A decade of data reflects only a marginal change in integrating female talent on parity with males.

According to the WEF's *Global Gender Report 2010*, the average number of women holding the CEO-level position in all countries surveyed was a little less than five per cent. The sectors attracting the greatest percentage of women overall also tend to have the greatest percentage of female board members or female CEOs. An exception is the agriculture sample, where the number of female board members is above average despite the low overall percentage of women employed by the industry.

It may well be asked whether this situation is a result of the socialisation of women, their low aspirations or their values, or is it because institutions need to be reshaped to accommodate them? Is there a prevalence of gender biases and discriminatory laws? The answer to all the questions would be, yes.

A prime reason why few women reach the top and are stuck at the lower rungs is a patriarchal culture, and social and cultural practices in both society and corporate workplaces, which militate against more women in the workforce and also against their achieving their full potential.

India is still very much a conservative, traditional society and a woman's role is seen primarily to be that of a homemaker, not a career woman. Family responsibilities must come first and personal fulfilment later. In order for this to happen they are socialised into seeing themselves as subordinate to men who will make all the important decisions, especially those related to the external world. Their self-perception, therefore, is that of a follower, not a leader. It thus becomes difficult for them to assert their rights or see themselves in leadership roles.

The gender-based roles they play in the family and in society, irrelevant though they are to the workplace, are carried into the workplace. Consequently, even though many young Indian women seek employment, their exit rates are high once they marry and have children, or have to care for elderly parents or other relatives, and they leave before reaching their rightful place.

Given the patriarchal social structure and mindsets, women are also faced with stereotypes and pre-conceptions—that they are fragile and lacking in the qualities that are considered useful to be effective managers. Traditional masculine traits have a higher value than feminine traits in the management world. Top posts are generally characterised by aggressive masculine values and suitability for these jobs is decided mainly by males, even though women's success in banking, financial and HR services shows that their innate qualities of empathy, intuition and other 'soft' skills are equally valuable in determining company performance. When they enter the workforce they face other obstacles, although the 'double burden' of holding a job and looking after the family is undoubtedly the greatest of these preventing women from moving up the corporate ladder.

In 2009, a study, 'Women Managers in India: Challenges and Opportunities' by the Centre for Social Research (CSR) finds that women are primarily placed in non-strategic sectors and have positions with titles but little real power or supervisory authority, rather than in those sectors that involve financial decision-making or revenue-generating responsibilities, such as sales and production, positions that are critical for advancement to the top. Since the position which an individual holds within the organisation shapes their traits and behaviour, they do not exhibit the qualities needed for leadership.

Other factors hindering women's career growth are: discriminatory appointment and promotion practices; male resistance to women in senior/top level management positions; absence of policies and legislation to ensure participation of women; absence of women in the boardroom; decision-making processes to ensure pro-women measures in companies/establishments; smaller numbers in a company which limit bargaining strength; absence/non-existence/non-participation of women managers in forums/unions/bodies within and outside the organisational structure; and limited opportunities for leadership training and demonstrating competence.

Women's career paths are apt to be more interrupted than those of men which are typically linear, and this impedes women's progress to top positions. Frequently, women take a break when they go on maternity leave and give up their careers to take care of their children. If companies don't have gender-sensitive policies and don't offer work with flexi-time, women usually don't want to return to work. Sometimes, they lose confidence in their abilities after a long gap, especially when their colleagues have moved on to better positions.

Women, unlike men, set greater store by a good work/life balance and, therefore, are willing to make compromises about their career growth. They want flexible work hours, ability to work close to home, or at home. At times, women don't want to work late hours for fear of personal safety, and justifiably so, as it turns out. They may also refuse promotions, if posted away from their families, in order to keep the family together. Since men do not have such compulsions and put careers before a life/work balance, companies see hiring men, especially at executive levels, as a less troublesome option.

Some companies, or at least some male managers, blame leadership styles adopted by women and their unwillingness to promote themselves as one of the causes for their stagnation in the company hierarchy, although both are not necessarily true or widespread.

Another reason for their exclusion from top jobs is their lack of informal networks: men have old-boys' networks which help them with contacts and conducting business over dinner and drinks at clubs. Typically, for women such socialising for business purposes does not come easily. They still bear the larger burden of family responsibilities than men and so have less time for such formal and informal networking which, moreover, is also often socially disapproved of.

Thanks to their socialisation, women managers also have their own inner battles to fight. They generally don't have fixed career goals, and many women do not aspire for higher management posts which will automatically bring in greater responsibilities, including late hours and travel, and they fear that they would not be doing justice to their family. Another result of this socialisation is a lack of determination to overcome the obstacles that keep them from accomplishing their goals. The lack of visibility to senior leaders and an insufficient investment in women leaders also hold them back. Mentoring plays an important role in the advancement of women into management positions, but often such mentoring is not available or is limited, as is the lack of access to training for career development.

In sum, women's double burden and the lack of gender-sensitive work policies are the major obstacles in their career path. Given the shortage of skilled workers in India, it is, nevertheless, important to encourage women to join a company, to enable them to achieve their full potential and to retain them once they have joined.

Gender diversity in the corporate workplace offers several benefits. It is universally recognised now that the quality of a country's workforce—its education levels, its skills and productivity—is its most important development resource and determines its competitiveness. But not so well appreciated is the fact that gender equality within the workforce enhances productivity, economic growth and competitiveness. Women have certain inherent advantages over men which makes them natural leaders if only they are *allowed* to lead.

Women can lead naturally without being authoritarian; they tend to be less egotistical; have higher degrees of efficiency, focus and pragmatism, as well as empathy for staff. Women have certain inherent strengths, honed by raising children and managing families with limited budgets—namely, relationship-building, empathy for clients and staff, multi-tasking and strong communication skills. They also have strong problem-solving and analytical skills, and an ability to listen which, if harnessed, can lead to substantial economic benefits.

In 2010, the United Nations Development Programme sponsored the *Asia-Pacific Human Development Report*, released in March 2010, which states that the lack of women's participation in the workforce costs the region billions of dollars every year. In countries such as India, Indonesia and Malaysia, conservative estimates show that GDP would increase by up to 2–4 per cent annually if women's employment rates were raised to 70 per cent, closer to the rate of many developed countries, and if women are given the same rights, responsibilities and opportunities as men.

A 2007 Mckinsey study, 'Women Matter: Gender Diversity, a Corporate Driver', too showed a link between a company's performance and the number of women serving on the Governing

Board. According to a 2003 study by Catalyst, a leading researcher of women in the workplace, Fortune 500 companies with the highest percentages of women corporate officers yielded, on an average, 35.1 per cent higher return on equity than those with the lower/lowest percentages. Clearly, the women in these companies were doing something right which steered their companies on the path of growth. Companies whose policies are more inclusive in approach and committed to gender equity, gender balance and diversity are also found to retain the best talent from both genders.

The good news is that with social change in the past two decades, this dim scenario has begun to change, opening doors for more women, especially in business sectors such as technology services, finance and banking, and retail. A significant change is that men and women are being employed in the same roles within a company, whereas earlier, even in the most diverse of organisations, there was clear demarcation as to what was a 'woman's job' and what was not. Further, with the increasing number of women graduates opting for technical and mainstream study courses—which were otherwise considered a man's domain—women are likely to increase their representation in several sectors considered non-traditional so far.

One of the major contributing factors has been globalisation, which brought increasing numbers of multinational firms into the country with their more progressive work practices. Alongside, the increased role allowed to the private sector, as a result of economic reforms begun at the end of the 20th century, has facilitated a slow but definite rise in the number of women in this sector. The emergence of service sectors such as tourism, hospitality, media, entertainment and BPOs has provided increased opportunities for women's success. The situation has begun to improve, particularly since 2011.

Today, there are a number of women CEOs and directors of companies, as well as women in senior management positions. Typically, women in senior management positions in the corporate world fall into one of several categories: women entrepreneurs such as Kiran Mazumdar Shaw of Biocon; Deepa Soman of Lumiere Business Solutions; Shahnaz Hussain of Shahnaz Beauty Products; Paru Jaykrishna, CMD of Asahi Songwon Colours; Meena Bindra, Chairperson, BIBA and many others have perhaps faced the hardest battle, especially those who have opened up non-traditional fields such as biotechnology, as demonstrated by Shaw.

A second category, that of women in family businesses, has perhaps had less of a struggle because they were often groomed for these positions by the family. Nevertheless, women such as Shobhana Bharatiya, Chairperson and Editorial Director of Hindustan Times Media; Mallika Srinivasan, Chairperson of TAFE, who also has the distinction of being the head of a company dealing with agriculture-related engineering products; Roshni Nadar Malhotra, Executive Director and CEO of HCL Corporation; Priya Paul, Chairperson of Apeejay and the Park Hotels chain of boutique hotels, have proved their own worth, taking family firms to new heights.

Perhaps the largest category is that of professional women whose rise has been a role model for countless women. Starting at the middle rungs they have risen to the top through merit to feature among Fortune 500's top global CEOs. They are found at apex positions of large banks—for example Chanda Kochhar, CEO of ICICI Bank; Shikha Sharma of Axis Bank and Naina Lal Kidwai, India Head of HSBC Bank—at the head of MNCs, with one of the most celebrated CEO's being Indra Nooyi, Chairperson and CEO of the MNC, PepsiCo., rated as number one on Fortune's list of the '50 Most Powerful Women' and sixth on Forbes' list of the 'World's 100 Most Powerful Women' in 2010. Other well-known women CEOs and directors of Indian firms include Sminu Jindal of Jindal Saw Ltd.; Reliance Infrastructure's Leena Srivastava; Radha Singh of Yes Bank; Renu Sud Karnad of HDFC Ltd.; and Vinita Gupta of Lupin.

Women professionals today are also directors of consultancy companies such as the Boston Consulting Group and Mckinsey, of PSUs and other public limited companies. They have all played an important role in India's economic rise, have vindicated women's potential to be as good in business as men, as well as provided inspiration for other women although there is no evidence, either positive or negative, that they have actively encouraged other women. What binds all these women is the fact that they have broken stereotypes and traditional mindsets, and have all managed to think out of the box while showing great leadership qualities.

Their success has stimulated a demand for increasing gender diversity at the workplace, with a focus on inducting more women in critical roles and on company boards. Some of India's top companies are reported to be giving specific mandates to head-hunting firms to fill senior and middle management positions with women. The change is being seen largely in potential CEOs, which is strengthening gradually. Reportedly, a global engineering major recently asked an executive search firm to hire a woman CEO for their India centre, indicating that new sectors are opening up to women. In some MNCs in particular, CEOs and top leaders are accountable for promoting and mentoring female talent.

While all this is good news, it should not lull one into thinking that the goal has been reached. On the contrary, there is still a long way to go. While governments must play a role in creating the right environment for improving women's economic participation, particularly through maternity-leave policies and childcare provision, it is primarily the responsibility of companies to create ecosystems where the best talent—both male and female—can flourish.

What is needed is commitment from top leadership, sensitising male managers and making men part of the solution, because men constitute 80 per cent of the workforce. Their mindsets will have to change. Companies also need to invest in training and confidence-building measures, flexible work schedules, and more mentoring, among other measures. Some companies have already put such measures into place.

For instance, British telecom major Vodafone India has started an executive committee level mentorship programme for high-potential women in middle management to propel them to the top spot. Additionally, it is mandatory for senior leadership teams to have one woman among their numbers—what the Telco calls the 'Plus One Target Programme'. Mahindra Satyam kicked off a programme 'Starting Over' last year, aimed at getting senior women associates aged between 35 and 40 years back to work. Encouraging women's talent should start right from the beginning and they should be supported and mentored throughout their careers.

In general, Indian companies prefer to put in what are called gender-neutral policies as against affirmative-action policies. Affirmative-action policies refer to quotas and targets and positive discrimination in favour of women, such as giving them extra marks in assessments. This is in line with the affirmative action taken to promote Scheduled Castes (SC) and Scheduled Tribes (ST) and minorities by the government. While UK and US companies have the most extensive spread of affirmative action, Indian companies have not adopted it widely, just as they have not in the case of SCs and STs. Instead, they favour gender-neutral policies.

Gender neutrality implies that companies should avoid distinguishing people by gender in order to avoid discrimination. Traditionally, organisations have unconsciously followed a male model of ambition defined by anytime/anywhere, i.e. high mobility and ability to work long hours. Such criteria show a positive bias towards male employees, putting women at a disadvantage.

A gender-neutral approach would emphasise delivery of results rather than hours put in, or mobility. Similarly, a gender-neutral policy would not expect career paths to be linear but take into account career breaks. This model would benchmark women employees coming back after a break, on the basis of their experience/achievements rather than when they joined and left. The concept of following a gender-neutral policy has gathered momentum because it is seen as a policy that provides *both* genders opportunities to balance work and personal/family life. Gender-neutral policies deal with unconscious bias rather than offer positive discrimination.

While gender-neutral policies for breaking the glass ceiling are welcomed by most women in the corporate sector, many women in top positions do not believe that diversity, especially at the Board level, should be mandated and quotas enforced. These women have made it to the top on their own merit. Like other women who have breached traditional male strongholds such as the senior administrative services, police, the army, or aviation through sheer hard work and merit, they believe that while back-end support such as coaching, mentoring and other facilitative measures should be put in at entry and middle levels, quotas and other mandatory measures would be short-sighted and counter productive for companies. A mandate should set the direction desired but should not be blindly followed, and only competency should guide the selection for highest levels. Focus should be on the large number of women executives who are stuck at middle level positions for years and budgets should be allocated to re-skill and re-train them for higher positions.

Nevertheless, taking in parallel the affirmative action debate for Dalits, Other Backward Castes and minorities, there are a few voices that urge some leeway for women even if they are not equal to a male candidate in terms of capability. So far, the government has refrained from mandating affirmative action for women at any level, and hopefully companies will see it in their own interest to increase the number of women at all levels and will take the action most appropriate for their companies. Results are what will matter, rather than any ideological position. Meanwhile, it is also up to the women who have made it to the top to go beyond being role models and holding out a helping hand to those left behind in a far more proactive manner than they have done so far.

◆

This chapter was first published in 2013 in the *IIC Quarterly*, Vol. 39, Nos. 3 and 4.

◆◆

7

LEADERSHIP FOR WOMEN'S EQUALITY AND EMPOWERMENT IN HIGHER EDUCATION

KARUNA
CHANANA[#]

OVERVIEW

Girls and women are entering schools and colleges in ever-larger numbers almost all over the world, although access to education remains a challenge in many countries. There are hopeful signs of change according to the *World Atlas of Gender Equality in Education* (UNESCO, 2012). It highlights the fact that dropout rates are higher for boys than girls in 63 per cent of countries. Additionally, women are a majority in tertiary (higher) education in two-thirds of the countries which provided data. But this is not so at the highest levels, namely, Ph.D. graduates and researchers in which men are 56 and 71 per cent, respectively; in other words, the higher the level, the lower the representation of women students. The situation is similar in India. At the research and Ph.D. level, Indian women are about one-third of enrolment.[1] Another trend is that there is a subject-wise variation in access, for example in law (25.6 per cent) and engineering (28 per cent) in which men dominate (University Grants Commission, 2011–12). Further, even if their enrolment at the undergraduate level in commerce and management is increasing, they may still not be taking competitive tests in equal proportion to men.[2]

In spite of these trends, women, though small in number, are entering the hitherto male-dominated professions, slowly and gradually. For example, in India, three women topped the Chartered Accountancy examination in 2011 and their pass percentage was higher than that of men. In 2010, the top two candidates and five out of the first 25 in the civil services examinations were women. These women are harbingers of change, no doubt, yet they remain a small minority and are not reflective of a broader trend. Women's near absence in top management positions across the board is now well known. In the higher education sector, too, they are almost invisible at the top. It is by now well established that a majority of the senior positions in the universities are held by men, while women are concentrated at the lower rungs. Men also hold most of the decision-making positions, namely, membership of executive, academic and administrative committees. Therefore, a pertinent question: why do women academics stagnate and remain relatively disadvantaged when it comes to promotions and leadership positions?

The search for the answer to the question led to research on higher educational institutions, or HEIs, their organisation and functioning. A critical outcome of these researches was that higher educational institutions are not gender-neutral in their organisation and functioning (Blackmore, 1999; Brooks and McInnon, 2001; David and Woodward, 1998). Researchers and activists have also highlighted socio-cultural factors such as the impact of socialisation and social expectations, which are internalised by women, which affect their goals and aspirations, on the one hand, and institutional barriers to women's advancement in education, on the other. Therefore, women's invisibility at top levels in the system also became a focus of study and research.

The capacity-building programme of the UGC, of which I write, is based on the premise that there are sufficient numbers of qualified women to take up leadership in higher educational institutions, provided they could be propelled and empowered to come out of their comfort zones and work toward a definite goal with a clear vision. Women have to see the structural and organisational barriers that prevent them from reclaiming their place, and to take up positions of administrative and managerial leadership. They have to be provided the capacity to perceive it, and to overcome it in the institutions in which they are located.

WOMEN IN THE ACADEME

Research on gender and leadership in universities has exploded two myths relating to higher education. The first relates to the objectivity and neutrality of organisations. However, the underlying assumptions about the objectivity of organisations, their functioning and the place of women in them have been re-examined from a gender perspective, which led to the understanding that the organisations are social constructions. Further, the system being gender-neutral is not enough, it has to be pro-women, i.e. make conscious efforts to integrate women into the system; neither access nor equal participation in leadership and management is possible. The second myth was that women who can access higher education are from privileged homes and, therefore, they do not have any problems in the academe. However, the gendered processes and structures in higher education are critical to the creation and reproduction of gender differences. The reality of academic life for women, irrespective of their class, is different from the ideal of academic institutions, and the universities do not promote merit and equality (Chanana, 2008: 8–9)

Several explanations are forthcoming to explain the inequalities in the career patterns of women and men in the universities. For example, women move up slowly because they face a 'chilly climate' in the universities; because they generally enter the profession at lower levels and stay there in spite of publishing and undertaking research and acquiring doctorate degrees, i.e. even when their academic profile fits in with the 'hypothetical' paradigm of a male professional. Others introduced the concepts of 'the greasy pole', the 'glass ceiling' and 'the man-centred universities' or masculinist institutions, which limit career patterns for women. Therefore, such patterns of inequality demonstrate that the negative effect on women's academic careers is not due to lack of capability (ibid.).

What, then, is it to be a woman in the academe? How do women negotiate the contradictions between the personal and the professional, which have to be resolved in order to move on as academics. They have been referred to as 'ambivalent academics'. The majority of women in universities are also regarded as the 'outsiders and the disadvantaged', 'the others' or 'double deviants' (Baglihole, 1994: 15–28). They are double deviants because not only are they working in the male-dominated world, but are also expecting equal rewards. Acker and Webber describe their position as 'liminal'—in the process of becoming something else. They are the 'outsiders within' ... they are unable to just 'be': they must always be something (2006: 486–96).

However, all women are not outsiders; nor do they all play subordinate roles. For example, although higher education is, by and large, dominated by men who wield power not only as heads of the HEIs, but also permeate decision-making bodies in and outside them, power is not equally distributed or wielded. Therefore, all women may not be equally exploited or subordinated. Some exceptional women get positions of leadership and responsibility by virtue of their merit and competence. They retain their distinctive style of functioning and interaction, while some remain mere tokens.

Male academics who join colleges and universities have the advantage of seeing men in positions of leadership, decision-making and authority. In addition, they are also under the tutelage and sponsorship of male professors who are their role models and mentors. It is also easy for them to get into the 'old boys' networks and to have access to these for support. The sponsorship of senior male professors has a positive impact on the self-esteem and confidence of younger men academics. All this helps men in the recruitment and selection process. They are also better placed in terms of promotion prospects; to gain research experience; to get invited to conferences for paper presentations and, ultimately, for publications. Networking is the key to academic success and is difficult for women to establish, especially across gender (Chanana, 2003: 381–90). All-male networks are effective for lobbying and facilitate exchange of critical information. They are also the platforms for converting 'informal visibility' to 'formal visibility', that is, securing memberships of important committees and leadership roles (ibid.). They are visible in a university's academic administration at the higher levels.

Women are not included in the all-male formal or informal networks in departments and universities, thereby excluding them from national and international networks. No doubt, women have started establishing girls' networks, yet such women are still a minority. They need the same socialisation into the profession that men get from male networks and sponsors.

The understanding that there are very few women in leadership positions in the administration and management of universities and about the gendered organisation and functioning of the universities, on the one hand, and the constraints of socialisation, dual careers and their impact on the goalposts of women faculty, on the other, led to the formulation of a programme to build the capacity of women faculty to enlarge their professional activities and to move up in the system. It was based on the premise that there is a glass ceiling and that women faculty have to understand the gendered nature of higher educational institutions, their governance and the male-centred academic leadership. Further, it is not true that there are not enough qualified women for top positions in higher educational institutions. Additionally, they had to come out of their comfort zone and make efforts to create or, if necessary, demand their rightful place in the system. In order for women to understand the system and themselves, the Capacity Building of Women Managers in Higher Education programme is a step in that direction.

CAPACITY BUILDING OF WOMEN MANAGERS IN HIGHER EDUCATION

The National Educational Policy, 1986, highlighted the role of education in promoting equality for women in the educational system as well as in empowering them. It recognised the fact that women needed special supports and programmes in order to bridge the gap between the participation and representation of women and men in the higher educational system. This programme is a very critical initiative in empowering women to claim due space for themselves and also move to the top.

The programme is about management and administration of higher educational institutions. It is also about enabling women to do management with a difference; to understand issues of leadership, power and governance and how they operate in the system. It assumes that these trained women will make a difference in the system when they occupy leadership positions.

The programme started in 1997 under the auspices of the University Grants Commission (UGC) in collaboration with the Commonwealth Secretariat, London. The initiative was taken by the then chairperson, Professor Armaity Desai. After the first collaborative workshop in 1998, the UGC took over the responsibility of training women faculty. Since 2004, it has been continuing with vigour and commitment in the different regions of India.

The focus of the workshops is dual, i.e. on the self and the institutions. On the one hand, the institutions do not provide an enabling environment and, on the other, women themselves also do not play a proactive role in moving up. It focuses on five dimensions: women's study perspective, governance, academic leadership, personal and professional roles, and on research—all with a focus on women. It encourages the participants to look inwards to go beyond the stereotypes of the self. It also moves away from an essentialist position regarding the differences between women and men with the expectation that women will find their place in the top administrative and managerial posts in higher education. Interdisciplinarity is the core of the programme because participants are invited from across all disciplines. It is also inclusive in terms of caste, tribe, religion, class, rural/urban and tribal locations.

THE TRAINING PROGRAMME

There are two levels of workshops which form the core.[3] The first-level workshops are Sensitisation, Awareness and Motivation, or SAM workshops. The second level are Training of Trainers workshops, or ToTs. Selected participants from SAM workshops are invited to ToTs. They become SAM trainers. Both these workshops are being held since inception in different parts of the country and have reached out to about 4,000 women in the furthest corners of the country. By now, the programme has trained a mass of local faculty members, or SAM trainers, who are pushing the programme forward at the local level.[4]

SAM workshops are residential in the main, while ToTs are all residential. In SAM workshops the focus is on understanding the self in a social context; to motivate the women and to reorient their thinking; and to help them understand the systemic barriers faced by them. ToTs give them the skills to become SAM trainers.

SAM workshops bring together quite a number of women who have never moved out from their homes and towns and also have had no academic interaction or exposure outside their institutions. Some of the participants have shared their experience either at SAM workshops, or at ToTs, of how their visions about their academic career and about themselves have changed due to the impact of the workshop.

OUTCOMES

While the purpose of the programme may seem to have well-defined parameters, namely the five dimensions around which the workshops revolve, the outcomes were several, which are emphasised and highlighted during the workshop. The positive responses of the participants came from across different disciplines. It is pertinent that they could relate to and understand the purpose and aim of the workshop. It is illustrated below with some cases,[5] cutting across disciplines and location. It was hoped that in order to build their capacities and in order for them to create space for other women and for themselves, they had to have self-esteem and confidence, the willingness to work beyond the classroom and contribute to the institutions' development, take on larger roles, proactively network with co-participants and, through them, with others.

> When I was invited to participate in a SAM workshop for Capacity Building for Women Managers in Higher Education in 2007, I had no idea that my entire life was to take a new direction. I expected it to be another welcome diversion like the seminars we routinely attended. The actual experience was a turning point in my life. Though the first two days of the workshop seemed to befuddle me with serious issues being diluted through games, energisers, chart-making and impromptu-talking, it sank in that these were a means to an end. While, on the one hand, I realised that the information I was struggling to gather from diverse sources was handed down to me in organised modules and manuals, on the other hand, I was surprised at the transformation I was undergoing. I was actually talking about my own self both in personal and professional spheres. I was busy interacting, connecting, overcoming inhibitions, putting forward opinions on a platform elsewhere denied to me. One of the greatest gifts of the SAM workshop was the network which it left in its wake. Even after the workshop, I reached out to the participants, read and wrote profusely for various opportunities it opened up for me. I gained confidence and took giant strides in decision-making. I realised I could become an able administrator too and then the SAM workshop and the ToTs with the many workshops, where I had gone as a Trainer, gave me opportunity to meet the great women whom I admired and wanted to emulate— independent, out-spoken, disciplined yet generous, egalitarian. I have never looked back since the workshop gave me the motivation to search for my true self. I have written, published, organised,

taught, trained, motivated, counselled, advised with a never-before effectiveness. I have faced interviews with greater command and determination. My selection and subsequent joining a University in 2012 is another stepping stone to help myself and others like me. My sincere gratitude to the SAM movement, which has made my life meaningful.

(Case 1, humanities, undergraduate women's college in a suburban location in the east)

Several faculty members reported that they had started using the interactive methodology of the workshops in the classroom for better outcomes. There were others who were already active teachers and researchers, had a good record of publishing and undertaking research projects when they attended the workshop. One of them was thinking of continuing her academic career after retirement at 58 (most state university teachers retire at this age). An administrative position was far from her thoughts.

I attended a SAM workshop in December 2010. I was due to retire from State government service as Associate Professor of Economics employed in an aided College. I wished to continue my interest in the field of higher education. But how? ... Maybe I can start a study centre of the university. Maybe I can join Central University. Or I can become a Principal of a self-financed College (private unaided for profit college). But the prospect of becoming a Principal was not an attractive option at that point of time.

At this juncture I attended a SAM workshop, which gave me a new perspective about the need for women to be in administrative positions. I became aware that there were very few women at the higher echelons of administration and leadership. I learnt that as an administrator one has the power to bring about changes. Very attractive indeed! The prospect of becoming a Principal, all of a sudden, became very bright and beckoning!

The change in attitude, which happened in my case, should happen to every faculty member and Principal. Now I am working as the Principal of a co-educational college in a rural area. I am in a position to instil self-confidence in my young women students and faculty. I take crucial decisions keeping in mind the

special needs of women students. I am very happy I attended the SAM Workshop.
(*Case 2, social scientist, undergraduate co-educational college in a rural setting in the south*)

Working in a small city or in a town with a secure job in a government-aided institution puts women in the comfort zone from which they do not want to move. They need a push and a reorientation to move out and up.

I was a typical college teacher who was involved only in the teaching of women undergraduate students in a women's college. I had studied in the same college. As such, I was living in a closed and secure environment. I had a comfortable life, both personal and work-wise.

Later in 2005, I got the opportunity to attend ToTs at Chennai. This was the first time I stayed away from home for six days, leaving my small children. I was feeling very guilty. But, to my surprise, I did not actually miss my family as much as I thought I would. On the contrary, I realised that my role was not limited to my family and teaching in college. I found a new world unfolding in front of me. I realised that women can, and need to, actively participate in the broader academic life. On my return, I took keen interest in the Centre for Women's Studies, which I was heading. From a time when travelling alone was an unthinkable task, I started travelling far and wide in the cities and interior parts, conducting awareness programmes. As a SAM trainer I also transacted manuals in colleges and universities as well as organised four SAM workshops in my college to motivate women faculty around the college. Later, I applied for the post of Controller of Examinations in a specialised Central University in a metropolis. I was selected for the post. This was a challenging situation. If I chose to accept this post I had to migrate from my home, where I was settled for the last 25 years. After long discussions with my husband, we decided that I should take the plunge and accept the appointment. Before 2005, I would not have dreamt in my wildest dreams that I would leave my home town and take up a position outside of my college and the city.
(*Case 3, economist, undergraduate women's college in an urban location in the south*)

They could balance their personal and professional lives better, even though they began to give some/more time to the latter than they had hitherto done. Again, the imperative of networking and not taking things lying down came home to a participant who was happy being a good teacher and an academic, irrespective of whether she had even considered administration.

I became a full professor in January 2002 and was eligible to be the head of the Department, as the current head had already completed three years. Headship is by rotation for the duration of three years. However, another male professor, who was promoted with me, was made the head in May 2002. I took it lightly, as I was of the nature that I accepted what was given to me. I was also satisfied academically. I had set up the first-of-its-kind labs and had also started a new M. Tech. programme in Electrical Power System Management.

In 2003, I attended a SAM workshop and that changed my perspective about taking things lying down. In 2005, when the Department headship was again to be decided, manipulations started at the highest level to deprive me of headship a second time. However, I could sense the undercurrents and discovered that the ordinance regarding the rotation of headship was being modified by the academic council of the university to give it to another male professor.

I mobilised enough support from the Vice Chancellor, the AC and EC members and the teacher's association of the University. The resolution to amend the ordinance was withdrawn from the AC agenda and I was given the Headship in May 2005. The advantages of networking that I learnt from SAM and also the confidence to reclaim what was due to me helped me in becoming proactive in my professional development. I have researched, published extensively and become a part of the international community of professional scholars.
(Case 4, computer scientist, in a central university in a metropolis in the north)

A scientist has become a very active SAM trainer and supporter. Although she holds the position of Principal of a medical college and is extremely busy, she always finds time to contribute to the programme. She, too, was perplexed when she was invited to attend the workshop.

> I attended the SAM workshop in 2006 in Chennai. I was already a professor and head of the Department. When I was invited to attend the SAM workshop the words 'Capacity Building' aroused my curiosity. Till then I had no experience of interacting with colleagues from social sciences and humanities. That was another reason for me to want to know what was in store for me. At that point I had already done my Ph.D. and was thinking of further research. The SAM workshop inspired me for leadership. I started thinking of becoming a Vice-Chancellor, but I knew that there was another stepping stone to achieve that. This made me think about aiming for the post of Principal. I worked for it and got it. I learnt several lessons from the SAM workshop. These were: inspiration for leadership; the will to balance my personal and professional roles and face any situation; how to manage my department; one must be knowledgeable to be able to hold leadership positions; the criticality of networking; the self-confidence to take decisions on my own (women have a tendency to react when offered a position, to react with, 'I will think about it', consult the family or the husband). I also learnt to recognise my capacity and my strength so that I could identify the role that I could play in a given situation. I have an established position within my profession due to my contribution to knowledge through research, publications and participation in professional conferences.
>
> (Case 5, pharmacognosy in the field of pharmaceutical science, principal of a medical college of a private[6] university located in a metropolis in the south)

Reclaiming one's due place in academia, balancing personal and professional lives and, in fact, becoming a confident member of the national and international academic community, thereby becoming visible: these are also the outcomes. Some participants may have experienced or gained from one or more of these dimensions. There are exceptions who underwent a holistic development.

> On getting nominated by the Vice-Chancellor to attend the SAM workshop in 2003, I wondered what there would be for me as a

Botanist and Environmentalist. This theme seemed to be suitable for social scientists. Nonetheless, I came and attended. After a day or so I realised its importance and was happy that I came. I could interact with faculty members from across disciplines. I understood that there were common issues and problems on which we can unite and also network. Here, my vision broadened and I came out of the narrow confines of thinking only as a scientist working within the narrow confines of the laboratory. As a result of this I have been able to do more and better quality research, effective teaching, and actively participate in academic governance and leadership. Subsequently, I have published many research papers in reputed national and international journals. I have also handled several research projects funded by different agencies in addition to organising a number of national and international seminars, conferences, refresher courses. I regularly attend national and international conferences, seminars and workshops. I have collaborations with many National and International Institutions. I have also received a national award.

SAM has also helped me in executing bold and daring academic decisions. I recall my experience of how the physical space, which was critical to the functioning of our Department, was being taken unfairly away by a very undemocratic decision of the institution. I networked in the university to win support and evolved strategies to thwart the attempt to give the floor of our Department to another. I even brought the media in to highlight the issue and succeeded in retaining the physical space. I might not have done anything had I not attended SAM.

I also learnt to balance my personal and professional life better. For example, I could withstand a crisis in my personal life and continue to work professionally without upsetting the former. I would say that the impact of SAM was holistic.

(Case 6, botanist and environmentalist in a state university in the north)

CONCLUSION

Overall, the gains have been multifaceted and have surpassed the expectations of those of us who were involved in the initial designing and implementation of the programme. No doubt, the takings have varied from participant to participant, yet the positive feedback and responses of quite a few instils confidence that the programme has made a difference and empowered the women faculty who have been associated with it. They begin to understand the systemic barriers and how to overcome them, along with the barriers ingrained in them through the socialisation process at home, which also underlie the educational structures and organisations.

For quite a few, teaching is no longer a routine activity. Being a teacher is not just confined to the classroom, but beyond. They have become aware of the larger role that they can play within their institutions. This perspective leads to their empowerment and propels them to leave the 'sticky floor' in order to realise their full potential in a larger network of women faculty from across the country. They can see the interplay of structure and power within the institutions and its negative impact on their educational careers. Some of them are very visible in the profession, have the leadership qualities and persona as well as a curriculum vitae that is required to be at the top. The question is: will they move to the top?

◆

This chapter was first published in 2013 in the *IIC Quarterly*, Vol. 39, Nos. 3 and 4.

NOTES

1. Overall, women formed 41.5 per cent of total enrolment of 169.75 lakh students enrolled in various courses at all levels in 523 institutions of higher education (including 30 Central, 130 Deemed, 345 State Universities, and five institutions of national importance) and 33,023 colleges.
2. In 2010, Indian women formed 24 per cent of candidates who sat for the global management test, GMAT, compared to 63 per cent Chinese women (Chhapia, 2011: 6). Further, there is not much change in their proportion since 2006 when it was 23 per cent.
3. There is a third category of workshops for skill training in specific areas and issues that are pertinent in higher education management. These are called MSEM, or Management of Skill Enhancement Modules. Eight areas have been identified and modules prepared. These are: stress and time management, ICT in higher education, sexual harassment, advocacy, financial management, communication, human resource management and team building.
4. The National Information Development Cell (Nidcell) has also been established under this programme. It provides several supports, but a salient one is the creation of a network through Google, thereby enabling all the participants to communicate with one another through email.

5. I am grateful to those of my colleagues who have willingly shared their thoughts and experiences with me. They are all senior academics and have well-established positions in their subjects or disciplines and are holding leading positions in their professions. Some have received national and international awards.
6. The programme also invites a limited number of participants from private, unaided (self-financing) HEIs.

REFERENCES

Acker, Sandra and Michelle Webber. 2006. 'Women Working in Academe: Approach with Care', in Christine Skelton, Becky Francis and Lise Smulyan (eds.), *The SAGE Handbook of Gender and Education.* London: SAGE.

Baglihole, Barbara. 1994. 'Being Different is a very difficult Row to Hoe: Survival Strategies of Women Academics', in S. Davies *et al.* (eds), *Changing the Subject: Women in Higher Education.* London: Taylor and Francis.

Blackmore, Jill. 1999. *Troubling Women: Feminism, Leadership and Educational Change.* Feminist Educational Thinking Series. Buckingham: Open University Press.

Brooks, Ann and A. McInnon. 2001. *Gender and the Restructured University.* Buckingham: The Society for Research into Higher Education and the Open University Press.

Chanana, Karuna. 2008. 'Women in the Indian Academe: Difference, Diversity and Inequality in a Contested Domain', *Journal of Indian Education,* National Council of Educational Research. New Delhi, August 2008, pp. 5–19.

Chanana, Karuna. 2003. 'Visibility, Gender and the Careers of Women Faculty in an Indian University', *McGill Journal of Education,* Vol. 38, No. 3, Fall.

Chhapia, Hemali. 2011. 'Chinese Women School Women in Business', *The Times of India,* Mumbai edition, 21 March, p. 6.

David, Miriam and Diane Woodward. 1998. *Negotiating the Glass Ceiling.* Washington D.C.: The Falmer Press.

The Times of India. 2012. 'Gender Atlas', *Education Times,* Delhi edition, 19 March, p. 3.

University Grants Commission. 2011–12. *Annual Report.* UGC: New Delhi.

◆◆

ANATOMY OF A CHANGE
Early Women Doctors

MALAVIKA
KARLEKAR[#]

I n 1901, Swasthya, a monthly periodical on health and medical treatment published from Calcutta, commented that while earlier, during marriage negotiations, lineage was a significant consideration, it was now important to have 'a thorough and detailed search' into the groom's educational background. In addition, cautioned the editor of the periodical, as 'arthritis, tuberculosis, asthma and venereal disease are often passed on to the offspring', genetic disorders within a family needed to be looked into while negotiating a match. A healthy couple would ensure healthy offspring to keep the line of inheritance intact. By the end of the 19th century, it is quite possible that among more enlightened families, some covert enquiries on such matters by those competent to do so were not regarded as being out of order. Early marriage, frequent childbirth, high maternal and infant mortality, and morbidity rates meant a demand for women in the field of health; only the most anglicised would ever consider consulting a male doctor; for the large majority, childbirth meant the services of dais or even older women in the family. Seeking—and being allowed—specialised medicare was empowering for Indian women as they quickly learnt that they had a right to control some aspects of their body. An entrenched patriarchy too realised that the ideal of a healthy, modern family necessitated quality care for women.

That the climate was clearly right for the emergence of medicine as an acceptable profession is well typified through the life stories of two quite exceptional women from different parts of India. Kadambini Basu was born on 18 July 1862 to the wife of Braja Kishore Basu, headmaster of a school in Bhagalpur in Bihar.

On 31 March 1865, Yamuna Joshi, who was re-named Anandibai by her husband, was born in Kalyan, a small town near Mumbai. Kadambini's family was a part of the migratory chain from East Bengal (present-day Bangladesh). The migrants came to Calcutta and the towns near it to seek their fortunes. Braja Kishore was committed to women's emancipation and set up an early women's organisation in Bhagalpur. He was also an active member of the reformist Brahmo Samaj and in 1876, his associates were able to persuade him to send Kadambini—a mere 14-year-old—to Calcutta, to the progressive Hindu Mahila Vidyalaya, the closest approximation to a girls' boarding school. Students were taught all subjects, contrary to the prevailing view that science and mathematics might overload their brain too much. The school adopted norms of Western social etiquette and students had to speak English during school hours, eat at the table with crockery and cutlery, and wear dresses. Music was taught, along with sewing and knitting, and girls took turns in being kitchen monitor and also learned to keep the school's accounts. They were taken in carriages on excursions and picnics by enthusiastic teachers who subtly used recreation as a learning experience. The school was run by Dwarakanath Ganguly and other like-minded Brahmos committed to the evolution of the well-educated, genteel Bengali lady, the *bhadramahila*.

In 1882, Kadambini and Chandramukhi Basu, a Christian from Dehra Dun, became the first women graduates of the University of Calcutta. By this time, nursing and medicine had started looking to Indian girls as possible recruits. The continued existence of the tradition of purdah and a decline in popularity of births at home made it essential to train Indian women doctors. Kadambini was excited at the prospect and after her graduation, decided to study medicine at the University of Calcutta. In those days, only a BA degree was adequate for admission to the course.

Despite an official commitment to expand medical education among women, the authorities grudgingly granted her a place. It was a momentous year for Kadambini as, on 12 June 1883, shortly after entering the Calcutta Medical College, she married Dwarakanath Ganguly, by now a 39-year-old widower with six grown-up children. Their marriage caused quite a stir even among the reformist Brahmo Samaj: not only had the couple made up their own minds, but the 21-year-old would now have to adjust to a household of motherless children—the oldest of whom was not much younger than she was—and combine housewifery with a difficult academic programme. Not an easy task, made more difficult by a lack of support from Dwarakanath's close friends and associates. It is not known how Kadambini's family reacted, but we can assume that they did not actively disapprove, as this would surely have been reported in the press—no doubt with some glee.

The Calcutta Medical College, where Kadambini was the first woman to be admitted, was established in 1835 and was the first Indian institution to teach Western medicine. Its elegant Palladian-style building, eminent teachers and elite students (they had to be competent in English) aimed at creating a cadre of young men committed to becoming well-educated professionals. Interestingly, in Bengal, where the 19th-century reform movement was involved with issues relating to girls' education, early marriage, polygamy and, by implication, marital relations (the Age of Consent debate in the 1890s, for instance), discussions on changing medical practices and the issue of women as doctors, neatly fitted into the extending discourse.

And so, in 1886, Kadambini became the first Indian woman doctor trained in India; in the same year, Anandibai also qualified in the US. By this time, the newly established Lady Dufferin Fund (formally known as the National Association for Supplying Female Medical Aid to the Women of India) to provide professionally trained Western and Indian medical practitioners for *zenana* women was rapidly expanding. It was the first systematic attempt at institutionalising Western medicine and its use among Indian women. Kadambini was quick to take advantage of the facilities being made available and, in 1888, was appointed a doctor at the Fund on a monthly salary of ₹300—an extremely generous amount at that time. In those days, both men and women who studied medicine and later became doctors had compromises to make with a traditional caste-based upbringing. Not only did they handle and dissect dead bodies, but they also treated people of all castes and religions. In addition, though there was no dress code, the men wore the white coat over their clothes and often abandoned *dhotis* and *chaddars* for a trouser and shirt. By this time, as dress reform for women had brought into vogue the contemporary sari and blouse, there are photographs of Kadambini wearing a sari in the style introduced by Jnanadanandini Debi, wife of Satyendranath Tagore.

With it, she has an elaborate long-sleeved blouse with ruffs at the wrist, and a shawl around her shoulders.

Kadambini, we know from her step-granddaughter Punyalata Chakravarty's memoirs, *Chhelebelar Dinguli*, had a flourishing practice and a variety of patients, including women from the Nepalese royal family; the Queen Mother loaded her with gifts, which included a pony. In no time, pony rides became popular with her two young children and step-grandchildren to whom Kadambini was a remote and busy figure, different from all the other women they knew. Her clinic-cum-study held many mysteries for them, including a human skeleton. As Kadambini commuted between patients in a horse-drawn carriage, she occupied herself with the ubiquitous feminine occupation of the times—making fine lace, for which she was also reputed. It is likely that nearly all her patients were women and delivering babies in hospital her major preoccupation; in those days, large families were common and the death of at least one infant or baby was not unusual.

Shortly after the establishment of the Indian National Congress in 1885, Dwarakanath Ganguly started agitating for women's representation at the annual sessions, and the 1889 Bombay session had a delegation of six women, including Kadambini. The following year, at the Congress session in Calcutta, she delivered the vote of thanks in English, becoming the first Indian woman to speak on such occasions. Kadambini was hailed by Annie Besant as 'a symbol that India's freedom would uplift India's womanhood'. Upset with her success and visibility, a conservative section of Hindu society launched a slander campaign against Kadambini; though she combined her roles of a doctor and a good wife and responsible mother very successfully, orthodox men viewed Kadambini's career with deep misgivings. In 1891, *Bangabasi*, a journal of the traditionalists, accused Kadambini of being wanton and wayward. Dwarakanath and other eminent Brahmos committed to women's emancipation—the latter appear to have overcome their objection to the marriage—launched a counter-offensive in the columns of a Brahmo publication, the *Indian Messenger*. Articles strongly criticised those who felt that the 'maintenance of female virtue is incompatible with their social liberty'. Dwarakanath was vindicated when the editor of *Bangabasi*, Mohesh Chandra Pal, was fined ₹100 and sentenced to six months' imprisonment.

At a time when women of her own class had barely started coming out in mixed company, riding on the crest of·success and public acceptance, Kadambini went to the University of Edinburgh for another degree. In the 1890s, the Edinburgh Medical School continued to be the Mecca of medical education and it would not be unreasonable to surmise that Kadambini's decision to study there was based on information gleaned through word of mouth, experiences of those who had returned, as well as newspaper reportage. By the beginning of the 19th century, it had started admitting foreign students and in 1874–75, a little less than a third of almost one thousand students were from other countries, of which 57 were from India. Over the years, more Indian men must have joined, though Kadambini was the first woman to be admitted. When she arrived in Edinburgh—no doubt after a long sea journey and then by train from London to the north—prejudice against women students had just about abated; in fact, women's medical education in the city had had a colourful past.

From the early years of the 19th century, Edinburgh had been actively involved in women's access to medical education, and a little research into the city's role in British medical history makes Kadambini's choice very clear. In 1812, James Miranda Stuart Barry obtained a medical degree from Edinburgh. Barry served for 46 years in the armed services, going on to be Inspector-General of Military Hospitals in Canada. When Barry died, it was discovered that the person was actually a woman, and thus, technically, the first woman medical graduate! Non-acceptability of women in a male-dominated profession was surely one reason for Barry's subterfuge, so carefully maintained. And this was not all: in 1869, Sophia Jex-Blake applied to study medicine at Edinburgh and together with six others, was accepted.

At the very outset, Sophia had made her reason for wanting to be a doctor quite clear in *Medicine as a Profession for Women*, a booklet she had published in the same year. She said, quite unequivocally, that women's health suffered at the hands of male doctors who did not have adequate information on health and hygiene practices and, of course, childbirth was a concrete instance that required a female practitioner. She continued, 'I know of more than one case where ladies have habitually gone through one confinement after another without proper attendance, because the idea of employing a man

Kadambini Ganguly
Courtesy: Malavika Karlekar

Anandi Gopal Joshi (31 March 1865–26 February 1887)
Source: http://xdl.drexelmed.edu/item.php?object_id=001128

Anandi Gopal Joshi with her signature
Source: http://commons.wikimedia.org/w/index.php?search=
Anandibai+Joshi&title=Special%3ASearch&go=Go&uselang=en

was so extremely repugnant to them.' Another popular myth was that women had less confidence in their own sex, and would rather be attended to by a man. Sophia contested this with more solid data. An alarmed London-based Society for Apothecaries passed a regulation preventing women from sitting for medical examinations. Clearly, feminine interest in medicine had to be nipped in the bud.

The medical profession was divided. Doctors, professors and the public had strong feelings about women's access to medical education. A visibly undecided University Board hesitated over the necessity of separate classes for women, though, as some teachers did not admit them, the seven young women had little option but to attend separate lectures. In no time, the media got involved and from the pages of *The Times* and *The Scotsman*, the debate soon spilled over onto the streets. In November 1870, there was a riot at Surgeons' Hall when a protesting crowd tried to prevent the seven from taking an anatomy examination. Sophia wrote, 'An angry mob were [sic] filling up the road! They abused us in the foulest language [and] slammed the gate in our faces!' This incident came to be known as the 'Surgeons' Hall Riot'. More obstacles followed and for six years women were not allowed to sit for their final examinations. Instead, they were to be awarded a certificate of proficiency that allowed them to practise. Sophia and her companions—now known as the Edinburgh Seven, or *Septem contra Edinam* (Seven against Edinburgh)—were understandably furious and went to court. It was not until 1877 that each woman in the group was allowed to qualify as a doctor with a degree.

When Kadambini came to the University of Edinburgh, in no time she would have heard of the histrionics over women's medical education, and of the Edinburgh Seven's success. It was a good time to be a woman doctor as an exciting, proactive role for medicine had begun. Not only could women be trained doctors, but also, by this time, interventions at childbirth were considerably enhanced by the use of ether. This was not simple either: its use was denounced by the Church, which believed that it was women's destiny to suffer pain. It was only in 1853, when Queen Victoria—who combined her many roles with rare clarity, if not panache—used it during the birth of her ninth child, that upper-class and conservative opposition to this great alleviator of pain abated. In 1892, Kadambini, who had decided against a degree (perhaps it was too expensive and would have meant a long time away from her young family) received two licentiates—LRCP (Edinburgh) and LRCS (Glasgow). No doubt her months had been eventful, packed with learning, discussions and debates on women's wider rights. She must surely have been impressed by what her predecessors had gone through in those very streets and buildings, melding her own determination and commitment with that of Sophia's intellectual and activist heirs.

It is likely that Kadambini wrote many letters to her children and her husband, the redoubtable Dwarakanath. Perhaps she even kept a diary in addition to her medical notes when she was a student in Edinburgh. However, practically no accounts survive of her many roles and identities during her long and eventful life. All we have to go by are family anecdotes and some factual information. How did a self-respecting Brahmo like Dwarakanath Ganguly garner the funds for his wife's education? Did he take loans from admiring friends? Though she had won scholarships for her education in India, there is no evidence that these were available for the expensive course abroad. Was the family cash-strapped as a result? How did she adjust to a different cuisine and the misery of surviving a sari-clad Scottish winter? Or did she wear long skirts and blouses—by then, emancipated Bengali women like Swarnalata Ghosh wore nothing but Western dress in conservative Calcutta, as did some younger women from the Tagore family. We know that Anandibai, on the other hand, wore only the nine-yard sari, draped not unlike a *dhoti*.

◆◆◆

If there is a tantalising silence that surrounds the life and times of Kadambini, Anandibai Joshi left behind a rich body of correspondence with her husband, Gopalrao, and others. Though there was Grant Medical College teaching Western medicine in Bombay, Anandibai did not attend it. Nor did she have any regular schooling. Her husband was her chief instructor and, in any case, it was not usual for traditional Marathi Brahmin girls to go to school until the last decades of the 19th century. Kashibai Kanitkar's 1912 biography, the first Marathi one in this genre to be written by a woman, quotes extensively from letters, information given by Gopalrao, and some family friends. On the other hand, the fictionalised *Anandi Gopal* (1962) by S. J. Joshi, which follows her life very closely, projects Anandibai more as a victim, a helpless recipient of all Gopalrao's depredations and untrammelled ambition. Joshi's novel was immensely popular, an English translation appearing 30 years later. Meera Kosambi's account of Anandibai's life strikes a keen balance between fact and myth: as a reputed historian of 19th-century Maharashtra, she was well placed to do so.

Though Anandi is the heroine, in Joshi's version, the postmaster Gopalrao's life-consuming obsession with women's education makes the reader focus on him—even in anger. Abuse of his child-wife and violence towards her—all in the name of making sure that she had a single-minded interest in education—are described in detail. So is a cringing, dominated Anandi. One day, when she was found helping her grandmother in the kitchen, Gopalrao flew into an uncontrollable rage and beat the young girl with a bamboo stick. The neighbourhood was agog: husbands beat wives for not cooking—but whoever had heard of a wife being beaten for cooking when she should have been reading? Soon after, a son was born to the couple—but died shortly thereafter. He had been treated by the local doctor, as the one who was trained in Western medicine was a Christian and an outsider; neither Anandi nor her child could be seen by him, lamented Joshi. Maybe this loss encouraged Gopalrao and Anandibai to think of medicine as a profession for women.

Soon, Gopalrao's fixation with educating his wife grew exponentially, and he decided that with the help of a Mrs Carpenter, a Philadelphian missionary, he would send Anandibai to America to train to be a doctor. Before she sailed for New York from Calcutta (where her husband was then employed), Anandibai addressed a full hall at a public meeting. This was in 1883, not long after Kadambini and Chandramukhi Basu had graduated from Bethune College. Anandi spoke of the lack of women doctors and added, 'I volunteer to qualify myself as one.' She went on to point out that existing midwifery classes were not sufficient, and in any case, 'the instructors who teach the classes are conservative and to some extent jealous'. Brave words from a mere slip of a girl who, Joshi writes, hid timorously behind her husband as loud applause broke out. But did she indeed do so? Or was she smiling proudly at the audience?

Anandibai's sea voyage was anything but pleasant. She had to share the cabin with a missionary, Mrs Johnson, whose attention was focused on converting the young girl. Anandibai resisted but was badly shaken by the time she reached New York. She was met in New York by Mrs. Carpenter, her mentor, who instantly bore her off to her family home in Roselle, a three-hour train ride away. Mrs Carpenter's calm disposition was a great relief and soon Anandibai became an honorary member of her family, and good friends with the three Carpenter girls. There was no question of conversion. The furthest Mrs Carpenter got to try and pressurise Anandi was when, on a cold and miserable New England winter's day, she arrived at Anandi's door with a skirt and blouse in hand. But to no avail—what would Gopalrao say, shuddered Anandi!

On a family picnic, a photographer was sent for and Anandi mailed the visual back to Gopalrao, to whom she wrote diligently every week. Gopalrao was not pleased; who was the man she was smiling at (the photographer, presumably), and why was her sari not covering her breasts adequately? Anandi was crushed, but overcame her sorrow by burying herself once again in her books at the Women's Medical College in Philadelphia. Moments of reflection on a tortured past were expressed freely in her letters to Gopalrao: 'I had no recourse but to allow you to hit me with chairs and bear it with equanimity'; these emotions were offset by her own motivation to study medicine. Feted by the Carpenters' friends at elaborate non-vegetarian meals, Anandibai did not change her dietary habit of not eating meat. And she even hosted a grand party for her friends with vegetarian fare that she had cooked. On ceremonial occasions, Anandi would wear a resplendent red silk sari, many sets of bangles, a bejewelled choker around her neck and a nose ring.

It was not long before the strain of a different culture, the cold and damp affected her and Anandi developed a persistent cough. To add to it all, Gopalrao decided to come to America. Latterly, Anandi had felt even more estranged from him; his sarcastic barbs about her having become at heart one of 'them', unbearable. By the time Gopalrao arrived in Philadelphia, he was met by Dr Anandibai Joshi. This was in 1886, the same year that Kadambini qualified to be a doctor in Calcutta. It was time to go home, and a visibly sick Anandi boarded the ship with her husband. Soon after returning to a heroine's welcome in Bombay, consumption claimed yet another victim, and the 21-year-old died without a chance of practising in her country. Her ashes were later sent to Mrs Carpenter, who had them interred in her family cemetery at Poughkeepsie.

Was Anandi a victim, or did she intelligently make space for herself in her all-too-brief life? The truth clearly lies somewhere in between. Patriarchal Chitpavan Brahmin society oppressed her—and yet, through her letters and diary, she expressed her deep anguish and conflict. At a fundamental level, Anandibai knew that she owed everything to her husband, tyrannical though he may have been. Her life has been dissected from several perspectives, unlike that of Kadambini, about whose life there is little available to dissect. We do not know whether Kadambini and Anandi were acquainted with each other or, indeed, knew of their respective achievements. Though their lives were very different, they certainly shared a deep commitment to better medical care for women, crossing the seas to do so. All clothing, shoes and books were transported with the two women on their long sea voyages. Not only did they become the first Indian women doctors but were also among the earliest women to travel abroad. Both knew all forms of existing locomotion— horse-drawn carriages, the train and now the ocean steamer.

They were amazingly empowered, strong women and, interestingly enough, both were married to widowers appreciably older than themselves—widowers committed to educating their wives. But was Dwarakanath as autocratic as Gopalrao? Did he quail when he felt that his wife was escaping from the mould he had carefully constructed? Was he involved in the minutiae of his wife's intellectual life—and barely concealed his jealousy at signs of any other existence? Perhaps not, as he was an active social reformer. As there is no way of knowing the answers, one is free to dream them up. Ultimately, it is up to the reader to form her private word-image of Anandibai—and fantasise endlessly about Kadambini, who escaped the posthumous fate of being at the receiving end of a biographical venture.

◆

This chapter was first published in 2013 in the *IIC Quarterly*, Vol. 39, Nos. 3 and 4.

◆◆

9
FROM DYNASTY
TO LEGITIMACY
Women Leaders in Indian Politics

SUDHA PAI[#]

An analysis of the role of women leaders in Indian politics reveals a paradox. On the one hand, India, both in the past and at present, continues to have a number of powerful women in top political positions, well-known nationally and internationally for their strong personalities and, in some cases, efficient governance. On the other hand, the number of women in politics—in national political parties and in Parliament—continues to be woefully few. It is also alleged that the former have been able to reach top political positions mainly because they are either the daughters, or wives, of well-known political leaders. While dynastic succession of women is not absent in other parts of the world, two features seem to characterise South Asia. The first is 'emergency dynastic succession' as a result of assassination or a military coup, which brought leaders such as Bandaranayake, Benazir Bhutto, Corazon Aquino or Aung San Suu Kyi to power in Sri Lanka, Pakistan, Philippines and Myanmar, respectively, gave their husbands/fathers dramatic martyrdom and provided them legitimacy (Richter, 1990: 528). The second is the dynastic continuation of a family, including its women members, over a number of generations rather than in a single instance, exerting family control over a political party, the Congress party in India providing a good example.

However, in recent years, this picture is undergoing a gradual change and an analysis of the emergence, role and impact of women political leaders reveals a more complex and nuanced picture. While the number who enter politics and reach the pinnacle remains very low, two developments point to the increasingly important role of women leaders in politics. First, the rise of political parties led by women, such as Mayawati, Mamata Banerjee or Jayalalithaa, that have captured power in their own states; second, as leaders of these parties, these women leaders today also occupy the national stage as regional allies that can determine the life of the central coalition in a fragmented, multi-party system. Against this backdrop, this chapter, analysing the political careers of some important women leaders, argues that while dynasty and family connections remain important variables determining entry and functioning of the large majority of women leaders in politics, a handful of women leaders have been able to enter politics on their own and emerge as independent and strong leaders in their own right.

A perusal of the existing literature suggests there are two angles from which the role of women leaders can be examined. First, whether women leaders work differently and bring in different skills from their male counterparts and, second, to examine their role in politics and record while in office. As gender is a socially constructed category, there are stereotypical images about women and men in public life, their leadership characteristics, their relative strengths and weaknesses. Many feminists point to the 'moral capital' argument which suggests that women are less corrupt[1] than their male counterparts; less likely to act opportunistically from self-interest; more likely to exhibit softer behaviour on social issues; score more highly on 'integrity tests'; take stronger stances on ethical issues with resulting benefits to the democratic governance of society.[2] Celebrating this difference they hold that women need not, and must not, change when they enter public life, a strategy that gives them an initial advantage. However, scholars belonging to the post-modern, Southern and Black feminisms criticise the gender-as-difference argument and point to the tremendous diversity in politics across the Indian subcontinent due to differences in identities based on region, religion, caste and class, which come together to create gender inequality in a number of ways (Spary, 2007: 263). The feminine category, they feel, is homogenised in accounts of white, middle-class women which does not provide space to the experiences of marginalised groups in society. Thus, one can argue that there are as many differences *among* women as *between* men and women, which have been lost in the internalisation of differences between genders that is part of the daily discourse on them.

This chapter, based on the second argument, focuses on the emergence and role of women political leaders in order to understand their impact on national politics and governance, though it recognises that the gender argument cannot be completely set aside, as women face many hurdles in their careers. Accordingly, it examines the paths through which women leaders enter politics, the hurdles they encounter, and the reasons for their small number despite sixty years of democratic politics during which women have enjoyed equal legal rights and a growing feminist movement that has tried to address the question of gender equality in public and private life. Against this backdrop, examining the mode of entry, style of functioning and achievements/failures of some important women leaders, the chapter discusses whether they work differently, are more honest, efficient and committed, than their male counterparts and whether, through hard work, they have been able to achieve an independent status and 'legitimacy' from the electorate.

CLASSIFICATORY FRAMEWORK: UNDERSTANDING WOMEN LEADERS

With the gradual emergence of a variety of women leaders, a classification helps us understand their role and impact on national politics. One method of classifying women leaders is the path they have used to reach the top, based on which three types of women leaders can be identified: dynastic succession, institutional climbers and proxy leaders.[3] The first consist of those who have emerged through dynastic succession, having succeeded their fathers/ husbands, good examples being Indira Gandhi or Sonia Gandhi, who inherited control of the Congress. But, increasingly, this category is visible in parties other than the Congress.

The second category consists of those who have climbed the institutional ladder and reached the top on their own, good examples being Mamata Banerjee or Uma Bharati. Leaders such as Jayalalithaa, Mayawati or Sheila Dikshit—chief ministers but with a national image—fall in-between, i.e. they had the initial advantage of being associated or related to a male leader, but have climbed the ladder of success due to their own hard work; 'transactional' career politicians who have overcome the dynastic marker (Spary, 2007: 253–77). The third group consists of proxy women who have occupied positions of power but have earned little respect or legitimacy, a good example being Rabri Devi, although we do find many examples in the Hindi heartland, elected as Panchs or Sarpanchs but, in reality, it is their husbands who take decisions and control resources (Pai, 1998).

Another method of classifying women leaders is on the basis of caste as upper-caste women find it easier to enter national politics, while those at the bottom suffer the double disadvantage of gender and caste. Most women who have had the advantage of dynastic succession are from the upper caste: Indira Gandhi, Sonia Gandhi and Jayalalithaa. Mayawati is the only example of a Dalit woman who has climbed the political ladder to emerge as a strong leader. Political parties often select women leaders to establish credentials as a party of the lower castes. Some good examples are Meira Kumar, the Speaker of the Lok Sabha; and Selja Kumari, a cabinet minister in the present UPA government. Two backward-caste women leaders are Uma Bharati and Rabri Devi, with the latter already mentioned as a proxy leader.

LOW PRESENCE OF WOMEN IN NATIONAL POLITICS
Despite women having become prime ministers and chief ministers, as Table 1 reveals, the number of women in the national Parliament remains low, the average over 15 Lok Sabhas being a meagre 560 members, or 7.08 per cent. The number of women leaders in political parties is also dismal. Two reasons have been proffered for this state of affairs: political parties are reluctant to give tickets to women as their ability to win is considered low (Omvedt, 2005). This is despite the fact that four political parties with a national presence are headed by women: the Congress by Sonia Gandhi; the Bahujan Samaj Party (BSP) by Mayawati; the Trinamool Congress (TMC) by Mamata Banerjee; and the All India Anna Dravida Munetra Kazhagam (AIADMK) by Jayalalithaa. The principal opposition party, the Bharatiya Janata Party (BJP), has a number of women leaders such as Sushma Swaraj, Uma Bharati and Vasundhararaje Scindia—the latter two have been chief ministers of MP and Rajasthan, respectively—but the number of seats it offers to women is low. In the 2004 Lok Sabha elections, major national parties offered a total of 110 seats to women: Congress, 45; BJP, 30; BSP, 20; Communist Party of India (CPI), 2; CPI (M), 8; and Nationalist Congress Party (NCP), 5. The winning percentage was above 25 per cent in all cases, except the BSP and

the CPI (Spary, 2007). A study of the 2004 parliamentary elections shows that a major factor in women's low winning percentage was at the political party level; the 'success rate' of the women who actually contested was 12.4 per cent compared to 9.8 per cent for men (Deshpande, 2004).

A second reason often pointed out is the failure of the Lok Sabha to pass the Constitutional Amendment Bill seeking to provide 33 per cent reservation to women in Parliament. The Bill was drafted and introduced in the Lok Sabha as the 81st Constitutional Amendment Bill in September 1996 during the tenure of the United Front Government, but could not be passed. Subsequently, it was introduced a number of times as the 84th Constitutional Amendment Bill by the National Democratic Alliance (NDA) Government, but could not be passed. In 2004, the UPA government included the Bill in its Common Minimum Programme, but it was only in 2008 that it was introduced in the Rajya Sabha where, amidst much din and shouting, it was passed on 9 March 2010, but it still needs to be passed by the Lok Sabha (*The Hindu,* 2010). The major source of opposition has been members of parties representing the backward castes such as the Samajwadi Party (SP), who argue that a quota should be kept aside for backward, minority and Dalit women without which it would allow the entry of more upper-caste/class women, most of whom are wives/sisters/daughters of members. But women members feel that it is gender bias as, over the years, the debate has been bitter, and they have faced violent abuse and been caricatured as '*bal-cutti* memsahibs' (short-haired memsahibs) or the '*biwi*' (wives) brigades, and their agendas described as divisive for the country (Rai, 1999).

Feminist scholars have also questioned the usefulness of quotas for women in Parliament.[4] Invoking Nancy Fraser, Shirin Rai articulates the feeling of many that political representation would be a strategy of 'recognition' rather than 'redistribution', thus limiting its transformative potential (Rai, 1999). The Bill has provoked serious debate in the country as to whether quotas are the best way forward to bring women into politics. Many argue that increased attention to improving female education, sex ratio, food security, the issues of divorce, adoption and share in family property, the gender-sensitive training of the police, bureaucracy and judiciary would create the conditions needed for women to enter politics.

CONTEXT OF PARTICIPATION

Equally important, the context within which women leaders emerge and participate has historically not been very conducive. During the anti-colonial struggle women did participate and were encouraged to do so, strengthening their legal rights and educational attainments. But it was largely upper-caste/middle-class women who participated, encouraged by their own families. This did not affect attitudes towards the traditional gender hierarchy; the enemy was not patriarchy, but foreign domination (Forbes, 2000). Consequently, in the post-Independence period, despite a liberal attitude towards the participation of women in politics, it remained low. It was only in the 1970s, especially in the light of the Report, *Towards Equality*, produced by the Committee on the Status of Women that attention was drawn towards the need for greater involvement. The women's movement attempted to empower women, but it remained fragmented along ideological lines, with few movements and most of them on specific issues such as dowry, alcohol, violence and economic opportunities, rather than gender equality. Since the 1990s, the Hindutva movement has attempted to mobilise women, but along conservative lines. Political parties have set up women's wings that have appropriated women without giving them much space in the higher echelons.

Nevertheless, since the 1980s, a number of developments have introduced some change. Democratisation and rising levels of politicisation, particularly in the Hindi heartland; improved literacy levels; decline of the Congress Party and the emergence of regional, backward caste and Dalit-based parties; and improved levels of growth in some states, have provided new avenues to women.[5] Since the mid-1990s, six states in India, including the national capital region, have been governed by women[6] and at least three women leaders of regional/state parties have acquired national status and been instrumental in supporting/maintaining national governments: Mamata Banerjee, Mayawati and Jayalalithaa. The entry of Sonia Gandhi into national politics, prior to the 2004 Lok Sabha elections, was because Congressmen, afraid of the declining position of the Congress, were keen to obtain support by using the name of the Nehru–Gandhi dynasty.

ROLE AND IMPACT

We now turn to an analysis of the methods of functioning and governance by some women leaders in India. Our investigation is based on the few existing studies on women leaders, media accounts and the public image of their honesty, administrative ability, capacity for political mobilisation, and the management of political parties.

Both Indira Gandhi and Sonia Gandhi owed their entry into politics because of their dynastic position. Subsequently, their paths have been quite different. Indira Gandhi, recognised as a strong woman leader, nationally and internationally, was made the prime minister by the Congress 'syndicate' which felt that the party would benefit from her image as Nehru's daughter during a period when the party was facing a number of problems. Famously described by them as 'goongi gudiya' (dumb doll), within a few years she was able to obtain control over the party, emerge as a strong leader and deal successfully with a number of crises: the defeat of the Congress in eight states in 1967; the Congress split in 1969, which led to the formation of the Congress (I) that obtained a parliamentary majority in 1972, based on the 20-point programme; introduction of the Green Revolution, which effectively dealt with the food crisis; and withstanding pressure from the US to introduce changes in foreign and domestic policies.[7] She has been described as a popular plebiscitary leader, i.e. one who could appeal directly to the people and not through her party or government. However, she has faced much criticism for an authoritarian style of functioning, imposing the Emergency and trying to centralise and personalise power, which also weakened the Congress party (Hart, 1976).

Her daughter-in-law, Sonia Gandhi, who today controls the Congress, is admired on some accounts as an Italian who has adjusted to Indian life and customs and who revived an almost defunct party in the late 1990s (Kidwai, 2009). Nevertheless, she has faced criticism over the Bofors scandal, for poor administrative capacity, policy paralysis in UPA-II, and preserving the party as a family-holding by promoting her son, Rahul Gandhi, as her heir. A study argues that, unable to earn her status as a leader in her own right, 'dynastic charisma' has been used as a 'cover' for image-building and creating 'celebrification in politics', although such manipulated attempts have limited impact as they become routinised (Chakravorti, 1999: 2842). Despite this, with her control over the Congress Party she may continue to derive support, considering the leadership vacuum in contemporary Indian politics and the emergence of Hindu fundamentalism which threatens the secular, liberal and socialist trends (ibid.: 2843). This category is not limited to Indira Gandhi and Sonia Gandhi, both of whom have enjoyed independent control of the Congress and have achievements to their credit. A younger generation of educated and capable wives and daughters are entering 'feudal' political parties, which are under the control of a patriarchal figure. Good examples are the Samajwadi Party (SP), Akali Dal, NCP and the DMK, in which wives/daughters play a subordinate role.

In contrast, the seminal achievements and honest image of Sheila Dikshit, the doughty Chief Minister of Delhi, has overshadowed the fact that she is the daughter-in-law of Congress leader Uma Shankar Dikshit. During her three terms in office she has dealt effectively with factionalism within the party; been able to expand the Delhi Metro; provide a new bus transport system under the Jawaharlal Nehru National Urban Renewal Mission (JNNURM); and improved roads, flyovers and other conveniences for the citizens, which have earned her much support. The rise and success of Jayalalithaa, a former film actress, is a more complicated story. While her association with popular film hero MGR enabled her to become leader of the AIADMK and the chief minister for two terms (1991–96 and 2001–06), she has also been described as a beautiful woman, a ruthless and authoritarian leader and an able administrator (Banerjee, 2004: 291). Beginning with a difficult apprenticeship under MGR, when she learned to survive in a largely male political arena, she successfully competed with V. Janaki, the widow of MGR, for control of the AIADMK, and has withstood attempts by the DMK patriarch Karunanidhi and his partymen to malign her image and misbehave with her in the Assembly. Popularly called *amma,* or mother, she has worked hard using an elaborate system of patronage and established herself as an independent leader (ibid.). But she still draws on MGR's charismatic, Robin Hood figure, which is portrayed in her campaigns. Despite corruption charges and an opulent lifestyle, she is equated with a modern day '*Tamiltaay*' a uniquely Tamil ideal, which appeals to men and women, combining the varied female attributes of mother, desirable woman, virginal goddess, while also personifying the Tamil language itself (Banerjee, 2004: 294).

Despite being a Dalit woman, Mayawati has overcome tremendous opposition to become the chief minister of UP, a conservative state where Brahmin men have long enjoyed power. Selected and mentored by Kanshi Ram, when he brought her into the All India Backward and Minority Communities Employees' Federation (BAMCEF) in the mid-1980s, many felt a woman would not be able to handle the rough and tumble of Dalit politics. In the mid-1990s, hired goons of the SP, it is alleged, made an attempt on her life and person in the well-known guest house incident, but she emerged stronger from this episode (Bose, 2012). Although the BSP was established by Kanshi Ram, building a strong organisation and achieving a majority in 2007 has been her achievement. Despite her authoritarian control over the party, the cadres respect and like their *Behenji*. In the mid-1990s, when she became chief minister for the first time, Mayawati emerged as a role-model for Dalit women in Uttar Pradesh (Pai, 1998). During her term as chief minister from 2007 to 2012, instead of her Dalit-oriented agenda she attempted to develop backward regions and all disadvantaged sections. Nevertheless, there is also trenchant criticism that Mayawati has failed the Dalit movement by compromising with upper-caste groups/parties and is a very corrupt politician whose family members have amassed fortunes (*The Indian Express*, 2012).

Uma Bharati, the fiery *sadhavi* with oratorical skills and religious training, has sacrificed everything for her political career and is recognised as a leader of the BJP. As a sadhavi, she does not have the usual image of a woman politician; owing to her loyalty to the Sangh Parivar and Hindutva ideology, only conservative Hindu women support her, but her greatest asset is that she is perceived as a backward-caste leader. She has a number of undeniable achievements: member of the Lok Sabha for five consecutive terms, no mean achievement with no family connections and in a party not very congenial to women leaders; ministerial positions at the Centre; and vice-president of the Madhya Pradesh unit of the BJP. However, as a maverick leader, she has often challenged party rules, leading to her expulsion in 2005, forming a party of her own and eventually returning to the BJP (*Frontline*, 2005). Although viewed as honest, Bharati's record as the chief minister of Madhya Pradesh was undistinguished, leading to her replacement. She is one of the most articulate and aggressive leaders of the BJP who made her mark, not as an administrator, but by leading the party's Hindutva campaign.

Mamata Banerjee also rose without any family connections, through sheer grit and determination, to become a recognised regional and national leader. She has a number of achievements to her credit: she was elected five times to the Lok Sabha from the South Kolkata constituency; she was a Youth Congress leader in West Bengal; she formed her own party—the TMC—which is positioned as both anti-Congress and anti-Left, an ally of both the NDA and United Progressive Alliance–II (UPA–II); she was appointed railway minister in both governments. However, the most seminal achievement has been defeating the Communists who were in power for almost 30 years, a feat that could not be achieved by the Congress opposition (Banerjee, 2004). Like Jayalalithaa—a colourful and unorthodox woman leader with huge public bases, flamboyant personality and 'populist appeal' (ibid.: 285)—Banerjee does not conform to public standards of feminine behaviour; she does not only have a reputation for unpredictability, ruthlessness, and a volatile temper, but also a mastery of the timing of public gestures, the manipulation of public sentiment, sycophantic loyalty from followers and complete control over the party. In contrast, her public image is clean; she is viewed as honest and supported by the poorer sections, especially women, although she has used both 'assertive and paternalist populism' to build her constituency and gain power (ibid.: 302). Unmarried and from a modest, lower middle-class family, she still dresses in inexpensive khadi sarees and slippers and lives frugally in her old house in a congested south Kolkata area. But Banerjee has displayed little capacity to effectively govern West Bengal. Rather, she is a 'street fighter' ready to *gherao* (ambush) political leaders, join marches and sit-ins on the streets, even as chief minister, for social and political causes. Her followers compare her to the goddess Durga and a tigress for the twin qualities of female courage and intolerance for injustice, which voters find rare in politicians (ibid.: 303).

Rabri Devi, in contrast to the other women leaders studied, has commanded little respect from voters as chief minister of Bihar, except for behaving as a model wife. Put into the office by her husband Laloo Prasad Yadav, a charismatic, backward caste leader who was arrested in a fodder scam in 1997, she held the post for three successive periods: July 1997–February 1999; March 1999–2000; March 2000–05 (Sinha, 2012). Rabri Devi was able to draw on her husband's popularity and the elaborate patronage system established by him for the Yadav community. It limited her strength and ability to deal with the bureaucracy and party workers; she lost the respect of the electorate and disappeared from the political scene after the defeat of the RJD in 2005 (Spary, 2007).

Our analysis shows that, although India is a functioning democracy and has experienced considerable democratisation over the last few decades, the number of women leaders in national politics remains abysmally low. Both historical factors, which point towards slow change in patriarchal attitudes towards women and poor development of women's agency after Independence, have been responsible. Consequently, dynastic succession or family connections remain an important avenue through which women leaders have emerged. This trend is true not only of women leaders soon after Independence, but a younger generation of better-educated women—wives and daughters of established male leaders—who have, in recent years, entered Parliament and established themselves in national/state parties. Subsequently, only a few have been able to gain recognition as independent leaders; most remain in the shadow of their husbands or fathers. One reason for this is the larger phenomenon of dynastic or feudal parties in which entire families under a patriarchal figure, including women members who have a subordinate role, are involved.

The brief perusal of the functioning of some women leaders who have reached the top shows that there is no one model which fits all women leaders; rather, there are considerable differences among them on all four counts discussed. Women leaders in India are as corrupt, or as honest, as their male counterparts. Mayawati, Jayalalithaa and Sonia Gandhi are perceived by the electorate as having amassed fortunes for their family members and court cases have been filed against the first two. On the other hand, both Mamata Banerjee and Uma Bharati are viewed as honest. Some women leaders have proved highly capable in political mobilisation, establishing their own parties, maintaining a strong control over them and capturing power.

But rule by these women leaders is not always better; they have not hesitated to use authoritarian and confrontational methods, or corrupt means to achieve power, or implement desired policies. They have also proved adept at shifting support from one coalition to another, of holding at ransom the central coalition and legislation in Parliament. Hence, leadership roles are transgendered and having more women may make no difference.

All the women leaders studied, including those who rose through dynastic succession, faced many obstacles and hardships and it took time and effort on their part to gain recognition as national leaders. Gender affects authority and women leaders—with a few exceptions such as Indira Gandhi—and commands less legitimacy, authority and respect from the electorate. Hindu imagery and stereotypes are invoked; they are seen as mother-figures, or behenji, or *didi*. There are different expectations from men and women, which put the latter at a distinct disadvantage making it necessary for them to work harder and prove themselves as efficient and capable in politics, even more so when in power. Failure in the case of women leads to fingers pointed at gender, but not in the case of men.

All this suggests that it is difficult for women to enter and build a career in politics in India. At the same time, in recent decades, significant changes have taken place in the states—rise in women's literacy, social movements, faster economic growth in many states, and reservation of seats for women in panchayats—which have provided a more fertile ground for women leaders in politics. In this situation, a small number of women leaders have emerged and, through sheer hard work and determination, achieved status, respect and recognition on their own. Nevertheless, this trend remains exceptional and difficult for other women to emulate. The shift from dynasty to legitimacy for women leaders has barely begun. Clearly, change is required at two levels. First, attitudes to women must change together with improvement in their economic position so that they acquire the potential to compete with men. Second, internal reforms of parties must take place so that they do not remain family concerns in which women are expected to be subordinate members with little voice of their own.

◆◆◆

APPENDIX

Table 1
Representation of Women in the Indian Parliament from 1st to 15th Lok Sabha

Lok Sabha Elections (yr)	Total Number of Seats	Total Number of Women Members	Percentage of Women Members
1952	489	24	4.91
1957	494	24	4.86
1962	494	36	7.29
1967	520	32	6.15
1971	521	27	5.18
1977	544	21	3.86
s1980	544	32	5.88
1984	544	45	8.27
1989	529	28	5.29
1991	509	42	8.25
1996	541	41	7.58
1998	545	44	8.07
1999	543	52	9.58
2004	543	52	9.58
2009	543	60	11.05
Total	7,903	560	7.08

Source: Election Commission of India, Relevant Statistical Reports.

◆

[#] This chapter was first published in 2013 in the *IIC Quarterly*, Vol. 39, Nos. 3 and 4.

NOTES

1. A recent study examined the relationship between female participation in legislatures and the level of perceived corruption in a sample of more than 100 countries. It concluded that higher rates of female participation in government are associated with lower levels of corruption. See Dollar, Fisman and Gatti (1999).
2. For the arguments put forward in the literature, see Spary (2007).
3. While the classification is used by Spary (2007), a number of scholars have used each of these categories, as the chapter shows.

4. For debates among feminist scholars see Rai (1999); Kishwar (1996); Menon (1997); Rajan and Retnakumar (2005).
5. For the multi-faceted changes in the states since the late 1980s and their impact on national politics, see Pai (2013), forthcoming.
6. The six women chief ministers were: J. Jayalalithaa in Tamil Nadu; Shiela Dikshit in Delhi; Uma Bharati in MP; Vasundhararaje Scindia in Rajasthan; Rabri Devi in Bihar; and Mayawati in UP.
7. For a detailed analysis of Mrs Gandhi's period, see Pai (2011).

REFERENCES

Banerjee, Mukulika. 2004. 'Populist Leadership in West Bengal and Tamil Nadu: Mamata and Jayalalithaa Compared', in Rob Jenkins (ed.), *Regional Reflections Comparing Politics Across India's States*. New Delhi: OUP.

Bose, Ajoy. 2012. *Behenji*. New Delhi: Penguin.

Chakravorti, Robi. 1999. 'Asia's Women Leaders and Dynastic Charisma', *Economic and Political Weekly*, 2 October.

Deshpande, Rajeshwari. 2004. 'How Gendered was Women's Participation in Election 2004?', *Economic and Political Weekly*, 18–24 December, Vol. 39, No. 51, pp. 3561–62.

Dollar, David, Raymond Fisman and Roberta Gatti. 1999. 'Are Women Really the "Fairer Sex": Corruption and Women in Government.' World Bank Development Research Group on Gender and Development. Working Paper. Series No. 4. October.

Forbes, Geraldine. 2000. *Women in Modern India*. The New Cambridge History of India. Second reprint. New Delhi: Cambridge University Press.

Frontline. 2005. 'Interview with Uma Bharti', Vol. 22, Issue 26, 17 December.

Hart, Henry, C. (ed.). 1976. *Indira Gandhi's India: A Political System Reappraised*. Boulder: West View Press.

Kidwai, Rasheed. 2009. *Sonia: A Biography*. New Delhi: Penguin Viking.

Kishwar, Madhu. 1996. 'Women and Politics: Beyond Quotas', *Economic and Political Weekly*, Vol. 31, No. 43, pp. 2867–74.

Menon, Nivedita. 1997. 'Reservations and Representation', *Seminar*, No. 457, September, pp. 38–41.

Omvedt, Gail. 2005. 'Women in Governance in South Asia', *Economic and Political Weekly*, Vol. 40, No. 44/45, 29 October–4 November, pp. 4746–52.

Pai, Sudha. (ed.) 2013. *Handbook on Politics in the Indian States: Region, Parties and Economic Reform*. Forthcoming. New Delhi: OUP.

Pai, Sudha. 2011. 'Electoral Politics and Party: Mrs. Gandhi's Congress: 1964–84', in Aditya Mukherjee (ed.), *A Centenary History of the Indian National Congress*. Volume IV, 1964–84. New Delhi: Academic Publishers.

Pai, Sudha. 1998. 'Pradhanis in the New Panchayats: Field Notes from Meerut.' *Economic and Political Weekly*, Vol. 33. No. 18, 2 May, pp. 1009–10.

Rai, Shirin, 1999. 'Democratic Institutions, Political Representation and Women's Empowerment: the Quota Debate in India', *Democratization*, Vol. 6, Autumn, pp. 84–99.

Rajan, Irudaya and J. Retnakumar. 2005. 'Women's Reservation Bill: Some Emerging Issues', *Economic and Political Weekly*, Vol. 40, No. 39, pp. 4190–92.

Richter, L.K. 1990. 'Exploring Theories of Female Leadership in South and Southeast Asia', *Pacific Affairs*, 63, pp. 524–40.

Sinha, Arun. 2012. *Nitish Kumar and the Rise of Bihar.* New Delhi: Penguin Viking.

Spary, Carole. 2007. 'Female Political Leadership in India', *Commonwealth and Comparative Politics*, Vol. 45, No. 3, July, pp. 253–77.

The Hindu. 2010. 'The 14 years Journey of Women's Reservation Bill', 9 March, New Delhi.

The Indian Express. 2012. 31 January, New Delhi.

◆◆

10
OTHER HISTORIES
Gender and Politics in the Fiction of Mahasweta Devi[1]

RADHA
CHAKRAVARTY[#]

'**Y**ears ago, when I was a child, my grandmother told me the story of the Queen of Jhansi. Heard in her gentle voice, by the dim light of a lantern, it did indeed seem like the most amazing fairy tale.' In these opening lines of her Preface to the first edition of *The Queen of Jhansi* (1956: ix), Mahasweta Devi recounts her fascination with the legend that inspired her first book. The fascination persisted into adulthood. She says: 'Later, after I acquired an education and a consciousness of history, my curiosity about our national life increased and a wish arose to write an entire book about the Queen of Jhansi' (ibid.). But the love of fairy tales did not go away. *The Queen of Jhansi* presents a spectacular blend of fact and fiction, history and myth. This book was the beginning of a long and prolific writing career, spanning more than 50 years to date. But Mahasweta Devi's talent for combining the real and the imaginary, the facts of history with the promptings of a visionary imagination, remains unchanged. Her creative writings inhabit the borderland between history and fiction, where 'truth' is constructed from a mixture of fact and make-believe. The role of gender in this process of construction is the subject of this chapter.

It is not insignificant that the inspiration for her first book came from Mahasweta Devi's grandmother. The art of storytelling is generally thought of as a woman's domain, belonging to the popular oral tradition rather than the mainstream field of written history which has for centuries been dominated by men. From her ancestress or foremother (to use a term from Virginia Woolf), Mahasweta learns the story of another foremother in history, the Rani of Jhansi. The gendered dimension of this communicative transaction forms the foundation of Mahasweta's abiding concern with the lives of women, and the intersection of gender and politics in her writing is the subject of this chapter. What happens when a woman like the Rani of Jhansi enters the domain of history, for so long a male preserve? What happens when another woman such as Mahasweta claims the right to retell that story? What happens when yet another woman, living in the USA, translates the story—with her mother's help—for a different audience (ibid.)? What forms of counter discourse emerge from such interventions, and what are their implications for historiography? These questions about gender and narrative haunt my reading of Mahasweta's fiction.

Mahasweta herself denies that gender is her primary concern. 'When I write I never think of myself as a woman,' she declares. 'I look at the class, not at the gender problem.'[2] She is popularly perceived as a champion of the tribal cause and decrier of class prejudice. Her global literary reputation has been reshaped by Gayatri Chakravorty Spivak, who places Mahasweta within the frame of the subaltern and links her activism with the struggle to emancipate other marginalised peoples of the world. So powerful is this reading of Mahasweta that Sujit Mukherjee has described the process as 'Operation Mahasweta', in which Spivak becomes 'the door to the Third World through which the First can enter, ushered in by an incomparable *dwarpalika*' (Mukherjee, 1991: 30–31). Such readings overlook the importance of gender as a constitutive category in Mahasweta's work, an importance which I attempt to establish in this chapter, arguing against Mahasweta's overt focus on class issues and Spivak's privileging of postcolonial discourse. Class and nation remain important defining categories as well, but I regard them, along with gender, as intersecting strands that weave together the complex alternative histories that Mahasweta's narratives unfold. After all, as Rajeswari Sunder Rajan says,

> The challenge to and of feminist writing lies in negotiating women's identity defined in these terms ... women *are* classed, caste and communal subjects ... at the same time, in the interests of a transformative politics, difference must be managed, if not transcended. (Sunder Rajan, 1999: 1–16)

Here I examine two texts by Mahasweta Devi dealing with two women situated differently in time and place. Lakshmibai,

Rani of Jhansi, inhabits the history of the 1857 uprising. Dopdi Mejhen in *Draupadi* is a tribal woman involved in the Naxalbari insurgency. Lakshmibai is a queen, engaged in the struggle to free the nation of foreign rule; and Dopdi is an outcaste, excluded from the mainstream on account of her tribal descent, yet determined to play her part in the political arena. By examining Mahasweta's representation of these two women, we may address some pertinent questions regarding the role of gender in the narrativisation of other histories.

As an avowed Marxist, Mahasweta acknowledges the importance of history. Her work reveals painstaking research to uncover concealed facts, in an approach she describes as 'forensic': 'My approach is forensic [...] everywhere, my search is for what lies behind.'[3] To write *The Queen of Jhansi* she travelled to Bundelkhand and gathered a fund of information from local sources, including oral and written versions. She also consulted historians and sought the help of the Rani's grandson, Lakshman Rao Jhansiwale. But alongside this concern for accuracy, she also indulged her interest in myth and folklore. Referring to the uprising of 1857, she says: 'I found evidence in folk songs, rhymes, ballads, and in various popular stories, of how local people viewed the rebellion in the places where it happened' (Devi, 1956: x). The first chapter, for instance, presents an elaborate family tree to explain Rani Lakshmibai's lineage as well as the history of the principality of Jhansi. But the 'Background', which precedes this chapter, also provides the local rhyme that mythifies the Rani:

> *She made soldiers out of soil,*
> *And swords out of wood;*
> *She picked up mountains and made horses,*
> *And off she rode to Gwalior* (ibid.: xiv).

The narrative is thus based on conventional as well alternative sources, presenting both British and Indian versions of the protagonist's role in the 1857 uprising. This method of narration challenges the idea of a monolithic 'truth', constantly reminding us instead that the Rani of Jhansi we think we know is actually a construct. In place of a reified truth, the narrative emphasises the elusiveness and indeterminacy of the Rani as a subject.

Seen through the prism of so many perspectives, the Queen of Jhansi emerges as a flesh and blood woman who is also somehow an enigma, combining the roles of daring warrior and tender mother, wily strategist and devout religious woman. She enjoys the feminine pastime of beautifying herself in private, but in public she appears in splendid male attire, sword in hand, riding her favourite horse. She is full of sympathy for the people, yet shows herself capable of ruthless political resolve. She defies gender stereotypes, showing herself capable of holding her own in the male-dominated field of politics, governance and war, without giving up the maternal instinct for care, nurture and love, especially in her interaction with her subjects and her affection for her adopted son. In the face of so much conflicting evidence, the figure of the Rani emerges as a site for contestation, and the role of the narrator/biographer/historiographer becomes crucial. The narrative voice in *The Queen of Jhansi* constantly foregrounds the intractability of her subject matter, often presenting conflicting reports on the Rani's various activities. This concern for factual veracity coexists with, and is sometimes undercut by, a textual impulse to endorse populist attempts to mythify the Rani.

Realism blends with fantasy in this rendering. History here comes to represent what Kumkum Sangari has called the politics of the possible, a narrative mode that combines 'a notion of history as a set of discoverable facts with a notion of history as a field of diverse human and cultural possibility' (Sangari, 1999: 7). In the popular imagination, the Queen of Jhansi lives on as an embodiment of possibility; she inhabits the national imaginary as a figure of transgression as well as integration, for she challenges the boundaries between the separate roles prescribed for men and women, usurping the domain of male authority even while demonstrating her capacity for tenderness and altruism. In her capacity to arouse loyalty, she unites men and women, Hindus and Muslims, in the struggle for a common cause. Such is her hold on the national imagination. That Mahasweta should seek to revive this figure almost a hundred years after her death is also significant. All texts, even histories, are produced by their specific contexts; the context for Mahasweta's representation of the Rani of Jhansi is perhaps the tendency in post-Independence India in the 1950s to contain women and to bring them back into the fold of convention and domesticity after their active participation in the public domain of nationalist struggles. To the mainstream discourse that sought to regulate women's lives in the 1950s, Mahasweta's narrative offers a counter discourse of female self-empowerment that insists on women's place in history. Such a method answers Kumkum Sangari's call for 'a more sensitive feminist historiography, a reinflection of culture that can keep radical alternatives open for an integrative political praxis' (Sangari, 1999: xlix). The roots of this counter discourse lie in Mahasweta's emancipatory, interventionist politics, and the sources for this version of the Rani's story are to be found most often in collective popular desire.

For, as Mahasweta declares, 'I have always tried to explore people's version of history.... In all my writings I have tried to present the subaltern point of view' (Devi, 1956: 275). The subaltern perspective, as Spivak reminds us, presents events from the point of view of those beyond the margins of the society, the outcasts and the dispossessed. Everywhere in Mahasweta's work is a keen desire to insert into history those who have always been excluded from it. Of particular interest to her is the plight of tribals, especially tribal women. Her writings about the tribal predicament are inseparable from her activism, for in Mahasweta's fiction, writing itself functions as a form of activism. As Spivak points out however in her essay 'Can the Subaltern Speak?' there are degrees of subalternity, and it is the underprivileged woman who often occupies the lowest position in this hierarchy of exclusions. The poor tribal woman, for instance, is thrice oppressed on account of her ethnicity, class position, as well as her gender. It is this extreme level of subalternity that particularly interests Mahasweta, and here gender functions as the crucial and ultimate marker of discrimination. Paradoxically, gender also often acts as an enabling factor, instrumental in the resistance and self-assertion of which Mahasweta's protagonists often show themselves capable.

We see this in the well-known short story *Draupadi*, for instance. The story of a woman who dares to challenge her destiny, *Draupadi* is a narrative of self-empowerment that invites feminist interpretation, despite Mahasweta's insistence on a class-based reading and Spivak's focus on postcoloniality. *Draupadi* is the story of a tribal woman who, along with her husband, joins the Naxalite movement. Caught by the police during a nocturnal operation, she is gang-raped by her captors through the night. In the morning, when produced before their leader, Senanayak, she refuses to cover her nakedness, bringing her tormentors to shame by exposing their crime. Class, no doubt, is an important feature in this story, which uses several characters to represent a range of ways in which hegemony can operate. We encounter Surya Sahu, the landowner who enjoys an unlimited supply of water from his five wells while the so-called untouchables burn with thirst during the drought. There is Surya Sahu's wife, who casually names Dopdi after the Draupadi of the *Mahabharata* in an act that may be read as an attempt to erase the tribal woman's pre-Aryan ancestry. The forces of State power operate through Captain Arjan Singh, who chases political fugitives concealed by their Santhal supporters in the forests of Jhadkhani. His guide and mentor is Senanayak, who pretends to sympathise with the migrant labourers even as he hounds them ruthlessly in practice. Also involved in the scenario of exploitation are the 'moneylenders, landlords, grain-brokers, anonymous brothel-keepers, ex-narks of the area' (Devi, 1990: 154).

At the opposite end of the spectrum are those oppressed by these dominant powers: peasants, migrant workers, outcastes and tribals. Resistance is also embodied in the city-bred intellectuals who join the Naxalbari movement, targeting police stations, stealing guns and attacking those who symbolise structures of authority. But speaking *for* the subaltern does not amount to speaking *as* the subaltern. With her degree in English literature, her experience as a college teacher, her culturally eminent family background and her long career as a Bengali writer, Mahasweta Devi cannot be dissociated from the world of the intellectual elite. Within the text, Draupadi's song may be unintelligible to the Bengali *bhadralok* and her ululation might signify a primitive, pre-lingual mode of communication. But the narrative voice of Mahasweta's text is far from naïve. We encounter, for example, references to Shakespeare's Prospero, Antonioni's 'highbrow' cinema and to the male principle in Sankhya philosophy. English words and phrases are scattered throughout the narrative. The ironic references to the Indian Constitution where 'all human beings, regardless of caste or creed, are sacred' (ibid.: 150), or to the 'law of confrontation' by which fugitives are 'shot at the taxpayers' expense' (ibid.: 153), reveal a sophisticated mode of verbal resistance of which the subaltern Dopdi would herself be incapable.

In this rhetorical sophistication lies the clue to Mahasweta's ambivalence about class. She remains implicated in the very class hierarchies she claims to challenge, using the linguistic and intellectual tools of the culturally privileged to attack the idea of cultural privilege. This is not to dismiss a class-based reading of *Draupadi*, but to argue for a more nuanced understanding of how class difference actually operates in the text.

A postcolonial reading of *Draupadi* demands a similar rethinking. In the Preface to *Imaginary Maps*, Mahasweta Devi describes tribal culture as a 'lost continent', a part of the ancient past that has been forgotten by colonialist as well as nationalist historiography (Chakravarty, 2004: 75–88). In the post-Independence world, according to her, tribals have been displaced and excluded from the process of decolonisation, and are often victimised in the name of 'progress' and 'development'. Mahasweta asserts that her activism is motivated by a desire to reclaim the rights denied to tribals, and to reinsert these marginalised groups into the mainstream. In other words, she claims to tell the 'truth' about the experience of tribals in India, replacing officially accepted falsifications with fact, and silence with speech. But there are some crucial contradictions in this truth-claim, and also some important differences between the stated aims of the writer and the way in which her work is interpreted for Western readers by Gayatri Spivak. Although Mahasweta insists on the need to emphasise historical specificity, she also claims to represent the '[g]eneral tribal as Indian, not only that. They are Indians who belong to the rest of India' (Introduction; Devi, 1995: xx–xxi). Rejecting official versions of nationalism, Mahasweta nevertheless implies the need to imagine other kinds of nationalism, in ways that would reinscribe the tribals into history.

Some critics, such as Alakananda Bagchi, assume that Mahasweta displaces the construction of an essentialised, spiritualised, 'Hindu-ised' India by evoking a remote tribal past that is not only pre-colonial, but also pre-Aryan and pre-Hindu. The role of the tribal Dopdi is played off, for instance, against that of her mythical namesake, the Draupadi of the *Mahabharata*. When Dusshasana in the *Mahabharata* tries to disrobe Draupadi, she is saved from dishonour by divine intervention. In Mahasweta's story, no god intervenes to protect Dopdi when she is stripped and gang-raped. While Draupadi in the epic retains her dignity by preserving her modesty, Mahasweta's Dopdi acquires an extraordinary dignity by refusing to clothe herself when she faces her captors in the daylight after her night of torment. She perceives this act as an expression of the indomitable spirit of her ancestors, a sign of her 'pure' Santhal blood, traceable to a pre-colonial past: 'Dopdi's blood was the pure unadulterated black blood of Champakbhumi ... Dopdi felt proud of her forefathers. They stood guard over their women's blood with the poison of the black kunch' (Devi, 1990: 158).

This 'pure' blood predates colonialism and Hinduism, challenging both the discourse of colonialism and the essentialist Hindu-ised version of nationalism. This apparently radical move, however, is undercut by its own essentialist underpinnings. The affirmation of a 'pure' tribal identity, powerful though it is, remains conservative in its nostalgia for 'pure' origins, a nostalgia blind to the forces of change and historical contingency. Dopdi, after all, is the product of a particular historical moment, embroiled in the politics of the Naxalbari movement and the dangers of a fugitive existence. Her courage and endurance could as much be a product of her training in collective insurgency as of her so-called 'pure' ancestral blood. Mahasweta's seemingly radical position is thus unmasked as another form of essentialism, one that is premised upon a reified notion of what constitutes 'true' or 'original' Indian identity. The discourse of nation thus does not provide here an adequate site for the articulation of history as possibility.

An examination of the ending of *Draupadi* demonstrates that it is gender, rather than class or nation, that offers us an appropriate reading strategy for uncovering the radical potential of this text. It is gender that marks the difference between Dopdi's treatment at the hands of her tormentors, and the fate meted out to her male comrades-in-arms, who are captured and 'countered'. Dulna Majhi, Dopdi's partner, is shot in the back as he drinks from a forest stream while on the run. Dopdi, by contrast, is sexually assaulted through the night, though the same death sentence must inevitably follow. The difference in their respective modes of punishment is determined by the politics of gender, rather than class, ethnicity, community or nation. But this gendered narrative is also unlike the feminist plot we often encounter in fiction by other Indian women writers, who generally favour the story of a middle-class housewife or mother rebelling against her stereotypical domestic role. Though married, Dopdi is neither housewife nor mother. Her marginal position as a tribal woman, paradoxically, affords her a degree of freedom that is denied her middle-class counterparts in fiction. And she is already a rebel when the story begins. As a political activist she challenges the institutional authority of the law and the State; her participation in the killing of Surya Sahu, the landowner, represents a class-based rebellion, though complicated by her anger at Sahu's lascivious gaze. Her final act of rebellion, though, is a specifically gendered one. Her body, the site of her subjugation by the men who rape her, also becomes the chosen instrument of her defiance. Confronting Senanayak in her nakedness at the end of the story, she figuratively forces her captors to confront an image of their own brutality, for which her exposed and mutilated body becomes a signifier. Contrary to Spivak's claim, the subaltern in Mahasweta's narrative can and does speak, and the vehicle of her resistance is her body (Spivak, 1994: 66–111).

In the final lines of the narrative, Dopdi undergoes a kind of apotheosis. She becomes a larger-than-life image of female self-empowerment, striking terror into the heart of her beholders. Is this apotheosis a form of 'truth-telling' as the author would have it, or is it, rather, a kind of myth-making, a glorification of the fearless tribal woman that would exhort us to dream of change? I suspect the latter is true.

Such myth-making does not stem from an escapist impulse, though. Its source is the 'white-hot anger' that impels Mahasweta Devi to write, anger against the forces that silence the subaltern, and also against the apathy and complacency of those in positions of privilege who do nothing to alter the existing state of affairs. Her ruthless, 'forensic' probing of facts and her refusal to accept official versions of the 'truth' underlie the uncompromising social realism that has come to be recognised as the hallmark of her writing. But this realism is also countered by a visionary dimension, seeking to imagine into being alternatives to the status quo. The target of this transformative vision is the reader. The protagonists of Mahasweta's texts are not always able to rise above their circumstances to analyse the conditions of their own subjugation. Jamunaboti's mother, Jashoda in *Stanadayini* and Douloti, for instance, are victims of their own specific circumstances. But the textual rhetoric frequently places the reader in a position of greater knowledge and awareness and, therefore, of greater responsibility. Her narratives are never merely descriptive, for at their core is a strong ethical charge that denies the reader any possibility of apathy or detachment. The uncompromising urge to expose the forces of oppression goes hand-in-hand with a powerful imaginative vision that arouses our conscience and calls for changes in the existing order. This interweaving of dystopian and utopian elements creates the vibrant fabric of Mahasweta's narratives. The act of storytelling, learnt from her foremothers, becomes for Mahasweta an interventionist, emancipatory practice.

What happens, though, when local histories travel via translation? What does Draupadi's story signify when translated by Spivak for the consumption of audiences in the West? The interfaces between local, global and national acquire crucial significance here. It is possible, for instance, to argue that Draupadi's self-assertion, or Rani Lakshmibai's leading role in the freedom struggle, enforce a questioning of the universalist claims of some brands of 'international' feminism emanating from the Anglo-American academy. This has been Spivak's mission, as also her attempt to place the plight of tribals in this region in relation to the struggle of indigenous peoples in other parts of the world: the Native Americans, for example; or the aborigines in Australia. These transpositions generate new ways of reading Mahasweta's texts, a process that Brinda Bose calls 'transformed transmission' (Bose, 2002: 265). Much indeed is lost in the process, especially in terms of cultural nuances, varying dialects and linguistic registers. The issue also raises questions about authorship and authority, and about the limits of the translator's freedom to interpret and transform. All the same, the translation remains a valuable way to enact cultural border crossings that have the potential to promote greater awareness and understanding between those situated in different cultural locations. And like storytelling, translation too is never innocent, for it always has a context. In the construction of other histories, the politics of translation can also possess transformative potential.

Such, then, can be the multiple and far-reaching effects of inserting women into history. For in Mahasweta's fiction, the narrativisation of history represents a mixing of memory with desire, an evocation of the past in order to articulate our desires for the present and our dreams of the future. Freedom, Sangari reminds us, can function in literature as an absent horizon.

> This may be an absent freedom but it is not an abstract freedom: it is precisely that which is made present and possible by its absence—the lives that people have never lived because of the lives they are forced to live or have chosen to live. That which is desired and that which exists, the sense of abundance and the sense of waste, are dialectically related. (Sangari, 1999: 18)

Tribal women have, for centuries, been silenced and erased from history, but in Mahasweta's narrative, the ravished Dopdi is transformed into a terrifying figure of vengeful female wrath. And the Rani of Jhansi does not die: in Mahasweta's alternative version of history, the vanquished queen lives on in the fantasies of the people, who swear that '"The Queen hasn't died! *Baisaheba jarur jinda houni*"' (Devi, 1956: xv). This, to Mahasweta Devi, is the true significance of the life of the Rani of Jhansi, an icon who signified the spirit of the people at a key moment in the nation's history:

> Rani Lakshmibai was an expression of what India felt in those times. One truth rises above the countless mistakes, flaws, weaknesses and defeats of those days, and that is of the first conscious rebellion taking place against the stranglehold of foreign rule... As long as people insist, '*Rani margay na houni*'—'The Queen did not die'—the Queen will be alive. (ibid.: xvi)

◆

This chapter was first published in 2013 in the *IIC Quarterly*, Vol. 39, Nos. 3 and 4.

NOTES

1. A version of this article was presented as the Sufia Kamal Lecture, delivered on 1 July 2007 at the Asiatic Society, Dhaka (Bangladesh).
2. Samik Bandopadhyay. Interview with Mahasweta Devi. 26 May 1993. Calcutta. Cited in Anjum Katyal (1997).
3. Mahasweta Devi. Personal interview. 8 August 1999. Calcutta.

REFERENCES

Bagchi, Alakananda. 1996. 'Conflicting Nationalisms: The Voice of the Subaltern in Mahasweta Devi's *Bashai Tudu'*, *Tulsa Studies in Women's Literature*, 15.1, pp. 41–50.

Bose, Brinda. 2002. *Translating Desire: the Politics of Gender and Culture in India*. New Delhi: Katha.

Chakravarty, Radha. 2004. 'Visionary Cartography: *Imaginary Maps* by Mahasweta Devi', in Malashri Lal, Shormistha Panja and Sumanyu Satpathy (eds.), *Signifying the Self: Women and Literature*. New Delhi: Macmillan.

Devi, Mahasweta. 1995. *Imaginary Maps*. Translated and introduced by Gayatri Chakravorty Spivak. New York: Routledge.

Devi, Mahasweta. 1990. 'Draupadi. *Bashai Tudu.*' Translated by Samik Bandopadhyay and Gayatri Chakravorty Spivak. Calcutta: Thema.

Devi, Mahasweta. 1956. *The Queen of Jhansi*. Original Bengali version. Translated by Sagaree and Mandira Sengupta, 2000. Kolkata: Seagull.

Katyal, Anjum. 1997. 'The Metamorphosis of *Rudali*', in Mahasweta Devi and Usha Ganguli (eds.), *Rudali*. Kolkata: Seagull.

Mukherjee, Sujit. 1991. 'Mahasweta Devi's Writings—An Evaluation', *The Book Review*, 15.3.

Sangari, Kumkum. 1999. *Politics of the Possible: Essays on Gender, History, Narrative, Colonial English*. New Delhi: Tulika.

Spivak, Gayatri Chakravorty. 1994. 'Can the Subaltern Speak?', in Patrick Williams and Laura Chrisman (eds.), *Colonial Discourse and Postcolonial Theory*. New York: Columbia University Press.

Sunder Rajan, Rajeswari. 1999. 'Introduction', in Rajeswari Sunder Rajan (ed.), *Signposts: Gender Issues in Post-Independence India*. New Delhi: Kali for Women.

◆◆

11
IN HER OWN WRITE*
Writing from a Dalit Feminist Standpoint

UMA
CHAKRAVARTI#

The women's movement in India since the 1980s has made for the emergence of a decisive feminist perspective in the social sciences, primarily from women scholars; it has also inspired a huge wave of creativity among women, leading to the appearance of the category of 'women writers' although not all of these writers might accept such a label. The languages in which women have written and the genres they have used to express themselves have varied. Collections of short stories, novellas, and on occasion poetry published by feminist presses have circulated widely and accessibly among a readership that the social science writings would not have been able to reach. This body of writing has also been able to enter university courses, especially in literature. Given that the social and regional location of women writing in India is also widely disparate, the nature of the audience itself would vary and translations into English and other languages play a key role in widening the reach of the writing.

While examining the body of work that has emerged and studying its audience would be an important project, I will focus here on a growing body of work by Dalit feminist/women writers. Almost all of them write in their mother tongue and have a dual readership comprising those who read the work in the original languages used and others who read them in English translations. With such a focus we may be able to think about a dialogue that has been opened up between scholars and activists on the unacknowledged universalist claims of the women's movement and the critiques of the movement that have come from Dalit scholars and activists. Dalit feminist writing might give us an idea of what may perhaps be 'shared' and what is distinctive in experiential terms in the making and breaking of identities. Since it is impossible to be exhaustive in exploring this category of writing, I will select some works for a close reading while drawing from others in broader terms.

It took some years for the caste question to 'hit' the consciousness of the largely city-based women's movement, even as the issues the movement took up in its first phase did focus on the 'subaltern' woman. The rapes of Mathura and Rameeza Bee, around whom the campaign against sexual violence by the police in custodial contexts triggered off country-wide protests at the judicial bias evident in the judgement which was understood as an imposition of normative standards drawn from upper-caste Hindu notions of female virtue. Since these notions were being widely challenged in the campaign, even though the activists, almost always constituted by middle class and upper-caste urban women, confronted the judicial bias against an Adivasi girl, their own social location was less visible to them. The marginal woman and the city-based activists were united in a common cause against the imposition of outrageous standards drawn from archaic 'Hindu' but decisively upper-caste notions of virtue. It took a decade for questions of caste to surface in the 1980s and early 1990s, especially when the Mandal agitation introduced what was perceived by urban India as the emergence of identity politics over the supposed unity of people forged by the Left. Once these debates appeared in the public sphere, suppressed or unacknowledged questions of caste began to fracture the consciousness of a single unitary woman subject that the women's movement had 'sort of' worked within an overarching call for 'women's solidarity'. Dalit feminist consciousness became a force to reckon with.

Literature on caste from a feminist perspective soon began to appear in the social sciences. At the same time, the distinctive experience that shaped the identity of Dalit women too appeared as an issue in social science scholarship (Guru, 1994). Before Dalit women began to speak to a wider national and international 'audience' through their own writing in English translations, a life history of a Dalit woman speaking through an interlocutor caught the attention of scholars. Viramma's recounting of her own life is significant for the graphic account of how her identity is shaped by the performance of labour, her caste location, the class relations that subject her to the power of landlords, and the workings of the State. It also vividly depicts the mythologies, histories and culture of the *paraya* community, the struggle for survival, the subversions, the refusal to consent to the hegemonic ideologies by which class and caste power are maintained and reproduced, and the attempts at resistance whenever possible (Racine and Racine, 1997). It mirrors, nuances, enriches and deepens the fine anthropological account of labouring women in Tamil Nadu (Kapadia, 1996).

A point that emerges from the account narrated by Viramma is her awareness that she is telling her story to someone who is not of her own caste or class, or indeed someone who shares her culture. Viramma not only constantly reminds Josiane Racine, to whom she is speaking, of this, but through this device the reader too is made aware of the huge gap between Viramma and us. She does this through the book in various ways, disguised sometimes and more consciously at other times, interspersing her speech with reminders of the different locations of the narrator and the interlocutor. An example is her allusion to *kaliyuga*, the traditional notion of dystopia in Brahmanic mythology and textual tradition, of which she makes very subversive use. The Brahmanical ideology of the kaliyuga as a time of normlessness because of its obsessive fears of it being a time of social upheaval is retained intact by Viramma; however, by using a strategically neutral voice, she continually draws attention to all the things that are now pro-paraya. In the time of kaliyuga, Dalits can go to school, become teachers and so make it possible for Dalit children to have teachers who are not biased against them, have access to dispensaries and hospitals, vote, and therefore be wooed by political parties. Now the government itself has brought in the kaliyuga. As Viramma tells 'Sinamma', her name for her biographer:

> Yes it was better for you in the past. You could employ us for a rupee or a rupee and a half and we'd eat what grew at the edge of the fields. Nowadays in this kaliyugam, ploughmen demand ten or fifteen rupees. The government steps in and sets wages. Would we have seen or experienced a government in the past that took care of us like that? (Racine and Racine, 1997: 252)

The separate worlds that Racine and Viramma inhabit is also tellingly brought out in a significant passage where Viramma points out that while Racine came to listen and collect the laments that Viramma sang for her study, she did not let Viramma sing them at Racine's father's death, because such a lament would have been culturally alien to her world. When Viramma tells Racine that she would have sung for her 'a most marvelous lament', it is a telling comment on the separate worlds the two women inhabit. It is also a comment on the difference between a relationship that must remain confined to one between scholar and native informant in the understanding of the scholar, but is regarded as a genuine friendship that is denied in a moment that otherwise could have bound them together in grief. The editors say that speaking gives pleasure to Viramma and 'is a form of self-assertion'; she uses it effectively to draw attention to the unbridgeable distance between her and her interlocutors. Later in this essay I will bring Viramma back as she speaks about the workings of caste in satirical ways, but also reminding us of the chasm between us and her.

Viramma's life history is based on her speaking sessions with Racine as she cannot write herself. There are other life histories where access to the written word enables Dalit women to tell their own stories, where they represent themselves and are thus their own interlocutors. A number of these memoirs were written since the 1970s and 1980s in Maharashtra, although they became available in translations in the last decade and have also been the subject of an important feminist engagement by Sharmila Rege.[1] Again, since the writing encapsulates a range of experiences, I will focus on a few issues that will help us to return to the debates on Dalit women speaking in a different way from upper-caste women who may never even reveal their upper caste-ness in their writing.

A stigmatised caste status and a permanent sense of its shaping of the world of the writers is the common thread in all of the works. As Kumud Pawade, who published one of the earliest memoirs in 1981 titled *Antahspot* (Outburst) writes:

> The result is that although I try to forget my caste, it is impossible to forget. And then I remember an expression heard somewhere: 'what comes by birth, but can't be cast off by dying—that is caste'. (Pawade, 1992: 97)

The irony is that the emphasis on Kumud Pawade's caste is doubly marked because though she is a Mahar by birth, she has forced her way into the sacred knowledge system by studying and then teaching Sanskrit; and compounded the transgression by making an inter-caste marriage with a man from a higher non-Dalit caste. This makes her more noticeable than other Mahar women and subjects her to veiled remarks, innuendos and blunt statements that are offensive.

Caste stigma is a running theme in all the autobiographical writings—the offending touch, the association with dirt, labour, 'unclean' occupations, and finally the quality of being polluting that inhered in certain castes. The most powerful exclusion that is ever present in Dalit writing is from access to the otherwise common resource of water, the very basis of life without which the possession of land itself would be rendered meaningless. Urmila Pawar refers to it simply, almost in passing, as she describes the structure of her house which was better endowed and therefore somewhat privileged in relation to other Mahar households:

> The houses of the Marathas and Brahmins were at some distance from our house. Bhandari and Kulwadi women could drink water from their wells but untouchable women were absolutely forbidden to do so. This was a permanent wound in father's heart. Therefore he had given strict instructions to my mother to allow the untouchable women to draw from our well. The rope and bucket were permanent fixtures to the well. These were never removed. (Pawar, 2003: 23)

It is not surprising that for Babasaheb Ambedkar, the right to draw water from the Chavadar tank at Mahad was more important than the temple-entry movement spearheaded by Mahatma Gandhi: in the scale of deprivation from resources, water was more important to challenge than the right to worship the Gods created by the Brahmanical system! As he said in his speech to those who had gathered in Mahad on the banks of the Chavadar lake:

> You will understand the significance of the struggle we have begun.... It is not as if drinking the water of the Chavadar lake will make us immortal. We have survived well enough all these days without drinking it. We are not going to the lake merely to

drink its water. We are going to the lake to assert that we too are human beings like others. It must be clear that the meeting has been called to set up the norm of equality. (Pawade, 1992: 223)

When Kumud Pawade married a man from a caste above hers, they had their first child with no support from anyone because they had been excluded from both families. This, despite the claim for equality and dignity, and even after the country became independent and the Constitution banned the practice of untouchability. The father-in-law was furious that his son had had a child by a Mahar woman. He sent his son a message through a friend that he would never accept the child of a Mahar woman into his family—he would rather swallow poison. 'I have been thrown out of my caste … I would rather burn down my property than give him anything', he raved. When he relented a little and went to see the child, he continued to humiliate Kumud. When he was approached in reverence by the little grandson he recoiled in horror from being touched by him, only handing over a five-rupee note to the boy. Unable to take the humiliation anymore, Kumud said to the boy: 'do not take the money in your hands. We too get polluted by money!' (Rege, 2006: 251).

We get a more satirical understanding of caste pollution from Viramma; perhaps she is in real form as she speaks to her upper-caste interlocutor about the contradictions in the way pollution is actually observed. When she is a young mother who is still lactating, the Reddiar mistress hands over her eldest son to Viramma when he is an infant: since they eat beef, the milk is rich. She says to her, 'here, give him a bit of your milk!' Years later when the child is a young man, Viramma asks him to pour out some water for her as she is 'dying of thirst'. He asks his mother whether he should do so. Viramma comments:

> He had drunk at my breast and now he is thinking twice about giving me some water! Now he doesn't respect me and if I'm in the house he says to me 'Aye! Stop there, you. It smells of paraya here!' (Racine and Racine, 1997: 76)

Apart from the spatial difference in the houses of the Dalits and the upper castes into the *ur* and the *cheri,* where the upper castes and the Dalits reside, making it obvious without being told that the Dalits are different from others, all Dalit children experience humiliating discrimination in the so-called impersonal institution of the school everywhere in India. Made to sit outside the schoolroom or at a distance at the back, that theirs is a stigmatised body is seared into the consciousness of children. A most powerful account of such discrimination comes from Urmila Pawar's memoir, *Aydaan*. When Urmila's father dies he exhorts his wife to educate the children so that they can get jobs and move out of the village and the humiliating life they are forced to live, subject to caste restrictions and servile obligations. Aai (mother) wheedles, begs and coerces Urmila to go to school, but she is reluctant for various reasons, including the beatings and humiliation that she receives from her teacher. Guruji insists that Urmila must sit in the last row, sweep the class after school and pick up the dung from the yard. One day Urmila refuses to pick up dung and the teacher slaps her hard across her face and tells her to get out of the school. Reaching home with a swollen and marked cheek, and crying miserably, Aai discovers the reason for the beating and is driven to take the Guruji on in front of others as he returns home in the evening. A furious Aai challenges his version of why the teacher hit Urmila. As Urmila writes in *A Childhood Tale*:

> 'Look here, I am not a respectable woman. I live here under a tree, by the roadside, with my children like an exile. Why? So that they can study...become important people, and you harass the girl like this?' Aai was speaking ungrammatically, incorrectly. In a loud voice she threatened Guruji, 'Look here, after this if your finger so much as touches my daughter, I will see to it that you will never walk on this road...'

> After that day many things became easier ... collecting dung and Guruji's beating were no longer part of my fate and destiny. But the main thing was that I began to see my mother as a tremendous support. And my life got some direction. (Pawar, 2002: 54–55)

Apart from describing the stigma and inequality experienced in school, Urmila also captures the strong investment in education that Dalits make, both as a means of countering the ideology of caste and as a means by which Dalits could hope to escape the prison-house of caste-based status and occupation that would keep them in the control of the landed elite for whom they must labour on degrading terms. Education was a means of social mobility through which the Dalits could at least partly break out of the stranglehold of caste. It had the power to transform the lived social reality of the Dalits, and so her father kept saying 'educate the children', like a mantra to their mother, even as he lay dying. Most importantly, Urmila translates through the act of writing or 'weaving with words' what her mother expresses through her silent and ceaseless weaving of baskets to make a living, and thus gives words to her mother's pain. Even though poverty and stigma have left an indelible scar on Urmila's personality, her subjectivity is also shaped by a new political understanding which enables her to make sense of the emotions she experienced as a child. Through the act of writing, Urmila brings the changed consciousness of both the mother and daughter into the public world.

Violence of different kinds hovers around the narratives, ever present and inescapable. Children grow up in its shadow. When Bama, the author of *Karukku* is 11-years-old, she witnesses the battle between her community of Dalit Christians and the dominant caste Saliyars which takes place in the local cemetery, the raids by the policemen who sided as always with the dominant groups, and their brutality against the men which leads them to escape to the hills and forests to save their lives. The women then have to face sexual abuse by the policemen which Dalit women face on a daily basis too. Bama's voice in this account is the narrative voice of the community as she recalls the days when she wrote her first book. Her recall of the events also shows how women thought of different ruses to escape the endemic police raids: one time they hung margosa leaves to ward off entry into a house because that is what is hung when someone has small pox, allowing a man to spend a night at home without fear of a raid. On another occasion, Bama's grandmother hatches a plan to dress a man who is hiding from the police in a sari so that he can attend his son's funeral. When Bama becomes an adult she joins the church as a nun, hoping to be able to do something for her people. But there too she discovers painfully that there is the violence of caste repression extracted in the form of unquestioning obedience; she leaves the church, writing somewhat bitterly: 'I don't know where the God has fled. For now it is the priest, nuns and their relatives who claim themselves to be Gods' (Pandian, 2003: 135). After her return to her own people she breathes freely and seeks to fashion a world of justice and equality. The title of the book *Karukku* evokes the pain she has suffered through the violence of poverty and stigma as she is seared by sharp double-edged leaves when collecting firewood. Now she uses words and ideas that will be sharp like the karukku to hit back at the oppressors (ibid.: 133).

There are three issues with which I want to close this essay. Dalit women's articulation of difference is evident in all the pieces of writing to which I have already alluded. There are two issues that I want to examine here that are suggestive of the areas of tension between the women's movement and the Dalit women's movement, and these have erupted at different stages of mobilisations and events in the last three decades. Early on in the 1980s when the feminism of Dalit women was less evident as a different voice—a stage that Rege refers to as the 'silent' or perhaps 'silenced' years of feminism[2]—Dalit women in the urban cities were part of women's groups that began to mushroom as the autonomous women's groups. But they soon began to feel that their experience of caste could never form the basis of the main campaign plank of the women's groups as their distinctive experience was swept under formulations such as 'all women are Dalits because all women were involved with cleaning jobs for their children!'[3] Thus, when Dalit women in Delhi sought to include an end to manual scavenging for an 8 March campaign, its non-inclusion in the campaign document led to some Dalit members falling out of the campaign. Over the years, Dalit feminists have formed their own organisations. They have also drawn attention to the Dalit woman as the thrice-oppressed: by class power and the exploitation of labour; by the stigma of the caste system and the oppression experienced through the power of dominant castes and on the basis of their gender through regular abuse of their dignity and endemic sexual violence. The distinctive social experience which upper-caste women in the movement failed or refused to understand surfaced sharply at a conference in 2007 over bar-dancing. Contentious issues arose around how feminists should view forms of contemporary labour complicated by gender and sexuality. There was anger expressed by Dalit feminists because the relationship between labour, caste and stigma was not recognised by the mainstream women's movement. These confrontations have led to the opening up of a dialogue between the two strands of the women's movement which is still ongoing.[4]

These dialogues may be deepened by the nuances of the literature produced by Dalit feminists in the form of poetry, short stories and other forms of writing being published now. Two have made a powerful impact on me: a short story by Gogu Shyamala on the practice enforced by the dominant castes of dedicating girls from the Dalit castes to a goddess and then making them available for sexual use by the landed elites and justified by tradition; and a powerful story by Saraswathy on manual scavenging. Shyamala's story, *Raw Wound*, is written in the first person and poignantly describes a Dalit family's struggle to save their daughter from being dedicated, which the rest of the village, led by the biggest landlord, is trying to enforce in the name of tradition. When he hears that the family is trying to place the daughter in school to be educated, the landlord says:

> In this village our word is law. We speak for the good of the village. Tomorrow we may have deaths, disease, drought and famine. To appease the gods after that would be futile. We should do our dharma—only then will god look after us.... If you don't do your duty and I mine, we are doomed. We have to follow what is written on our foreheads. Who are we change our destiny? You know the fingers of the hand are not equal, don't you, my man? (Shyamala, 2012: 142)

When the family against all odds manages to secretly take the daughter away to a residential school for admittance, they face the severest of violence. The whole family is beaten viciously and then banished from the village; so they must leave it, giving the land to the landlord in return for their lives. As they leave the village lamenting the cruelty of caste power, the father exhorts his daughter not to cry, to study and become a big officer, and that is what gives the daughter courage to continue with her education. She writes about the struggle:

> My childhood, marked by a refusal to become a jogini, and by my father losing his land, is a raw wound for my family and for me—a throbbing memory even today (ibid.: 258).

Saraswathy's story weaves together two axes of difference that have become points of criticism for the mainstream women's movement: caste and disability. In a marvellous story, *Bacheesu* (Tip), that Saraswathy has read at conferences, she describes the life of the manual scavengers, the filth that they must carry away for the city to remain clean. A pregnant daughter of such a family who has come home for her delivery decides to cook a nice meal for her parents who work so hard and have little time for themselves to prepare meals, just drinking coffee to get past the tiredness of the day. But, when the parents return home the mother is unable to eat; she cannot swallow anything after having dealt with the stink of the rotting remnants of the everyday life of (upper-caste) people, the dregs of the city, dead dogs and cats. She has just come back from dealing with the remnants of a dead puppy which has disintegrated in her hands. Before the daughter can notice that her mother is not eating, the baby decides to herald its arrival. But the baby has a deformity—he does not have all his fingers. The boy has only two fingers in the right hand and three in the left. The doctors reassure the grandparents that they can do corrective surgery in three months but that it will cost money, something the parents do not have. They are deeply distressed. The mother tries to console the daughter and says to her that if God has put an obstacle in their lives, He will find them a way out too. That reassurance is not needed as the daughter has found her own way:

> Why should I bemoan my fate? Amma, I am not sad, only recalling how much you tried to make me go to school and I never heeded you. Now there is no way but to send this child to school. You ask why? This child can only hold a pen in two fingers and never a broom. God has given a gift. Why should I refuse it? (Saraswathy: forthcoming)

◆

* The title of this chapter is inspired by a collection of short stories published in Pakistan by Nighat Said Khan for ASR Lahore.

This chapter was first published in 2013 in the *IIC Quarterly*, Vol. 39, Nos. 3 and 4.

NOTES

1. I will also include *Karukku*, which functions as a part-memoir by the Tamil writer Bama (2001) with a noticeable slide from the narrative voice of the community to the narrative voice of the author and back.
2. See Rege (2006) for a discussion on the amnesia that has written out the years of serious engagements by Dalit scholars and writers on Dalit feminist standpoints and the critiques of mainstream but also the possibilities of a more incorporative politics.
3. Personal communication from feminist friends in Delhi.
4. This paragraph is based on debates that have been taking place around women's groups in Delhi.

REFERENCES

Bama, 2001. *Karukku*. Chennai: Macmillan.

Guru, Gopal. 1994. 'Dalit Women Talk Differently', *Economic and Political Weekly*, 14 October, pp. 2548–50.

Kapadia, Karin. 1996. *Siva and Her Sisters*. Delhi: Oxford University Press.

Pandian, M.S.S. 2003. 'On a Dalit Woman's Testimonio', in Anupama Rao (ed.), *Gender and Caste*. Delhi: Kali For Women.

Pawade, Kumud. 1992. 'The Story of My Sanskrit', in Arjun Dangle (ed.), *Poisoned Bread*. Bombay: Orient Longman.

Pawar, Urmila. 2002. 'A Childhood Tale,' in Tapan Basu (ed.), *Translating Caste*. Delhi: Katha.

Pawar, Urmila. 2003. *The Weave of My life: A Dalit Woman's Memoirs*. Kolkata: Stree.

Racine, Josiane and Jean Luc Racine. 1997. *Viramma: Life of an Untouchable*. London: Verso.

Rege, Sharmila. 2006. *Writing Caste/ Writing Gender: Narrating Dalit Women's Testimonios*. Delhi: Zubaan.

Saraswathy, D. (forthcoming). 'Bacheesu', in Susie Tharu (ed.), *Steel Nibs Are Sprouting*.

Shyamala, Gogu. 2012. *Father May Be an Elephant and Mother Only a Basket, But....* Delhi: Navayana Publishers.

◆◆

12
CATALYSING CRAFT
Women Who Shaped the Way

RITU SETHI#

Mahatma Gandhi's powerful call of *swadeshi* and *swaraj* to his fellow Indians not only created the radical shift that led to the crumbling of imperialism in India, but the call was also equally a beacon to spinners and weavers, the makers by hand, spread across rural India. His vision for a self-reliant, free India closely linked to its resurgent village industries and its village roots laid the foundation stone of women's leadership and empowerment in the craft movement. In parallel, in Bengal, the visionary Nobel Prize winner Gurudev Rabindranath Tagore initiated a search into the indigenous roots of culture, setting the bedrock, inspiring others to follow.

Over the almost seven decades since India's independence, many women contributed to change, walking the long road to try to convert the vision of a revitalised crafts and handloom sector into reality. While it is hard to single out names, as their histories are largely unrecorded, the aim of this short essay is limited. It is, first, to briefly examine and identify those women who led the way, shaping the journey, creating invigorating patterns of impact and influence. Whether working pan-India or in localised spaces, these authors of development created and empowered crafts[1] and craftspeople.[2]

The second aim is to signpost the changing mandates that led to directional change. These were models of development which, whilst rooted in a similar ethos, metamorphosed and adapted to fit the rapidly evolving social, cultural, political and economic landscape in which crafts and craftspeople were situated.

A fitting starting point of the journey is Kamaladevi Chattopadhyay, whose pioneering work in the decades after

Independence rejuvenated and vitalised crafts and craftspeople across India. She was appointed the Chairperson of the All India Handicrafts Board (AIHB) in 1952 and served till 1967. The situation she faced on the ground is hard to imagine today. With a nascent polity, an uncharted territory, crafts and craftspeople displaced and unsettled in the turmoil of Independence and the partition of the country, it was an enormous mission that the then Prime Minister Jawaharlal Nehru entrusted her.

> This was a challenging task for there was no previous experience on which to build the work. It meant the creation of a new economic order for a newly independent country which would nurture and support the existing structure and skills. (Dhamija, 2007: 69)

The task of formulating policy, the setting up of institutions, and the designing of a framework for crafts to flourish and develop in, was the vast undertaking faced. Her holistic view of the sector wherein 'She saw crafts not in isolation, but as part of the rich fabric of our life involving all the creative expressions of a people' (ibid.: 69) was the grounding of the vision. The Ramon Magsaysay Award Citation which she received in 1996 stated:

> Among the architects of modern India few have been so broadly effective as Kamaladevi Chattopadhyay ... in an era when great traditional crafts and artistry often are submerged by mass production of standardised products, Kamaladevi has led in mobilising for new generations these ancient skills.[3]

The creation of support systems and frameworks such as the Regional Design Centres, the infrastructure she put into place and the organisations she seeded included the Indian Cooperative Union (ICU), which she founded in 1948, providing tools, loans and directions in a new way of living.[4] The ICU managed the then iconic handicrafts and handloom store—the Central Cottage Industries Emporium (CCIE), where:

> Teji Vir Singh and Mrs Prem Bery with their experience of Marketing of Refugee Handicrafts and with the guidance of Kitty Shiva Rao and Mrs B.K. Nehru and the support of dynamic and

talented Sina Kaul were responsible for building it up ... the best of
handicrafts, with its buyers such as Gulshan Nanda,[5] Nakara sisters
and many others travelling the length and breadth of the country,
searching for crafts and craftsmen.... (Dhamija, 2007: 78)

The furthering of the craft movement, the process of revival and
empowerment, continued through her lifetime. She brought new
ways of looking at the crafts, challenged hierarchies and reached
out to craftspeople. Herself a prolific writer and spokesperson,
she initiated research and documentation on the crafts and its
practitioners. Her interest and her ability to galvanise others led
to the seeding of organisations across the continuum of art, culture
and heritage. In the field of craft, she served as the Vice President of
the World Crafts Council, an endeavour that she initiated in 1964.
The backing and encouragement she provided to many furthered
the cause—from Rukmini Devi Arundale whose efforts in the area
of natural dyes and weaving at Kalakshetra have continued to
be carried forward, to the setting up of the Crafts Council of India
(CCI), which now has chapters across several states and is largely
women-led and women-run.[6] The Paramparik Karigar Trust was
established in Mumbai in 1996, when master craftspeople from across
India met with her and Roshan Kalapesi to create the first registered
body of craftspeople responsible for their own future. 'It is in this
context that Paramparik Karigar is so important. Its active core "with
full decision-making rights" is the now around 1,000-strong crafts
community.'[7] These were just some of Kamaladevi's many activities
and achievements in shaping, empowering and revival.

In parallel, in the 1950s, Pupul Jayakar was appointed the
Chairperson of the All India Handloom Board by Prime Minister
Jawaharlal Nehru, with a short break in-between. Her role in
influencing culture and craft policy continued under the prime
ministership of both Indira Gandhi and Rajiv Gandhi.

The building of the Weavers' Service Centres, the marketing
frameworks and institutions supportive of the sector, the formation
of the Handloom and Handicraft Export Promotion Corporation
(HHEC), where she was the Chairperson from 1968 to 1977, and
other initiatives were a response to the shifting economic and
social situation, a directional change that recognised the need for
repositioning Indian handmade products for the world. The Sona

shop in New York, the emphasis on design and design education, the introduction of internationally known designers, including Pierre Cardin to Indian culture, crafts and textiles, the Festivals of India, all worked towards a global repositioning of Indian crafts and textiles as valued, timeless, cultural artifacts.

Pupul Jayakar initiated the idea of a national school of design in 1955, when she met Charles Eames in the United States. Subsequently, Eames was invited by the government to outline a proposal.

> He came to explore the actuality of India before preparing his blueprint. He and his wife Ray travelled through India ... observing the landscape, the people ... the rural capacity for attention, their skills and the intensity of their minds. He prepared out of this raw material his blueprint, an integral view of the Indian scene ... his report was placed before Manubhai Shah, the then Minister of Commerce and Industry; ... also present, was Gautam Sarabhai.... The Minister was confused but trusted Sarabhai's acute business sense and was aware of my down-to-earth approach to development. Finally, the report was accepted and the National Institute of Design (NID) came into being and was built in Ahmedabad.... (Jayakar, 1995: 150–51)

Similarly, the creation of national-level institutes of fashion and accessory design was mooted and the National Institute of Fashion Technology (NIFT) came into being in 1986. There are now 15 NIFTs located at different centres across India. These institutions, and the many others they spawned, changed forever the design landscape in India. The many design graduates and the increasing emphasis on design in the country are a product of this foresight.

The establishment of INTACH was similar:

> While in England I had met the senior representatives of the National Trust in London and discussed the possibilities of establishing an all-India society concerned with heritage and its preservation ... there was no major all-India body to concern itself with identifying, listing and conserving manmade and natural heritage. Indira was enthused with the suggestion. In spite of all

manner of obstacles, the Indian National Trust for Art and Cultural Heritage (INTACH) was registered in early 1984 with Indira Gandhi as its patron, Rajiv, its first Chairman. (Jayakar, 1995: 437)

Her interests in rural arts and crafts, her ability to see potential and translate it into action, sparked change in many areas of craft. One such incident was recounted by L.K. Jha:

> ... another field of high achievement ... is the popularisation of Madhubani paintings ... when in the mid-'60s, during the famine which threatened Bihar, she went there to discover ways in which new incomes could be generated for those whose crops had failed, with the result that they neither had the food which they used to grow for themselves nor the income to buy it from others. The problem was that since Madhubani paintings were done on walls, there was no way they could be transported or sold.... Pupul Jayakar was the first person to persuade them to do their paintings on paper.... Soon, their quality caught the fancy of those with a discerning eye.... Madhubani paintings are in many museums as well as homes of the art lovers all over the world—thanks more to Pupul Jayakar than to anyone else. (Chandra *et al.*, 1986: xxviii)

In a period before ethnic became chic, Pupul Jayakar connected the crafts to their cultural underpinnings. As a Chairman of CCIE, she initiated policies that widened their reach. As a Chairperson of HHEC, she introduced Indian crafts to the global market. It was, however, as a Chairman of the Advisory Committee of the Festivals of India, held in Britain, USA, Japan and France that her creative and organisational activities were brought to the fore. The Festivals were a major series of events, a unique cooperative effort between the Government of India and the host country, designed to bring to the attention of the world the greater understanding of the complex life and 'the vibrant manifestations of Indian culture ...' (Doshi, 1982: 4). In the wide-ranging presentations on art, culture, performance, scientific achievements included 'Vasna', a portrait of a contemporary village, and The Living Arts Exhibition with demonstrations of crafts skills. Several years in the making, the Master Weavers Exhibition, a part of the Festival, 'projected the great contemporary textile arts of the country and focused on the continuity of tradition' (Jayakar, 1982: 5) with Martand Singh as conceptualiser, exhibition director and curator. The exhibition—Aditi—inspired by the rural and ritual arts, with Rajeev Sethi as the Project Director and Curator—centred on the growing-up of the child, from womb to adulthood.

While received with glowing tributes, '... and as Mrs (Indira) Gandhi said it had "succeeded beyond our wildest hopes". It did not serve just as a "show window" for India but had actively created interest in India' (Doshi, 1982: 6). When this shift in priorities and strategies led to trenchant disapproval with traditionalists, Mrs Jayakar countered these by saying, 'There may be much criticism today but I am confident that the events as they unfold will bring in the bouquets. We hope these festivals will reveal the great strengths of a young nation with an ancient culture and heritage' (Singh, 1986: xvii).

The early foundational figures had worked in synch with a farsighted political class and bureaucracy, who backed their initiatives. From Prime Minister Jawaharlal Nehru to Indira Gandhi and Rajiv Gandhi, there was the recognition that the arts and crafts, the second largest sector of employment in India after agriculture, were not only an invaluable cultural asset but, equally, an economic force.

From the late 1980s onwards, government institutions became less responsive to the needs of craftspeople. Political will now shifted gear, with prioritisation and an almost exclusive focus on the urban, the industrial and digital; crafts and craftspeople were now relegated to the backwaters. Their neglect reflected in the phrase used by politicians and policy-makers to describe the sector as a 'sunset industry', and viewed through the lens of sops and subsidy, rather than as a muscular economic activity contributing to GDP. This mindset made the task of those who worked in this sector much harder.

The major question that arose was: How to equip and empower craftspeople for the changing times? While there was a burgeoning middle-class market that demanded goods that fit into their lifestyle, there was a growing schism between rural and urban India. The opening up of the economy, globalisation, loss of traditional markets, increased competition from mass-marketers and declining incomes were just some of the many challenges being

Block printing. Akola, Rajasthan.
Courtesy: Chinar Farooqui. CRT Pictures

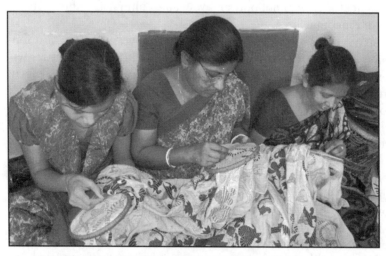

Collectively embroidering a Kantha spread. Kolkata, West Bengal.
Courtesy: Upal Sengupta. CRT Pictures

faced. Craftspeople too were looking for change, being aware that economic empowerment, development and other transformations occurring in modern India were not trickling down to them. Priorities and strategies were needed to change to suit this rapidly altering scenario. It was in this context that a new generation of activists matured; their direction, both a response and a reaction to the shifts in circumstances confronting craftspeople. Mandated to empower and improve the economic and social status of craftspeople, pan-India and regional non-governmental organisations (NGOs) heralded a new wave of women from dissimilar backgrounds who, drawn to the sector, had a pulse for its needs and changing priorities. Working to create sustainable economic models and, equally significantly, going beyond economics to fulfil social development agendas, these NGOs focused on a wide range of actions. Measures included seeking sustainable employment, collectivisation, generating income, economic self-sufficiency and social equity—all human development aspirations.

To review the impressive line-up could risk producing a mere laundry list of achievers, but it needs to be done. Each name could be accompanied by a roll call of achievements although, given the exigencies of space, the mention here is pithy and brief.

One such organisation, among others with a wide mandate, is SEWA in Ahmedabad—registered in 1972—with its trade union of self-employed poor women workers, led by Elaben Bhatt, Renana Jhabvala and Mirai Chatterjee. The struggles it undertook strengthened women to organise for social change, making it equally 'both an organisation and a movement'.[8] Its emphasis on creating self-reliance and employment included those engaged in craft activity and was led by Reema Nanavati and Lalitha Krishnaswami.

In 1972, Bunker Roy set up the Social Work and Research Centre (SWRC), popularly known as the 'Barefoot College', in Tillonia, Rajasthan. He was joined in 1974 by his wife, Aruna Roy—who now heads the Mazdoor Kisan Shakti Sangathana—both working to improve the lives of the rural poor by addressing basic needs for water, electricity, housing, health and education. The Hatheli Sansthan wing works with artisans across Rajasthan, and Saharanpur in UP.

Non-governmental organisations interknitted the concerns of the sector, creating self-sufficiencies, improving the economic status of craftspeople and promoting the survival of traditional

Spinning. Phulia, West Bengal.
Courtesy: CRT Pictures

Pattachitra Artist. Midnapur, West Bengal.
Courtesy: Ritu Sethi. CRT Pictures

craftsmanship. They developed a momentum as well as foci of their own—maturing and transforming along the way to resolve the problems of their time. Through successful experimentation, crafts were introduced to urban India, demonstrating that skills were alive and the products of craftsmanship in demand for a new, rapidly evolving middle class.

Set up in 1981, Dastkar was headed by Laila Tyabji with its groundbreaking exhibitions, where craftspeople could interact with their customers, learning new skills and developing markets. Their programmes provided support, whether in design or in accessing credit and raw material, from training in entrepreneurship to providing technical assistance. With year-on-year bazaars held across India, craftspeople developed direct links to new markets, leading to improved incomes, social equity and empowerment.

These concerns were echoed at Dastkari Haat Samiti, established in 1985 and chaired by Jaya Jaitley, which worked closely with craftspeople from across India, expanding their markets, developing cutting-edge design, and giving the strength and support required in each area. Jaitley's innovative and breakout idea of a permanent craft bazaar, the Dilli Haat, was conceptualised, blue-printed and pushed through with the government with great perseverance by her. This landmark achievement has been hugely successful and duplicated across India and, indeed, in other countries.

Working closely with the concerns of the sector at large, NGOs adapted programmes to needs, reinforcing efforts while constantly pushing the boundaries to growth, empowerment and change. Weaving together a network of mutual interests and collaborations, they attempted to make an impact and bring change for those whom they were serving. From Anita Reddy working with the Kalamkari craftspeople in Sri Kalahasti (Dwarka, Delhi); Sally Holkar's work with the weavers in Maheshwar (Women's Weavers); Gita Ram and Neelam Chibber's developmental and marketing initiatives with natural fibre craftspeople in South India (Industree Foundation); Uzramma's path-breaking work with cotton handloom and Malkha weavers in Andhra (Dastakar Andhra and Malkha Marketing Trust); Mukti Dutta in Panchchuli and Rashmi Bharathi in Uttarakhand (Avni); the work of the Craft Revival Trust in creating the largest online encyclopaedia on the arts, crafts and textiles, and its practitioners; Ujwala Jodha of

Dastkar, Ranthambore, are only some of the many examples that abound in the sector.

Working to preserve traditions, creating employment while ensuring income and livelihoods for its members, Chandraben Shroff at Shrujan, Meera Goradia at Khamir, Neena Raaste at KMVS, and Judy Frater at Kala Raksha, work in Kutch. While in West Bengal, the late Dr Phulrenu Guha of Karma Kutir worked to rehabilitate refugees from erstwhile Bangladesh, providing training in skills and reviving handicrafts; Ruby Pal Choudhuri at the Crafts Council; Sarba Shanti Ayog—SASHA—set up by the late Subhashini Kohli and its stewardship by Roopa Mehta, working now with more than a hundred crafts groups. Ananya Bhattacharya at Banglanatak.com; Sumita at Rangasutra; Adithi, established by the late Vijii Srinivasan, operate across Bihar and Jharkhand. The MRMRM Cultural Foundation, set up by Visalakshi Ramaswamy in Chettinad; the late Lalitha Prasad of Crafts Council of Andhra; SEWA Lucknow formed with the agenda of doing away with the middleman under the able guidance of Runa Banerjee, providing viable and sustainable livelihood opportunities to *chikan* embroiderers—the list goes on.

Diverse, spread out, kaleidoscopic in character, responding to the beat of development and opportunity, craftspeople[9] across clusters quickened to change. Their response echoed across the country. From the first women craftspeople to step out of the confines of home, whether it was women chikan embroiderers from Lucknow, Ahir and Rabari women from Kutch, or Banjaras from Sandur, these remarkable pioneers broke the mould, setting examples for others to follow. Madhubani artists from Mithila, Gond women from Jharkhand, women weavers from the North-east took the step, their standing-up to be counted having a multiplier effect on others in their community. Their personal growth was linked to social change and economic progress. These craftswomen seized the opportunity to enter the economic sphere, asserted their rights, and developed a voice within the social and contractual sphere of their lives.[10] In interviews, their reactions covered a range of affirmative responses from '*ghore bosa kaaj*' (Sethi, 2012: 73), to '… this is a boon to my craft' (Jangid, 2005: 64), their engagements and interactions creating a social and economic ripple effect on their communities.

Alongside the NGO movement was the parallel growth of commercial and entrepreneurial activity that brought to markets across India products of traditional craftsmanship. Improving livelihoods, opening up markets, introducing design adapted for the 'new' consumer, and, critically for the craftsperson, sustaining and increasing demand for their products. The most well-known of these remains FabIndia, founded by the charismatic John Bissel, its solid foundations have been multiplied a hundredfold under the stewardship of his son, William; Anokhi, a venture of John and Faith Singh in Jaipur; Suraiya Hassan in Hyderabad, who successfully combined revival with commerce—both in *ikat* and with the *himroo*-weaving skills; Bandhej by Archana Shah in Gujarat; Sunny and Meeta in Kala Dera; and other entrepreneurs across India, who clearly demonstrated that it was possible to run successful craft-based businesses with a social agenda. These commercial interdependencies between entrepreneurs and craftspeople worked in the best interest of both, reviving techniques, empowering craftspeople, introducing and innovating with new designs, and opening fresh markets so successfully that a steady demand for crafts skills is sustained year after year.

Designers, working with the crafts, served as a bridge, mediating between craftspeople and their evolving urban markets. Shona Ray, textile designer, 'introduced craft into people's interiors'; Prabhaben Shah and Malti Jhaveri, sisters, who worked with hand-block prints in the 1950s and 1960s; Iola Basu, with her 'understanding of product design as a process and marketing, well before others';[11] Sina Kaul and Ratna Fabri, whose design careers started at CCIE; Bina Das, who worked with the potters in West Bengal.[12] This connection and interaction has strengthened and multiplied four-fold over the decades, with designers working with craftspeople across the country and in varied traditions.

In museums, education, and writings on crafts and their cultural contexts, women continued to play a significant part. The Calico Museum of Textiles, set up in 1949 in Ahmedabad, is among the foremost textile museums in the world. It was inspired by Dr Ananda Coomaraswamy, and founded in 1949 by Gautam Sarabhai and his sister, Gira Sarabhai. Guided over the last several decades by Gira Sarbhai, its exceptional collection educates the curious and the scholar, besides being an invaluable reference source for practitioners. Its publication programme, encompassing both the historical, scientific and technical aspects of craftsmanship, has pushed the boundaries of scholarship in the subject.

Located in Paris, the Association for the Study and Documentation of Asian Textiles, established in 1979, was based around the textile collection of Krishna Reboud, its founder. It '... is a centre which was created to foster the study and research in Asian textile' (Introduction. *Marg,* June 1987: viii).

Praful Shah and Shilpa Shah's Tapi Collection of Textiles in Surat that grew from 'Shilpa's eager-eyed forays into our small town bazaars' (Barnes *et al.*, 2002: 8), began as a resource centre for design to become 'what must be one of the finest private textile collections in India today' (ibid.: Introduction). This formidable collection comprises textiles covering a wide range of techniques, materials and patterning, dating from the 14th century onwards. The Tapi Collection also supports an ambitious research and publication programme.

Dakshina Chitra, the museum of living traditions, set enroute from Chennai to Mammallapuram, was founded by Deborah Thiagarajan in 1996. It promotes, revives and preserves the arts, crafts and traditions of South India. This living heritage centre has given great impetus to crafts and craftspeople. Its activities include demonstrations of craftsmanship, seminars, workshops and other participatory activities for its many visitors, creating an awareness of everyday culture and the living practices of arts and crafts.

The Anokhi Museum of Hand Printing in Jaipur, an initiative of Rachel Bracken-Singh and her husband, Pritam Singh, is dedicated to the collection, preservation and interpretation of block-printed cloth, strengthening the appreciation for this living heritage.

Led by Dr Stella Kramrisch, the prolific writings of Kamaladevi Chattopadhyay on crafts influenced many who came after her. Pupul Jayakar's contributions to *Marg, Journal of Indian Textile History*, and to other publications, and Dr Lotika Varadarajan's scholarship and research on traditional knowledge systems, led to her publications in the fields of textiles, tribal cultures and maritime ventures. Jasleen Dhamija, who worked with the AIHB in the 1950s and subsequently internationally, has travelled, researched and written extensively on textiles and costumes.

Rta Chisti's work in the area of handloom, Janet Rizvi, and the many others, all pioneers, led the way in developing an Indian idiom in researching, documenting and publishing.

In Bengal, Gurudev Rabindranath Tagore's innovative and far-sighted initiatives vitalised and reformed education through the setting up of the Visva Bharati at Santiniketan.

> In every nation, education is intimately associated with the life of the people. For us, modern education is relevant only to turning out clerks, lawyers, doctors, magistrates and policemen.... This education has not reached the farmer, the oil grinder, nor the potter. No other educated society has been struck with such disaster.... If ever a truly Indian university is established it must, from the very beginning, implement India's own knowledge of economics, agriculture, health, medicine and of all other everyday science from the surrounding villages. Then alone can the school or university become the centre of the country's way of living. This school must practise agriculture, dairying and weaving using the best modern methods.... I have proposed to call this school Visva Bharati. (Das Gupta, 1983: 9–10)

In 1919, Kala Bhawana, as part of Visva Bharati, was established in Santiniketan. Under the guidance of Tagore's daughter-in-law, Pratima Devi, the French artist, Madame Andree Karpelees, and Mrs Sukumar Devi (Subramanya, 1982: 37–41), crafts were introduced into the curriculum,[13] resulting in the revitalisation of various traditional crafts.

In the area of educational reform and change, an extremely significant transformation occurred in October 2005. Judy Frater founded the first institution of design for traditional artisans—Kala Raksha Vidyalaya (KRV) in Kutch. Laila Tyabji expressed, very eloquently, what many felt:

> Twenty years ago, a Mithila craftswoman, Shiva Kashyap, bewailed that 'We may be wage earners but we are still walking on someone else's feet. Because we lack the tools of education and language we are still dependent.' It is a cry that many otherwise skilled traditional craftspeople have echoed. So Kala Raksha Vidyalaya is truly an answer to a dream ... of hundreds of craftspeople.

Hopefully, it will be a module for many other similar local design schools in craft pockets all over the country.[14]

Developing learning material, a modular curriculum that allows for flexibility and a pedagogy focused on acquiring knowledge and skills that are relevant to craftspeople, the KRV is now in its seventh successful year. Sally Holkar's small, yet significant start of the Handloom Weaving School in Maheshwar teaches sustainable dyeing practices, weaving techniques, use of alternate yarns, design, and has a curriculum that is expected to grow and mature with its students.

The change-makers were not only the women who were directly working in the sector with craftspeople, but also additionally those who shaped and influenced our professional values. These women in public life were politicians, artists, bureaucrats, doctors, lawyers, educationists and others, exuding authority, dressed in traditional attire, leading modern lives. The focus of attention in the 1980s was Prime Minister Indira Gandhi. At meetings of the Commonwealth Heads of Government or with other world leaders, whether in India or abroad, Mrs Gandhi made a powerful statement. Images relayed across India on cinema newsreels, Doordarshan and in the press, were of an Indian woman holding her own—dressed in handloom, conveying authority. It was a pan-Indian look, both distinct and original, and power dressing at its best.

> She chose her clothes to reflect the traditions of the different regions of the country. Thus she not only made a fashion statement but also gave an impetus to the development of the khadi and handloom sectors in India. (Bhagat, 2005: 150)

It is a powerful example continued by her daughter-in-law, the President of the UPA, Sonia Gandhi, and other political leaders.

The highly influential world of cinema also made its contribution with the diva Rekha, magnificently draped in sumptuous, glamorous Kanjeevaram silks and traditional handcrafted jewellery. Shabana Azmi, Aparna Sen, Vidya Balan, the mega-stars of south Indian cinema and others were seen, on screen and off, in handloom cottons and silks, in settings that showed the best of Indian crafts.

A view of the sector, of its empowerment, development and change would be unsatisfactory, deficient and incomplete without paying tribute to the many who worked and continue to do so in the sector. The fundamental debt owed to foundational figures like the late L.C. Jain—Gandhian, economist, social activist and builder of the framework for handicrafts—and John Bissel, cannot be forgotten. The immense contribution of Ashoke Chatterjee (former Executive Director, NID; former President, Crafts Council of India); Martand Singh (Founder Member, INTACH; author; textile revivalist); Rajeev Sethi (Founder Chairman, Asian Heritage Foundation); Brij Bhasin (Chairperson, Barsana); Bunker Roy and others, illumined the path.

At the policy level, meetings and committees in the last decade have done little to resolve the issues of the sector. Its fractured polity divided into the KVIC, handlooms and handicrafts. The craftspeople themselves were dealt with by innumerable Ministries, the threads of interventions and schemes not interlocking to produce on-the-ground deliverables. Yet, under the stewardship of Dr Syeda Hameed, Member, Planning Commission, thought and debate, along with concrete action, have since been initiated to bring about a much-needed relook at the sector as a whole.

While much has been realised since Independence, not enough has been done to achieve the watermark level for real empowerment, inclusion, and economic and social equity. As Ashoke Chatterjee vividly puts it:

> We all took for granted that this Indian advantage needed no special attention for its sustenance—all part of the landscape like the Himalayas and the Ganga...[15]

Issues of the paradox of value continue to confront craftspeople—while the products of craftsmanship are highly valued craftspeople, themselves the holders of knowledge, are relegated to obscurity and anonymity. Additionally, while much has been done, there are still large numbers who remain out of the ambit of change and development.[16] Access to markets, credit schemes and programmes, and social security remains elusive for many.

The urgent need to codify the traditional knowledge systems of the crafts and, furthermore, to research and contextualise the products of craftsmanship is still in its nascent stage. The study of the intersection of craft techniques and technology is an imperative for us to build on for the future. Additionally, the task to bring craftspeople on equal footing into the educational system as teachers and trainers, continues to defy us. The issue of intellectual property and the protection of community knowledge looms large. The faking and copying of traditional crafts products remains rife. There is a need, in addition, to revisit the ethics of engagement with craftspeople, bringing in the larger issues of rights (Chiba and Sethi, 2012). The questions of certification of skills, the need to collectivise to build strength, are also on the agenda. Development initiatives need to reach out to larger numbers, to deliver to those who need it most; for all this to be achieved, continuous, sustained and determined efforts by many more is needed.[17]

◆

This chapter was first published in 2013 in the *IIC Quarterly*, Vol. 39, Nos. 3 and 4.

NOTES

1. The term craft has been used here in a generic manner to include both traditional handicrafts and handlooms.
2. The term craftsperson/craftspeople has been used here to refer to the holders of traditional knowledge and includes weavers (including pre- and post-loom) and traditional craft practitioners (pre- and post-production).
3. Citation: Ramon Magsaysay Award for Community Leadership. 31 August 1966. Ramon Magsaysay Award Foundation. www.rmaf.org.
4. Ibid.
5. Gulshan Nanda has served with CCIE since 1952 and returned, after retirement, as Chairperson from 2005 to 2010.
6. With the honourable exception of Ashoke Chatterjee, who was President of CCI for over a decade and continues as Advisor.
7. *The Hindu*. 24 March 2002.
8. See www.sewa.org.
9. Highlights: Third National Handloom Census of Weavers and Allied workers. 2010. NCAER. Pp xxii. Of the over 38.46 lakh handloom workers in India, 77 per cent are women. A similar percentage can probably be expected from the results of the handicraft census that has been conducted, though the figures have not been released yet.
10. See Tyabji (1997). Also read Sethi (2012).
11. In conversation with Ashoke Chatterjee.
12. Information from Gulshan Nanda.
13. The pedagogy adopted by its first director, the artist Asit Kumar Haldar, was continued over the decades through the commitment and wisdom of Nandlal Bose, Benodebehari Mukhopadhyay and others.

14. Tyabji, Laila. *Dream Come True: Being a Jury Member at the First Graduation of the Kalaraksha Design School.* www.craftrevival.org.
15. Correspondence with Ritu Sethi. 5 January 2013.
16. National Commission for Enterprise. Arjun Sengupta Report. 2007. *'Condition of Work and Promotion of Livelihood in the Unorganised Sector'.*
17. Thanks to Ashoke Chatterjee for reading the draft and giving valuable suggestions.

REFERENCES

Barnes, Ruth, Steven Cohen and Rosemary Crill (eds.). 2002. *Trade, Temple and Court: Indian Textiles from the Tapi Collection.* Mumbai: India Book House.

Bhagat, Usha. 2005. *Indiraji Through My Eyes.* New Delhi: Penguin Viking Press.

Chandra, Lokesh and Jyotindra Jain (eds.) 1986. *Dimensions of Indian Art: Pupul Jayakar Seventy.* Vol. 1. Delhi: Agam Kala Prakashan.

Chiba, Moe and Ritu Sethi 2012. *Co-creating: Revisiting the Ethics of Engagement between Designers and Craftspeople.* July. www.AsiaInch.org.

Dhamija, Jasleen. 2007. *Kamaladevi Chattopadhyay.* New Delhi: National Book Trust.

Doshi, Saryu. 1982. 'Continuity and Change. Festival of India in Great Britain', *Marg,* Vol. XXXV, September. No. 4.

Jangid, Vishnu Kumar. 2005. 'Tarkashi Craftsmen', in *Designers Meet Artisans: A Practical Guide.* New Delhi: UNESCO–Craft Revival Trust Publication.

Jayakar, Pupul. 1982. 'Continuity and Change. Images and Tradition. Festival of India in Great Britain', *Marg,* Vol. XXXVI, December, No 1.

Jayakar, Pupul. 1995. *Indira Gandhi: A Biography.* New Delhi: Penguin.

Marg. 1987. 'In Quest of Theme and Skills—Asian Textiles', Introduction, Vol. XXXX, No. 4. June.

Sethi, Ritu (ed.). 2012. *Embroidering Futures: Repurposing the Kantha.* Banglore: IFA Publication.

Shah, Praful. 2002. 'Collector's Note', in Ruth Barnes, Steven Cohen and Rosemary Crill (eds.), *Trade, Temple and Court: Indian Textiles from the Tapi Collection.* Mumbai: India Book House.

Singh, Malvika. 1986. 'The Tapestry of her Life', in Lokesh Chandra *et al.* (eds), *Dimensions of Indian Art: Pupul Jayakar Seventy,* Vol. I. Delhi: Agam Kala Prakashan.

Subramanya, K. G. 1982. *The Craft Movement in Shantiniketan in Arts of Bengal and Eastern India.* Crafts Council of West Bengal. West Bengal.

Tagore, Rabindranath. 1963. *Addresses by Tagore.* Santiniketan, Visva Bharati. English translation by M. Das Gupta. 1983. Santiniketan and Sri Niketan. Calcutta: Visva Bharati.

Tyabji, Laila. 1997. *From Stones to Stitches—A Life Transformed.* 25 December. Craft Revival Trust.

◆◆

13
LEADERSHIP IN THE ARTS
Rukmini Devi Arundale

ASHISH MOHAN KHOKAR[#]

The traditions of the Indian performing arts are like flowing rivers that often replenish themselves at the font of inspiration and innovation. While many gurus (or Masters) provided Indian classical dance (and music) forms with concept, content and context, a few also proved to be path-breaking leaders whose example inspired others and made them take such narratives further.

Indian classical dance forms were the preserve of traditional gurus, whose art was almost hereditary. Though not castes in themselves, these artistes were a class in society with distinct attributes of lineage, role and a place in the temple milieu, where these art forms mostly flourished, or in the royal courts (Curtiss, 1974).

Consequently, in the case of Rukmini Devi Arundale, the first major context was the caste system itself. In this case, it worked in reverse. Traditionally, while Brahmins retained and promoted scriptural knowledge (in the fields of astronomy, astrology, vedic or non-vedic rituals), in the context of Indian classical dances, until the 1930s, teaching and dancing were the preserve mostly of a *class* (not caste) of total or 'complete' artistes (so-called, as they were well-versed in literature, music and dance in totality, and not piecemeal, as we see practised today), called variously as the *devadasis* on the south coast, the *maharis* in the east, the *mohinis* on the west coast, or the *vilasinis* on the upper-east coast. These arts were transmitted orally, as in Brahminical traditions, from guru to *shishya*—a master to a ward.

Each class of dancer—including court dancers, often called Rajdasis or Rajnartakis—had an assigned role in the power and patronage structures of Indian temples, where these traditional

Rukmini Devi
Courtesy: Mohan Khokar Dance Collection of India

forms were manifested. While all classical dancing in India can be attributed to divine origins and sources, its setting too was bound by religious moorings, i.e. within the temple precincts (Khokar, 1979; 84).

While classical dance forms—forms which have a structured or codified grammar, a fixed mode of musical language and a bedrock of literary texts derived from historical or mythological treatises—such as Bharatanatyam, Kathakali, Orissi, Kuchipudi, among others—thus survived centuries, mass forms such as community dancing—loosely termed as folk, tribal or even ritual—carried on without much evident organised patronage, as these dances were done by, and for, an agrarian collective.

Centuries of traditions, based on codified grammar and language, made Indian temple-related dances, classical. These were backed by treatises and texts ranging from 2nd BCE–2nd ACE, ascribed *Natyashastra* and Abhinaya *Darpana*. In each age or era (such as the Sangam Age; 500 BCE–500 ADE), a significant work was added that referred to dancing and music techniques, as in *Silappadikaram* and *Manimekhalai*.

It was not just the southern kingdoms that promoted dance and music, but various kings from Kashmir and poets such as Kalhan (1149 ADE) who wrote *Rajataranigini,* wherein he described dancing girls and patrons; or Damodargupta (9 ADE), who wrote *Kuttanimata,* on the life of courtesans; to Somedeva's *Kathasaritasagara* (1063–1091 ADE), give us proof of this important activity in daily lives. This clearly established the adage that, Kashmir to Kanyakumari, dancing and music did connect and bind India even before the *idea* of India was born!

The very definition of the long colonial rule from the 16th century onwards that lasted till 1947 meant a certain State strategy to divide and rule, and to marginalise local cultures and learning processes. As a consequence, many traditional Indian value systems in education and the arts were delinked from one another, making for a mixed palette of cultural conundrum. A good example is yoga and its practice. Or Sanskrit. Both these traditional Indian cultural and spiritual pillars were marginalised under Lord Macaulay's educational thrust, which delinked Indian language and cultural moorings from school or college-level educational systems. Its decline today can directly be traced to this measure and delinking.

In order to revive our classical arts, they must be brought back into the school curriculum.

◆◆◆

The advent of the 20th century and world explorations and experiences of ideas, both in science and in society, led to an Industrial Revolution in England which ushered in many ripple effects that could be seen in its colonies and Empire. Naturally, gradually, these advances helped connect people and trends, ideas and machines, and soon a slow desire for independence from foreign rule emerged. Into this scenario was born our protagonist, Rukmini Devi.

Born on 29 February 1904, in Madurai, to Sanskrit scholar and retired government engineer Nilakantan Sastry, Rukmini Devi was his sixth child. Her upbringing was traditional, as was the vogue those days, and there was nothing uncommon, except perhaps, a latent fact that soon, to seek a better livelihood, Nilakantan Sastry left his native Pudukottai and came to Madras in 1912.

After the Sastry family moved to Madras and owing to the proximity to many foreigners who frequented the Theosophical Society, Rukmini Devi became attached to a young English lady, Eleanor Elder, who had studied dance with Margaret Morris in London. Morris was now directing her attention to reviving ancient Greek dance, as set by the redoubtable Isadora Duncan and her brother, Raymond. To conduct her experiment and enquiry, Elder roped in some of the European and American residents at the Theosophical Society. Elder put up shows from time to time and in one of these, a Tamil version of Tagore's *Malini,* Rukmini Devi appeared briefly and sang a song! This was in 1918 (Khokar, 1996). Soon, in 1920 (according to her acolyte-biographer Leela Samson), she married George Arundale, her senior by many years, and settled into domestic life in the midst of the growing nation-wide clamour for Independence. She travelled with him far and wide; and it was on one such journey to Australia by sea that her cabin was next to Cleo Nordi, the famed ballerina. To pass the long hours on the journey, Rukmini Devi began studying Western ballet under Nordi. But Nordi, returning from Java and India, chided her for her interest in ballet while not knowing any Indian classical dance form, especially the one closest to her provenance, Bharatanatyam.

As a consequence, upon her return, Rukmini Devi decided to pursue this form of dance. The legendary Mylapore Gowri Ammal, a devadasi then attached to the Kapalieshwar temple in Mylapore, Madras, taught her nuances of *abhinaya,* while Muthukumaran Pillai of Kattumanar Koil taught her basic steps and foundation. Subsequently, Pandanallur Meenakshi Sundaram Pillai became her main dance guru.

On 30 December 1935, to celebrate the Annual Convention of the Theosophical Society, a short dance performance was planned. The venue was the headquarters of the Society in Adayar, Madras, and it was the first appearance of a woman who had no real background in the dance of the *dasis.* It was unheard of that a Brahmin woman would publicly dance the art of the devadasis, sullied and shunned by polite society. While the dance form itself was valued, its dancer was not, largely because some of those artistes, who had fallen on bad days, had taken to the world's oldest profession. Over a thousand aficionados had assembled for the event, more out of curiosity than real interest, and all of them sat transfixed. A handful of die-hards, bent on boycotting the event, sneaked in to condemn the dancer, Rukmini Devi (Khokar, 2000).

Bharatanatyam, an ancient art form, had evolved to become one in which teachers were mostly males, and dancers, females. By convention, a devadasi could keep one patron, or more. Sons born of such alliances took to *nattuvangam* and daughters took to dance. Nattuvangam is the art of conducting a dance recital by keeping rhythm and reciting syllables, while wielding small cymbals. The *nattuvanars* were the heads of the clan, or family, and each devadasi was normally attached to a temple. Patronage thus came from the temples, its natural moorings. It was this environment in which the dance form took birth and developed. However, the long years of colonial rule gradually eroded local and district-level patronage and this, in turn, slowly but surely, began affecting the fortunes of the artistes as well.

Polite society shunned devadasis, mistaking the symptom for the disease. One daughter of such a devadasi became a barrister— Dr Muthulakshmi Reddy—and fought for its abolishment. She succeeded in 1947, when India became independent. At the same time, another activist-lawyer-dancer, E. Krishna Iyer, had also espoused the case and cause of the devadasis. Iyer danced dressed as one, and presented them on prestigious platforms such as the citadel of Brahmin culture, the Madras Music Academy. The last great devadasi of Madras, Balasaraswati, gave a befitting account of her mastery and art by singing and dancing in the Music Academy 'yaaruku bhayama ('Of whom am I afraid? Or, I fear none...'). She also stood her ground and inspired several who did not possess the tools of the English language to hold forth or present their point of view. Balasaraswati, therefore, represented a world that was vanishing and an art form that was gradually becoming a reference point and also undergoing a class metamorphosis (Sundaram, 2000).

At the time, Rukmini Devi herself had no revivalist agenda, or any save-the-dance-from-the-devadasi crusade that, soon after, became the discourse. She, willy-nilly, became the eye of the storm.

In the 1930s, when Rukmini Devi took to the stage, she was not delinking a tradition or sounding its death-knell, but merely taking on an existing tradition and moving it into a more public domain. A traditional classical dance form like Bharatanatyam had already been seen at weddings of important chieftains and local rulers called zamindars (Subramaniam, 2008). Rukmini Devi's association with, and usage of, a form like Bharatanatyam positioned her in a unique role as a catalyst of change. Did she plan it? Knowing her personally for long and my father, the late Mohan Khokar, being her first male student from north India, one can authoritatively say, no.

She was beyond self-projection; she was on another plane and dimension; she was a mere receptor and preceptor. Rukmini Devi was destined to make, and rewrite, the history of the dancing arts in south India, although many others had preceded her by a good five to ten years, especially male dancers such as Ram Gopal and Uday Shankar, who were already touring Europe in the 1930s when she made her debut. Her example made many take to Bharatanatyam; thus, indirectly or directly, Rukmini Devi provided a leadership role and empowered many women. Overnight, new stars such as Baby Kamala (Laxman), Kausalya and Shakuntala were 'born' and feted. Films, in which compositions of classical dance were used, became a regular feature and later-day stars like Rajilakshmi, Vyjayanthimala Bali and E.V. Saroja added lustre and celebrity-standing; many gurus such as Vazuvuhor Ramaiah Pillai directed sequences for film-makers such as the director Subrahmanyam (father of renowned dancer, Dr Padma Subrahmanyam), whose dance films gave several dancers in general and Bharatanatyam, in particular, a wider outreach.

However, the grand success of the performance on 30 December 1935 proved to be a turning point for many: for Rukmini herself, of course, but also for the development of Bharatanatyam and the setting up in 1936 of the greatest of all such institutions for teaching Bharatanatyam—the Kalakshetra. This unique dance community had been conceived as an integrated one, a family. The residential cottages, the classrooms, the rehearsal hall, mess and administrative block were all cheek by jowl and there was energy in the air. There was Western discipline, to be sure, but after classes, old-timers recall how they could freely assemble, and converse and bond as a family.

Initially set up as the International Academy of the Arts, in 1939 it was rechristened Kalakshetra, temple of the arts. In June 1940, Kalakshetra was registered as a Society. In the beginning, classes were held only in Bharatanatyam and vocal music, the fee being ₹15 and ₹10 per month, respectively. Only two girls joined for dance, and both were from families in the Society estate. Lessons began under a tree! The first two teachers were both giants in the field—Kattumannar Koil Muthukumaran Pillai for Bharatanatyam, and Papanasam Sivam for music. In fact, Muthukumaran Pillai brought his star student M.K. Saroja, then a child of nine, to show Rukmini Devi what his teaching and training standards were. She immediately engaged him and he was appointed as the first dance teacher of Kalakshetra. Within a year, 20 more girls had joined and, by the next year, the number had risen to 40.

Kalakshetra-*bani* or style is formed by a group of successive gurus beginning with the senior-most Meenakshi Sundaram Pillai, to Muthukumaran Pillai, to Ellapa, Kittapa, and many others who followed. Most traditional nattuvunars taught at Kalakshetra as there was really no other formal institution in Madras then, although a plethora of personal, individual-run institutions flourished. Many gurus, such as Dandayudhapani Pillai (guru to Mangalore Alva, Vyjayanthimala Bali), Vazuvoor Ramaiah Pillai and Nataraja Shankuntala, became popular outside of Kalakshetra due to their work in films, which ensured that they could survive, even thrive. Films gave them regular exposure and their students multiplied and some of them, such as Kamala, Vyjayanthimala Bali and E.V. Saroja, went to work in the film industry.

In 1948, Kalakshetra received an eviction notice from the Theosophical Society on the grounds that its dance and music activities were alien to the tenets of the Society and thus it could not continue to host the institution. Kalakshetra's unceremonious delinking with the Society meant a certain loss in funds, much in the nature of abruptly severing a teenager from its parents and expecting the child, literally disowned, to fend for itself. Rukmini Devi's genius lay in taking up the challenge and creating an institution that has stood the test of time, despite many ups and downs. She realised that, to survive, teaching was the mainstay, and tours. In that, she created corps de students that fed the corps de ballet. Generally, a ballet, or a dance-drama production, needs a group of well-trained dancers. The question was: where was one to get these from, especially when no real fee could be paid?

Kalakshetra is a unique model that has functioned without monies, or very little monies. It is interesting to note that, until two decades ago, its faculty was still drawing monthly salaries in the hundreds, not thousands. The average salary of a teacher and staff was only ₹400, until its 50th anniversary! Kalakshetra was so staunchly unprofessional where money matters were concerned that it returned unutilised a grant of ₹25 lakh from the Ford Foundation on the grounds that, never having been a wealthy institution, it was at a loss as to how best to utilise the funds (Peria Sarada, 2008). This is not an incident from its inception, but one that took place in the late 1980s. Kalakshetra's creed was to do with art, not the business of art, as has now become common with most dance institutions.

Carnatic music also remained a pillar of the institution with Tiger Varadachariar, Vasudevachariar, Karaikudi Veena Sambasiva Iyer and Papanasam Sivan, themselves lending their musical services, when required, often without charging any fee. Rukmini Devi's generosity was such that she always compensated the artistes. Kalakshetra benefited immensely with fine inputs from many musical giants and geniuses and a list of its staff speaks for such alliances. Every eminent doyen of Carnatic music was associated with this institution for decades.

With such musicians and dance inputs, and as a daughter of a great Sanskrit scholar, it was only natural that Rukmini Devi focussed on the revival of *Kuruvanjis* (temple dance-dramas) and when *Kutral Kuruvanjis* (temple-drama) was first produced by her in 1944, the audiences were amazed. Sri Krishnamachariar, brother of Tiger Varadachariar, provided the necessary *varnamettus* (song-patterns) and Rukmini herself devised the dance-patterns. *Bhishma* was amongst the first; it was followed by Kalidasa's *Kumar Sambhava* in 1947 that was produced under such circumstances, as were many others, which are performed till date.

Sita Swayamvaram in 1955; *Usha Pariyanam* in 1959; the list is endless. In all, about 25 major dance-dramas, some as varied as the last one, *Meera of Mewar* (1984), and one based on martial arts (*Meenakshi Vijayam*, 1977) were made. These are full-length productions, with many sets and characters and costumes.

Rukmini Devi is remembered for creating and sustaining Kalakshetra with her untiring and dedicated efforts; but dance was not her sole passion, although it took up the major part of her time. She was a champion of both animal welfare and of vegetarianism, with both these causes dear to her, and, had she had her way, she could have well made animal welfare her life's mission. Her life has been many dimensional, though dance and Kalakshetra remained the red thread, the connecting link. She served on many boards and committees and was twice nominated to Parliament.

In 1977, a peculiar situation occurred when the then Prime Minister, Morarji Desai, promoted and proposed her for the position of the President of India. Had she accepted, she would have been the first woman President of India. This was the first time a dancer was being offered the highest post in the land but Rukmini Devi, with characteristic integrity and on principled grounds, declined, saying that unless all parties support my candidature, there is no point in holding this august office.

Rukmini Devi Arundale was a very quiet, reticent person and in the few biographies on her, one by her colleague S. Sarada, and one more recently by Leela Samson (2010), she comes across as a philosopher. She often thought long and hard before taking any action and some aver she thought too much. Sensitive to the point of becoming withdrawn, if the situation did not suit her, Rukmini Devi fought many battles and weathered many storms with dignity.

When a group of artistes within Kalakshetra led by Dhananjayans ('Malyalee union-bazi'; Peria, Sarada, 1986) went on strike for better and higher salaries, she took affront to this approach. Sadly, in her own lifetime, Kalakshetra became divisive and fractured into many factions.

Sankara Menon, her right-hand man, friend and associate, remained a constant support. Menon, the brother of the equally illustrious musicologist Narayan Menon, ensured that Rukmini Devi was provided the atmosphere and environment to run the institution as she deemed fit. He was her first line of defence and protected her from many ugly battles, taking upon himself the role of her protector. It is entirely to his credit that the institution continued to function years after she passed away on 24 February 1986. As she wrote in a letter to Mohan Khokar, 'The only treasure we have in India is Art. Otherwise this is not a happy country....' (Khokar, 2011)

R. Venkatraman, a former President of India, was Kalakshetra's Chairman for a long spell and he provided continuity in troubled times. As a veteran politician, he brought in his abundant experience in statecraft to bear on this troubled institution of art. The fact that Kalakshetra possessed hundreds of acres of land in a metropolis like Madras made it a sitting target for many sharks, and it was only a skilled politician, with cultural leanings and moorings, who could have provided some direction.

Sankara Menon oversaw the survival of the institution long after Rukmini Devi's passing, despite many eyeing Kalakshetra's extensive land assets. Menon and three associates were also assaulted by land sharks, although the attack itself was blamed on local fishermen. Menon orchestrated the smooth transition and its functioning and he ensured that Kalakshetra survived. Rajaram (grandson of Tiger Varadachariar) was appointed intermittently as director for many years until a suitable candidate could be found. The choice ultimately fell on Leela Samson when, in 2005, she was appointed its director. As an alumnus, she had a close bond with her alma mater; to serve it became a life mission. In the last seven years, Samson revived and revitalised a moribund, near-comatose institution. She served it well and saved the institution from certain collapse. Leela Samson can also be called Rukmini Devi's true follower and has furthered her ideals and cause. The State has, in recent years, given her multiple responsibilities such as the Chairmanship of the Central Sangeet Natak Akademi, Chairmanship of the National Film Censor Board, and of several

Leela Samson
Photo: Prasanna

Mallika Sarabhai in *An Idea named Mira*
Courtesy: Darpana

other organisations and bodies. She sits on many important committees and panels.

A totally different talent is that of Mallika Sarabhai. Daughter of the famed scientist, Dr Vikram Sarabhai, and doyenne of dance, Mrinalini Sarabhai, she cut loose from assigned roles of routine dancing and domesticity, and has introduced the feminist discourse to her art of dance-theatre-films. A multi-talented dynamo of dance-theatre, she has actively taken up social and political issues and provided leadership to art and education, emancipation and empowerment. Her solo productions, such as *Sita's Daughters*, have been path-breaking works, where mythology was re-questioned and in which new nuances provided a platform for women's rights and empowerment. She has done many more women-specific productions to highlight her concerns as an activist ('an activist who uses art for change') such as *An Ideal Named Meera*, *In Search of the Goddess* and *Sva Kranti: The Revolution Within*. Mallika Sarabhai has maintained the same vision politically, openly taking up causes that concern civil society, including contesting in the general elections against incumbent and presiding State political deities.

Kalakshetra has proved to be the Bolshoi of India because of its rigorous training and demands on the dancer. The idea of a gurukul—where one rises early, stays with dance all day, learns related dance forms such as music, literature and stage presentation—hones a Kalakshetra dancer as a performer. It is indeed a complete education in dance.

Amongst its best-known alumni are all world famous names in Bharatanatyam beginning with the Dhananjayans. 'Even if we had differences with our alma mater, we see no inner difference with its creator, our guru, *atthai* (aunt)' (Dhananjayan, 2011). C.V. Chandrasekhar says, 'Kalakshetra made me what I'm today. I came to learn music in 1945 but ended up learning dance.' Krishanveni, Janardahan, Yamini Krishnamurthy, even Orissi divas—Sanjukta Panigrahi and Minati Das—learnt Bharatanatyam at Kalakshetra, as did Orissi guru Mayadhar Raut. Teachers at Kalakshetra such as Perai and Chinna Sarada (Hoffman), Jayalakhmi, Padamasini are all part of the lore of Kalakshetra. Among the next generation were Laskhmi Vishwanathan, Shanta Dhananjayan and Leela Samson. They were followed by younger star students Ananda Shankar Jayant, Anuradha Shridhar and Urmila Satyanarayana.

Jyostsana Jaganathan, Meenakshi Srinivasan and Navia Natarajan are part of the current generation of star-performers.

Did Rukmini Devi empower just women? Is her legacy safe? What did she achieve? Any such assessment is almost subjective, unless the entire narrative above is seen in the light of the various turns and twists of her own life and example, showing how she empowered minds and provided leadership, that helped more women from among polite society to take to an art form.

Victor Dandre, popular Russian ballet master and married to the ballerina Anna Pavlova, lamented in 1922: 'We came to India to see its famed dances but except for some stray Nautch, we see nothing' (Haskell, 1947). But by 1942, in 20 short years, Rukmini Devi and many before her, like Uday Shankar (whom Anna Pavlova 'discovered' in London and Paris), Ram Gopal (whom American dancer La Meri 'discovered' in Bangalore) and Gopinath (whom American dancer Ragini Devi 'discovered' in Vallathol's Kerala Kalamandalam) had helped re-establish the classical Indian arts in a major way (Devi, 2010). This was not true merely in the field of dance but in the allied arts of music, costumes, backdrops, among others.

Thus, in the performing arts, Rukmini Devi remains the most important woman who helped empower not only women, but the arts and society itself. Her, we salute!

◆

This chapter was first published in 2013 in the *IIC Quarterly*, Vol. 39, Nos. 3 and 4.

REFERENCES

Devi, Ragini. 1950. *Dance Dialects of India*. Delhi: Manoharlal Munshi.

Devi, Rukmini. 2000. Ashish Mohan Khokar (ed.), *Attendance*. Bharatanatyam Issue.

Dhananjayan, V.P. 2011. Ramnarayan (ed.), *Sruti*. Chennai.

Haskell, Arnold (ed.). 1947. *The Ballet Annual*. London, UK.

Khokar, Ashish Mohan. 2011. *A Century of Indian Dance: 1901–2000*. Delhi: ICCR.

Khokar, Mohan. 1979. *Traditions of Indian Classical Dance*. Delhi: Clarion.

Khokar, Mohan. 1996. 'Kalakshetra: Then and Now', *The Hindustan Times*, 1 January.

Peria, Sarada. 1986. *Sruti*, Nos. 27/28, and assorted quotes in various articles. Chennai.

Samson, Leela. 2010. *Rukmini Devi: A Life*. Delhi: Penguin Viking.

Subramaniam, Padma (ed.). 2008. *Bhakta of B.N.–M.K. Saroja*. Bangalore: Ekah Bios.

Sundaram, B.M. 2000. 'The Legator and the Legatee', *Attendance*. Delhi.

◆◆

Sulochana
Courtesy: National Film Archive, Pune

14

RECASTING BODIES AND THE TRANSFORMATION OF THE SELF

Women Performers in the Bombay Film Industry (1925–1947)

SARAH
RAHMAN NIAZI[#]

The turn of the century in India saw the emergence of a newly configured public sphere dotted with the presence of women. Bombay, Lahore, Calcutta and Madras at this time were spaces consciously invested in a process of modernisation. This kinesis of modernity was accentuated by new technological inventions like automobiles, airplanes, telephone, gramophone, radio and cinema. Public life had acquired dimensions previously unknown as the cities made possible new modes of cognition and articulation. Though colonialism played a crucial role in the way cities shaped up, there is no denying that these cities were rejuvenated by a peripatetic labour force that transformed its topographic landscapes. In this changing demography of towns and cities, the public woman became a crucial presence. Women in this period were employed in a variety of professions. Colonial rule had dislocated and transformed the traditional economic systems to allow new, modern sites of production such as industries, mills and offices[1] to take precedence. With education and emancipation effected by the social reform movements, other professional opportunities were made available for women. They entered employment as teachers, lawyers, doctors, secretaries, typists, salesgirls and telephone operators.

In the matrix of the modern city, cinema was slowly and steadily creating a strong foothold. And, in the most fascinating ways, cinema marked the spatial and mental registers of the cities through its myriad sites of production (studios), circulation (posters and journals) and exhibition (theatres).[2] This indomitable presence of the cinema in the public sphere created a crucial nexus between cinema and city. For women, cinema became one of the many sites for change and transformation. The possibility of reinvention enabled by cinema was essential to the way in which women's selfhood was refashioned and articulated in the public sphere. The ubiquitous presence of women in the public sphere activated a series of frenzied regimes of affect. Women shared a contentious relationship with the public sphere, which was catalysed by their presence. However, the public sphere also worked in myriad ways to contain them. Women's experiences were constituted by a plethora of agents. Their interaction with modern modes of entertainment displays the diverse ways in which women actively used the technologies emerging in the late 19th through the first part of the 20th century to participate in the public sphere.

Women came to cinema from a variety of backgrounds looking for work, survival, fame and self-transformation. Cinema was an attractive vortex that drew peripatetic groups into its transformative processes. It allowed for the possibilities of self-refashioning the previously unknown. The prevalence of women, peppered on and off the silver screen in various generic combinations and permutations, was astounding. The role that women were to play in the film industry in the 1920s–40s was defined by an ambiguous unease. It is common knowledge that in the initial years women who worked in the film industry were considered to be from 'dubious' backgrounds. Though cinema was barely respectable, as the 'film world' was deemed as the den of vice and evil-doers, these numerous disputations were embroiled in a symbiotic relationship that bordered on fascination and suspicion. Thus, initial hesitations put on hold, the film industry had many women employees working in various capacities as actresses, dancers, character artistes, extras, directors, producers and, in the sound period, also as singers, composers and musicians.[3]

In the period 1925–1947, three kinds of women dominated the screen. In some ways, the first group of women to join films without inhibition were the women from Anglo-Indian, Jewish and Eurasian communities. The second group of women who came to the film industry were part of a long-standing tradition of performance—*nautanki*, theatre, *nautch* and *gana*. The anti-nautch movement was gaining momentum and in the wake of the weakening power of princely states and the gradual decline of older forms of patronage, women from these traditions came to the cities looking for new sources of livelihood and hoping in the process to reinvent themselves. The coming of sound, in the late 1920s and early 1930s, had created a demand for singers, musicians and dancers. Cinema needed these women, as much as they needed cinema, as these women from older performative backgrounds were known for their prowess in music and dance; they brought to cinema their repertoires of performance which transformed film music and film aesthetics. The third group of women to join films were the 'educated' society ladies who were to endow their 'charm' and 'chastity' to cinema and alleviate it to bourgeoisie taste and approval.

◆◆◆

Gender is the repeated stylization of the body, a set of repeated acts within a highly rigid regulatory frame that congeal over time to produce the appearance of substance, of a natural sort of being. A political genealogy of gender ontologies, if it is successful, will deconstruct the substantive appearance of gender into its constitutive acts and locate and account for those acts within the compulsory frames set by the various forces that police the social appearance of gender. (Butler, 1990: 33)

Judith Butler, in her highly influential text, *Gender Trouble,* suggests that the categories of gender are performatively enacted and stabilised through acts of reiteration and re-citations. Gender identities are constructed and constituted by language; Butler draws from Foucault's notion of power as discursive where the body is not a 'mute facticity', i.e. a fact of nature and, like gender, it is produced by discourse. But because there is no 'interior' to gender, the law cannot be internalised, but is written on the body through a 'corporeal stylisation of gender'. For Butler, like gender, there is no body prior to cultural inscription. Sex and gender can be performatively reinscribed in ways that accentuate its constructed factitiousness rather than its 'facticity', i.e. the fact of its existence. Such reinscriptions, or re-citations, as Butler will call them in *Gender Trouble*, constitute the subject's agency within the law: in other words, the possibilities of subverting the law against itself. Butler collapses the sex/gender distinction in order to argue that there is no sex that is not always already gender. All bodies are gendered from the beginning of their social existence (and there is no existence that is not social), which means that there is no 'natural body' that pre-exists its cultural inscription. This seems to point towards the conclusion that the '[s]ubstantive effect of gender is performatively produced and compelled by regulatory practices of gender coherence' (ibid.), into not something one *is*, it is something one *does*, an act, or more precisely, a sequence of acts, a verb rather than a noun, a 'doing' rather than a 'being'. Thus, in Butler's words, '[w]ithin the inherited discourse of the metaphysics of substance, gender proves to be performative, that is, constituting the identity it is purported to be' (ibid.: 24–25).

Actresses enjoyed freedoms unknown to women from other socially sanctioned respectable professions in this period. The actresses, by virtue of their publicness, elicited an ambiguous response as they presented different models of behaviour and codes for others to emulate and refashion themselves. Their unconventional work, lifestyle and the intimacy with which actresses circulated as cinematic entities produced deep-seated moral indignation and anxiety. These women performers occupied tenuous boundaries of repute and disrepute. Cinema held a certain kind of appeal for women, which allowed for the performativity of gender. Cinema allowed for the construction and production of images of women, not merely mimetically as symptomatic of a narrative regime, but also as performative bodies. This enabled women to reinvent and redefine their subjective experience of being in a modern world.

The notion of reinvention, however, holds within its crevices the struggles and hardships of women as well. It highlights the precarious balance between women's hopes and claims in modern society. This chapter attempts to engage with women performers who tried to negotiate societal constraints and found ways to refashion themselves through cinema. Cinema overshadowed the differences between women through processes of masquerade and disavowal which flattened hierarchies of ethnicity, class, caste and lineage. The possibilities of reinventing themselves that were intrinsically linked to the interaction of women with cinema provided them with the opportunity to work and earn a living.

◆◆◆

Ruby Meyers was working as a telephone operator when she was spotted by Mohan Bhavnani of the Kohinoor Film Company. Though excited by the offer, she turned him down because of the social opprobrium against working in films. Bhavnani persisted with his offer and Meyers finally agreed. She was rechristened as Sulochana under Bhavnani's direction at Kohinoor and later moved on to the Imperial Film Company. Sulochana was the highest paid star in the country in the 1920s, surpassing even her male co-stars.[4] Such stories of rise to spontaneous fame were innumerable and attracted a large number of pretty and not-so-pretty girls to the industry. In her evidence to the Indian Cinematograph Committee, Sulochana mentions how often she got letters from girls seeking advice on possibilities of work in the film industry. She said:

> I receive many letters from up-country asking to join … from their letters they must be of a very good class. From Muhammadans mostly, and I have had one or two Anglo-Indian girls who wanted to join.[5]

In the period between the 1920s and 1940s, many Anglo-Indian, Eurasian and Jewish women worked in the film industry: Ermeline Cordozo; the Cooper sisters—Patience, Violet and Pearl; Madhuri (Miss Beryl Claessen); Seeta Devi; Sabita Devi (Miss Iris Gasper); Rose; Manorama (Miss Winnie Stuart); Indira Devi (Miss Effie Hippolite); Iris Crawford; Kumudini (Miss Mary); Lalita Devi (Miss Bonnie Bird); Vimala; Mumtaz (Miss Queenie); Yasmin (Betty Gomes); Nadia; Pramilla (Esther Victoria Abraham); and Romilla (Sophie Abraham) were some of the women who played with, and played out, the fantasies of the Indian populace on screen. But nobody could really match up to the success of Sulochana. Among her popular films were *Telephone ni Taruni/Telephone Girl* (1926); *Cinema Queen* (1926); *Typist Girl* (1926); *Balidaan* (1927); and *Wildcat of Bombay* (1927) where she essayed eight roles, including that of a gardener, a policeman, a Hyderabadi gentleman, a street urchin, a banana-seller and a European blonde. Three romantic super hits in 1928–'29 with director R.S. Chaudhari—*Madhuri* (1928), *Anarkali* (1928) and *Indira B.A.* (1929)—saw her at the peak of fame in the silent-film era. In fact, so widespread was her fame that when a short film on Mahatma Gandhi inaugurating a khadi exhibition was shown, added alongside was a hugely popular dance sequence by Sulochana from her film *Madhuri* (1932).

Women from Anglo-Indian, Eurasian and Jewish backgrounds, by virtue of their particular ethnicity, occupied a distinct place in the public domain. This familiarity with urban space was crucial to adapting to modern modes of entertainment and employment. Publicness and performativity were crucially tied together. The contrast between the habituation of Anglo-Indian and other Indian women of the time was more than apparent. Despite impressive reforms in the social sphere, *purdah* and an increasing seclusion of Hindu and Muslim women was perceived as a sign of respectability. It took 'shy', 'educated', 'Indian' ladies under stringent norms of decorum and propriety almost two decades after the birth of cinema in India to appear on screen. Until then, cinema exploited the possibilities opened up by the greater degree of freedom of dress and action that was allowed by Anglo-Indian actresses like Sulochana.

With the advent of the Talkies in 1931,[6] the nebulous film industry was in a chaotic process of conversion and expansion. The Talkies had opened up the field of performance to a variety of performers. It was assumed that Anglo-Indian/Eurasian actresses would be wiped out as the discord of tongues would necessitate actresses who could 'talk, sing and dance'. Women from these backgrounds, however, continued their journey well into sound cinema. They were accompanied by another kind of professional public woman. These women, from a variety of performative traditions and lineages such as the *kotha*, the theatre, *nautanki* and music recording companies, came to cinema with similar hopes for self-fashioning and transformation.

An examination of archival material from the 1920s onwards reveals the overwhelming number of women who came to cinema from the performative traditions of the kotha and the theatre that had been capitalised on by the gramophone industry. In fact, it was the star order already set up by the theatre and gramophone companies into which cinema hoped to tap. Fatema Begum's daughters Sultana, Zubeida and Shehzadi; Jahanara Kajjan; Miss Mushtari; Goharbai Karnataki and Amirbai Karnataki; Mukhtar Begum; Sardar Akhtar; Miss Moti (Sushila); Miss Bibbo; Miss Anvari; Ratan Bai; Khursheed; Miss Gulab and Zebunissa were some of the singing stars of their time.

Despite the influx of new stars and performers, Sulochana continued to be a popular actress. In fact, in 1933, a film titled *Sulochana* was released. It drew a fair amount of hype in the press and film magazines because of its leading lady's popularity. Sulochana's silent hit films were remade with sound such as *Indira M.A.* (1934), *Anarkali* (1935) and *Bambai ki Billi* (1936) which were fairly successful at the box office. During the mid-1930s, Sulochana established her own film studio, Rubi Pics, but it did not do very well. Sulochana's unique star appeal, however, persistently outshone the others. She was sexy, provocative and fashionable, and the modern woman seemed to have emerged most spectacularly in her films.

◆◆◆

Jaddan Bai had shown great potential as a singer and performer from an early age. Her mother Dilipa, who was also a *gaanewali*, realised that a rigorous training in music would reap rich dividends. She therefore entrusted Jaddan's musical *taleem* to the legendary doyen of the Banares *gharana*, Ustad Moijuddin Khan. Jaddan was also taught music by Ustad Barkat Ali Khan of the Patiala gharana. The instructions by her mentors shaped Jaddan's musical expression and the various inflections in her singing. According to Kishwar Desai, Jaddan made her public debut in Banaras as a teenager.[7] From then on, she became a popular songstress and invitations for *mehfils* and performances began pouring in from wealthy patrons and connoisseurs of art.

Jaddan Bai was one of the many women from a *tawaif* background who had sensed that a career in cinema would bring possibilities of reinvention devoid of social opprobrium that the kotha had come to represent by the 1930s. She clung to her roots to create a niche for herself in the Talkies. She played on her identity as a courtesan to strengthen her foothold in an industry which was, to a large extent, influenced and vitalised by the tradition of the kotha. In 1932, she received a rousing welcome from the industry when she decided to join Playart Phototone in Lahore. Journalist Amjad Hussain wrote 'the film industry is to be congratulated on enlisting the services of such an eminent songstress of India as the famous Jaddan Bai' (Hussain, 1932: 10). Jaddan Bai was extremely shrewd and understood that opportunities lay ahead in this new

Jaddan Bai
Courtesy: National Film Archive, Pune

medium, not only in terms of achieving financial security at a time when her resources were drying up, but also that cinema held the promise of social recognition and respect. She did not shy away from experimentation. Prior to her tryst with cinema, she had tried her hand at recording discs for gramophone companies. She joined the film industry in her mid-thirties in 1932, an unusually late age to make a debut as a heroine. She was driven by a fierce need to succeed and to transform conditions for her family. In a move of expediency she set up her own production house, Sangit Movietone in 1936, and became a composer, a director and a producer. She did very few films, but her ambidextrous talent is apparent in the various roles she adopted throughout the production of many of these films. She was the lead heroine and sang her own songs. In addition, she was also a music composer, scriptwriter and producer. The films produced by Jaddan Bai at Sangit Movitone did not fare particularly well at the box office. The films, however, did well enough for her to sustain and maintain her household. The central theme in her films like *Nachwali* (1934), *Talash-e-Haq* (d. Chimanlal Lahore, 1935), *Hriday Manthan* (1936) and *Madame Fashion* (1936) was the travails of the modern woman in her various avatars as a tawaif/prostitute/wife. In this imaginative universe, the modern woman inhabited the ambiguous space of desire and sexual agency. These films complicated the problematic splitting of the image of the modern woman—as a carnal prostitute and the modest wife— through the 'fallen woman' routine that was a popular trope in the films of the 1930s.

Cinema was aligned to the discourse of nationalism and reform in the 1930s. This produced an inherent ambivalence within cinematic discourse and around cinematic work. Cinema strove to be adopted within the bourgeois cultural order and be recognised as a legitimate form through the manufacture of star discourses, mechanisms of genre differentiation, characterisation and realism. The body of the actress became a contested site for a plethora of subterfuges to be enacted for the recasting of cinema. As reiterated throughout many contemporary sources, the Talkies were tied up aesthetically to the desire for verisimilitude/realism and this was connected to the demand for 'respectable' labour. Simply put, in order to represent middle-class respectable 'reality', actors from the same 'cultured' class were sought out. Devika Rani,

Durga Khote, Leela Chitnis, Shanta Apte, Renuka Devi, Sadhona Bose, Nalini Turkhud, Enaxi Rama Rao, Shobhana Samarth and Maya Bannerjee were among the few who were celebrated as the first crop of educated, cultured actresses. Their entry into cinema was publicised and their 'respectable' lineage was a constant topic of discussion in newspapers and journals as part of the industry's attempt to forge new perceptions about film work. Prior to this discourse of respectability, we see that in the absence of players from an apparently 'respectable' class that cinema strove to represent others, like those from the Anglo-Indian community or women from the kothas who were groomed and trained to masquerade in place of this class. As the Talkies did not destroy older traditions from the silent era, women from a variety of backgrounds kept coming to the film industry in search of work and reinvention.

The ease with which Jaddan Bai shifted careers from the kotha via the gramophone to cinema makes us see her as a fiercely independent woman who never seemed hesitant about taking risks. Women like Jaddan Bai were negotiating the spectrum of performative idioms to craft an identity for themselves, articulating their presence both in professional practice and in day-to-day self-presentation. Her status as a producer enabled her to establish a strong foothold in the industry, and she commanded a lot of respect in the film world. Like the *baijis*, with their matriarchal gharana system where daughters were trained by their mothers as performers, Jaddan Bai turned her energies to preparing her daughter Nargis as an actress in the film industry. Ironically, even though her sons joined the business, they came nowhere close to their mother's or sister's success.

◆◆◆

Search engines on the internet without hesitation herald Durga Khote as 'one of the first women from respectable families to enter the film industry thus breaking a social taboo'.[8] In her autobiography, Khote herself repeatedly reiterates her lineage with the 'respectable' elites of the Marathi community; she belonged to the Laud-Khote clan in Maharashtra.[9] Khote, through her status and tag of respectability, was believed to dilute the stigma attached to cinema; her association with cinema was to endow it with 'charm', 'beauty' and, most of all, 'chaste' sensibility providing the spiritual basis of Indian femininity and nationhood to legitimise the film industry.

Khote's first film, J.B.H. Wadia's *Farebi Jaal* (1931), the first sound production of Mohan Bhavnani, who had directed the Imperial action-hit *The Wildcat of Bombay* (1925) was sold through advertisements as 'Introducing the daughter of the famous solicitor Mr Laud and the daughter-in-law of the well-known Khote family'. Her role in the film was minute, lasting for only ten minutes; she played the heroine's older sister who gets beaten up by her drunken husband in a fit of anger and sucumbs to death. She was made to sing in a 'weepy voice', and she confesses she wept a lot in the scene, pouring her heart out to perform. She was paid ₹250, which was perhaps insufficient, but it took care of her 'immediate problems' (Khote, 2000: 34). The film flopped at the box office, charged with morally poor content promoting decadence and debauchery; the Maharashtrian community tore her to shreds; newspapers attacked her for being 'falsely pampered' (in Marathi 'laud' is translated as pampering and 'khote' as false) bringing disrepute to her family name and status. But it was her parents who stood by her and she writes how her father complimented her by saying, 'I don't care what the rest of the film is like. But you have shown a way for women to earn a living' (ibid.: 35). She was 26 years old, a mother of two, a housewife with a home and family to run—such a woman would hardly be considered suitable for the heroine's role in Bombay. It was director V. Shantaram who was scouting for new talent for his new Marathi–Hindi film for Prabhat Films who chanced upon the sequence in *Farebi Jaal* and, impressed with her performance, he offered her the lead role in the film *Ayodhyecha Raja* in 1932.

The dawn of Prabhat in her life seems to have turned Durga Khote's fortune in the film industry. After the disaster with *Farebi Jaal*, her family was determined to hear no more about the film industry. V. Shantaram was conscious of the dominant perceptions about film studios and so he set out to carefully construct an image of his studio as a family, trying to reassure Mr Laud into allowing Durga Khote to act in his film, he says, as narrated by Khote:

> Mr Laud, it makes good business sense in our profession to get the best work out of our artists. [Y]ou can make any arrangements you

like for a companion to ensure her comfort. It is unfortunate that Durgabai's first encounter did not turn out well. [W]e will treat her like one of the family. (ibid.: 57)

Mr Laud relented and Durgabai became the new 'star' for Prabhat Films. The studio in Kolhapur was indeed organised around a joint family setup. Khote's anecdotal stories of her experience in Kolhapur and the way that work was organised reveal just that.

> The shooting and every other part of the work was done in such a warm and congenial atmosphere that one was filled with sadness when it was over. It was not the owners of Prabhat alone but also their families and the Company workers in general who had treated me with great respect and love. They would inquire solicitously after my food, health and other arrangements. [W]hen Bakul and Harin (her two sons) visited Kolhapur, they made much of them. With what words can I express my gratitude to them all? (ibid.: 61)

This romaticisation of Prabhat through various anecdotes feed into the myths that circulated about various studios and their working procedures.[10] This was part of the grand narrative that sought to restore the film industry from notoriety to respectability. Locating work and career within the domain of the home, the studios were cleansed of their excessive vulgar associations with sex and scandal to allow respectable women like Durga Khote to venture into film work.

After the success of *Ayodhyecha Raja,* Khote worked in Prabhat's *Maya Macchindra* (d. V. Shantaram, 1932). The film was based on the mythical story of princess Kilotala, the queen of a kingdom of men-hating women. In the end, her kingdom turned out to be only an effect of *maya* (magic). Although the ending of the film reinstated social patriarchal order, it allowed for some amount of gender bending through the figure of Kilotala. Prabhat was not the only studio that Durga Khote worked with in the 1930s at the height of her career. She writes that during 1934 and 1935, she acted in four films in Calcutta. She worked in *Rajrani Meera* (d. Debaki K. Bose, 1933); *Seeta* (d. Debaki Bose, 1934); *Inquilab* (1935); and *Jeevan Natak* (d. Debaki Bose, 1935). She signed a four-month contract for each film and was paid ₹2,500 per month. At the end of each shooting schedule she would return to her family in Bombay.

In that period she says, 'I earned ₹40,000.'[11] But work was beginning to take its toll on her family life. Khote refused offers from Lahore and Calcutta as she wanted to stay close to her family in Bombay. In 1936, she started work in Shalini Studio at Kolhapur. The studio was owned by the Princess Akkasaheb, Chhatrapati Rajaram Maharaj's sister. Work at Royal Studio was regal in style and pace and was governed by whim. She acted in two films in Kolhapur— *Ushaswapna* and *Pratibha* (both d. Baburao Painter, 1937).

Khote started a production house Natraj Films with director Parshwanath Atlekar, music director Govindrao Tembe and actor Mubarak as production manager. Associated Productions, owned by a wealthy solicitor, Natwarlal, was to handle all the financial responsibilities and according to the contract, would not meddle in the creative process of film-making. *Soungadi* went on the production floor. There was a lot of speculation in the press with regard to the film, as expectations were high from the 'illustrious staff'.[12] Work was progressing; with half the film already shot, a series of mishaps stalled the production of the film. Durga Khote's husband had a heart attack and passed away while he was sitting in a parked car at Grant Road Market. Natwarlal promised her, on behalf of the company, that she would be released from the contract without demanding compensation for losses. She was in shock, but there was work to be finished. Her father was there to comfort her; she gathered herself and shooting was resumed. In 1938, *Soungadi* was released and was a moderate success. According to a review, the film held a particular appeal to 'the intelligentsia from the society'.[13] By the 1940s, Durga Khote had established herself firmly within the top star order. She was a freelancer and worked at her own pace. In a broadcast for All India Radio, she said '[E]very role, I played, had a higher purpose in it and I liked everyone of them for one reason or the other' (Abbas, 1940: 39).

◆◆◆

The induction of women into films signalled their emergence and participation into an economic sphere which was very different from other spheres of work like education, medicine and social work that were becoming popular arenas of employment for women in the 1930s. Women chose to be part of the film industry for many different reasons. Some came looking for sheer survival, some for the promise of luxuries like fashion and travel, and some for a passion for the performative. Cinema became a means through which women could articulate themselves and participate in public and social life. While they brought to cinema their own charms, skill and talent, cinema conditioned their experiences and the way they lived their lives. This chapter, through a discussion of women performers, highlights the vital ways in which cinematic intervention and work reinvented women's experience of modernity which has been varied for women, as the three stories suggest. Cinema became a means through which women earned a livelihood, survived and took part in activities of leisure. They were allowed access to the public sphere in new and radical ways. Even though this relationship to the public sphere was fraught with complexities, they made an indelible mark on the public through their work and personae.

◆

This chapter was first published in 2013 in the *IIC Quarterly*, Vol. 39, Nos. 3 and 4.

NOTES

1. As pointed out by Geraldine Forbes (2009), these new spaces of employment for women cannot be viewed without criticism due to the harsh circumstances women were pushed into in these fields of work.
2. This point is reiterated in and through many writings on this period in various issues of *Filmland;* in the work of Erik Barnouw and S. Krishnaswamy (1980: 59–121); Stephen Hughes' work on exhibition spaces in Madras (2000: 39–64); and Kaushik Bhaumik (2001).
3. Phalke's wife Saraswatibai and his daughter Mandakini, Saraswati Devi—music director and composer; Fatma Begum—producer and director; Jaddan Bai—also producer and director; Gauhar Jaan—actress and producer. See Mohan and Choudhuri (1996: 4–14).
4. Myths around Sulochana propose that she was drawing a salary of ₹5,000 per month which was more than what was received by the Governor of Bombay. The journal *Filmland* reported that Sulochana was one of the highest paid actresses of her time. Her salary was '₹750 per mensem', interestingly more than her male co-stars Dinshaw (₹500) and Eddie Billimoria (₹300), Prithviraj (₹450) and Jamshedji (₹500). See 'Searchlight' in *Filmland*, 18 June 1932, Vol. 111, No. 114, 22; and *Filmindia*, December 1938, Vol. 4, No. 8, p. 22.
5. See *Report of the Indian Cinematograph Committee 1927–28*, Evidence V, 2.
6. Ardeshir Irani's *Alam Ara* was the first Talkie to release in Bombay at Imperial's Majestic Theatre on 14 March 1931. Along with Irani there were several others who had also been struck by the possibilities of sound technology for their own industry. Among them was another leading figure of the times, Calcutta's J.J. Madan, exhibitor, distributor, producer, director and one who had a virtual monopoly on theatres in the eastern region. On the very same day as the release of

Alam Ara in Bombay, 14 March 1931, the Madans screened about 31 short films at the Crown Theatre, Calcutta. The Madans followed up Ardeshir Irani's first film with six more Talkies in the same year. By 1933, most of the other leading studios had fallen suit and the Talkies had come to stay.

7. Her date of birth is highly contentious, while Desai writes that she was born sometime in 1897, there are accounts that specify her birth date as 1900. See Desai and George (2007).

8. http://en.wikipedia.org/wiki/Durga_Khote.

9. The translation of her autobiography *I, Durga Khote: An Autobiography* from the Marathi by Shanta Gokhale is published by Oxford University Press in 2006. Most of the references I make to Khote's writing are from this edition.

10. The Bombay Talkies is another studio that immediately comes to mind. For anecdotal details by other actresses, see Leela Chitnis (1981) and Lubna Kazim (2005).

11. *Filmindia,* 30 June 1935, Vol.1, No.3, p. 40.

12. *Filmindia,* 1 October 1937, Vol. 3, No. 6, p. 31.

13. *Filmindia,* 1 April 1938, Vol. 3, No. 12, p. 48.

REFERENCES

Ahmad Abbas, K. 1940. 'Indian Films and Stars on the Air', *Filmindia,* February, Vol. 6, No. 2.

Bhaumik, Kaushik. 2001. *The Emergence of the Bombay Film Industry, 1913–1936.* Diss. Oxford University.

Barnouw, Erik and S. Krishnaswamy. 1980. 'Discord of Tongues' and 'Studio', in *Indian Film. 2nd Edition.* New York, Oxford, New Delhi: Oxford University Press.

Butler, Judith. 1990. 'Subjects of Sex/Gender/Desire', *Gender Trouble.* New York: Routledge.

Chitnis, Leela. 1981. *Chanderi Duniya.* Pune: Shri Vidya Prakashan.

Desai, Kishwar. 2007. *Darlingji: The True Love Story of Nargis and Sunil Dutt.* New Delhi: HarperCollins.

Forbes, Geraldine. 2009. *Women in Modern India.* Asian Reprint. Cambridge University Press. India.

George, T.J.S. 2007. *The Life and Times of Nargis.* Chennai: East West Books.

Hughes, Stephen, P. 2000. 'Policing Silent Film Exhibition in Colonial South India', in Ravi Vasudevan (ed.), *Making Meaning in Indian Cinema.* Delhi: Oxford University Press.

Hussain, Amjad. 1932. 'A Brief Biographical Sketch: Jaddan Bai', *The Cinema,* September and October, Vol. 6, No. 1, p. 10.

Kazim, Lubna (ed.). 2005. *A Woman of Substance: The Memoirs of Begum Khurshid Mirza 1918–1989.* New Delhi: Zubaan.

Khote, Durga. 2000. *I, Durga Khote: An Autobiography.* Translated from the Marathi by Shanta Gokhale. New Delhi: Oxford University Press.

Mohan, Reena and Dibya Choudhuri. 1996. 'Of Wayward Girls and Wicked Women: Women in Indian Silent Feature Films, 1913–1934,' *Deepfocus,* Vol. VI, pp. 4–14.

Rajadhyaksha, Ashish and Paul Willemen (eds.). 1999. *Encyclopaedia of Indian Cinema.* New revised edition. London: BFI and Oxford University Press.

The Report of Indian Cinematograph Committee, 1927–'28.

◆◆

Nilima Sheikh
Gathering Threads. 'Each Night put Kashmir in your Dream' series. 2004–'10.
Scroll painted on both sides. 305×183 cm. Casein Tempera on Canvas.
Courtesy: Nilima Sheikh

15

ASCRIBING FEMINIST INTENT

The Invention of the Indian Woman Artist

DEEPTHA ACHAR[#]

In the course of discussions before the seminar 'The Issues of Activism: the Artist and the Historian (2003)' at the Faculty of Fine Arts, Baroda, Nilima Sheikh commented on the close relationship that the body of her work has with the concerns of the women's movement in India. In fact, Sheikh has, several times, invoked the feminist context in which her work was shaped. She has argued that her practice of painting could be seen as a resistance to 'the inherent pressure to engage with the political life of a nascent democracy, where there seemed to be little space left, within the definitive terms of radicalism, for a quest as personal, as the search for a feminine voice'.[1] In fact, she has sketched the slow processes through which the quest for the feminine voice as radical practice was thought through with definitively feminist tools. However, the discussions of Sheikh's work have tended to focus on what is called her 'lyrical' language and its implications.

There is a sense in which this focus on the lyrical in the discussion had an unsaid dimension that gestures to the feminine. While the lyrical as a description of a style and a mode can and has been used in the context of other genres and styles of art and even in the discussion of contemporary male artists, the term certainly carries implications of the sensuous and the sinuous, of the dominance of affect over thought, which, in the context of the woman artist seems to connote the feminine, particularly so when women are explicitly thematised in the work. It would appear as if a concept derived from music in the classical Greek context and which has been the dominant mode of poetry-writing in the West from at least the 18th century has almost acquired a gender connotation in

Nilima Sheikh
When Champa Grew Up, 6 and 7. 1984. 30.5×40.5 cm each, gum tempera on Vasli paper.
Courtesy: Nilima Sheikh

this context. Here, it appears as if the lyrical is posed against the rigorously analytic, the sharply historical, precluding any possibility of harnessing it to the political tasks of Indian feminism.

Why does art historical/critical language need to overwrite questions of gender through the deployment of categories such as the lyrical? On the one hand, the lyrical seems to invoke a notion of the feminine; on the other, it appears to be evidently informed by categories of feminist thought. This is not to suggest that the feminine and the feminist are oppositional categories; indeed, feminisms the world over have sought to theorise femininity in multiple ways. How is an understanding of the lyrical useful in this context? Instead of setting up a discussion around whether the lyrical is feminine (or feminist) or not, might it not be more productive to examine what the function and effect of terms such as 'lyric' have on the manner in which we read a work? What are the readings that it enables? Is it possible to work across the notion of 'lyrical' in order to formulate an engagement that allows a feminist dimension to emerge? The issue, as I see it, is not so much whether Sheikh's work is lyrical or not, or even traditional or not. Rather, its significance lies the manner in which she restructures a language designated as lyrical and practices designated as 'traditional' by the broad framework of art-writing to make it available for a political praxis; and a personal idiom that can acknowledge and politicise the representation of a world shaped in complex ways by gender and community. In working away from a conventionally masculinist modernist idiom, relocating 'traditional' techniques to the site of the contemporary, energising them with a new charge that engages questions of the minor, Sheikh's work offers a powerful reading of our time.

What I attempt to do in this chapter is to locate Sheikh's paintings in the realm of the political by establishing linkages between her work, feminist thought and the women's movement in India. In this, I will refer to the processes that consolidated the category 'Indian woman artist', a term, which, as one reads the writing on modern Indian art in catalogues, articles, books, enters the lexicon only around the mid-to-late 1980s. My intention, therefore, is to look at the moment and the manner in which this category 'Indian woman artist' was put together in the sphere of modern Indian art. I argue that the reshaping of this elite site took place in the context of the women's movement in India, particularly in the way the movement reformulated popular ideas about women and instituted a new kind of visibility about violence in women's lives. The category seems to have emerged across a range of factors, partly art-institutional, partly art-historical/art-critical and certainly in conjunction with feminist thought and the women's movement in India while having a quite decisive effect on the art market. And although one is aware of the key role played by international capital in the arena of the art market, it would be too reductive to tie down movements in art to a simple instrumental relation with capital.

◆◆◆

It is clear that the Indian woman artist as a category does not seem to exist before the mid-1980s. If one looks at the curriculum vitae of art practitioners who now fall under the purview of the term—Arpita Singh, Madhavi Parekh, Nalini Malani and Nilima Sheikh—it is evident that they begin to practise and show well before the 1980s. Singh exhibits in group shows from the early 1960s, and has solo shows by 1972; Parekh starts painting in 1964, participates in group shows in the 1960s and has solo exhibitions in the early 1970s; Malani participated in group exhibitions and had solo shows by the 1960s and Sheikh too had started showing by the early 1970s.[2] However, the art-critical discourses, which frame them at that time, are those regarding the debates occurring around modernism in the post-Independence context. They are positioned as 'young artists' or 'new contemporaries' or seen as players in the debate around tradition and modernity as in the 'Pictorial Space' exhibition.[3] They could be characterised as 'naïve' (Madhvi Parekh) or 'expressionist' (Nalini Malani), 'traditional' (Nilima Sheikh) or 'decorative' (Arpita Singh): nevertheless, their thematic choices and concerns, though recognised as women-centred, even feminist in the case of Malani, were not seen as belonging coherently to a cogent body of work that could be theorised under the rubric of the Indian woman artist.

In 1978, Gulammohamed Sheikh curated 'New Contemporaries': the show was a passionate assertion of an artist's right to draw on a visual stock that was not circumscribed by a simple nationalist 'rejection' of the West. In his catalogue essay, in an authoritative intervention in the then current debate on the 'derivative' status of modern Indian art, he argued that the contemporary artist came into a multi-layered visual inheritance that ranged from traditional art in India, to mural-making in Mexico, to Pop Art of America. The impact of this visual exposure, he maintained, was 'largely catalytic than decisive', and the engagement with these other (Western) art movements took a trajectory that led to 'the reinterpretation of Western norms in the non-Western context' (Sheikh, 1978: n.p.). It is with this as his frame, that he had noted that

> ...the most distinguishing feature of the art of the younger artist is its growing involvement with the local environment, its shift from generalities to specific areas of interest. This has led to an approach which is more realistic and intimate. A pronounced interest in print making and emergence of a number of women artists too ought to be recognised as important developments. (ibid.: n. p.)

These comments have the value of underlining at least two dimensions crucial to the constitution of Indian women artists: firstly, they gesture towards the question of the professionalisation of the woman artist. The recognition of the emergence of women who were professional artists and not hobbyists paved the way for the construction of the modern woman artist in India and, indeed, of a tradition of women artists. Amrita Sher-Gil's relentless characterisation of herself as a professional painter allowed her to be easily taken over as an iconic figure in the tradition of the Indian woman artist that was being invented. In addition, the re-evaluation of the monumental sculpture of Piloo Pochkhanawala, the innovative and pioneering print-making of Devayani Krishna, new recognition of the manner in which Meera Mukherji problematised the question of village artisanship allowed the constitution of a post-Independence trajectory of women artists.[4] Not least, these early moves placed under question the unmarked category 'artist' which, as the very nomenclature 'women artist' showed was, in fact, gendered. While such recognition as well as the problematisation of the site of the professional practice of art was important, the constitution of the category and the tradition of the 'Indian woman artist' did not materialise solely through the collectivisation of the newly emergent professional class of women artists. Rather, one can see it getting formulated across and through pressures of the women's movement in India.

Secondly, Gulammohammed Sheikh's framing of the question of the impact of Western art movements on modern Indian art as catalytic rather than decisive foresees and, to a certain extent, preempts the charge that the collectivisation of women artists in India was the result of a simple reduplication of Western feminism. Feminist intervention in art history in the West can certainly be plotted in terms of the second wave of feminism which powerfully engaged with the question of representation of women; literary and visual representation were privileged sites of feminist investigation. The thrust of many of these efforts was in challenging disciplinary canons and early work concentrated on addressing patriarchal art historical assumptions about women artists. The construction of a tradition of women artists and their new visibility also reorganised the art market in significant ways and surely one outcome of second-wave feminism was a new awareness of women artists from non-Western spaces.

At the same time, the UN Declaration of the years 1975 to 1985 as the International Decade of Women globally, the setting up of the Department of Women and Child Development as a part of the Ministry of Human Resource Development in 1985 locally, also consolidated the validity of moves that thematised women and gender. This acknowledgement of the invisibility of and discrimination against women that can be read in the UN Declaration and the Government of India's creation of the specialised Department was clearly a consequence of the force of the women's movement all around the world.

◆◆◆

Arguably, the contemporary women's movement in India was born in the mid-1970s. The women's movement in the 1970s was quite successful in raising the issue of dowry deaths, rape and women's health, orchestrating a sustained campaign at the national level. These drives were accompanied by an aggressive media campaign which allowed these 'women's issues' to enter popular consciousness. Moreover, each of these issues centred on the woman's body in a way that rendered conventional representations of women problematic. Notably, the body in pain became an important motif. The 1980s marked a shift in the women's movement in India: from its beginnings in the 1970s where the movement for women's rights focused on one or two issues such as dowry and rape, operating with a social welfare-based ideology and with a quite straitjacketed understanding of women's problems, it shifted to positions where the focus was on a range of issues systemically interrelated with explicitly feminist ideology that allowed more complex understandings of the issues involved. The idea that women were systemic victims made room for a more individual approach that emphasised the 'creative' aspects of women's life.

While such a reading of the women's movement is debatable, one can certainly track a new feminist interest in the arts, as also history, during this period which crucially focused on the question of representation. One key effort in this direction was Susie Tharu and K. Lalitha's project on women's writing [1989–1991] (Tharu *et al.*, 1992). At this juncture, Tharu and K. Lalitha were setting out a position which strained against simple notions of the loss and recovery of women's cultural productions and, more importantly, sought to work through 'the problem that arises as the concept of experience which, in feminist practice, has a critical deconstructive charge, is uncritically conflated with an empiricist privileging of experience as the authentic source of truth and meaning' (ibid.: 26). It is in these moves to work out an aesthetic of the personal that engaged with the themes of the women's movement that one could productively locate the consolidation of the category 'Indian woman artist' in the 1980s.

The invention of the tradition of the Indian woman artist can partly be tracked to the critical and artistic decisions by Singh, Parekh, Malani and Sheikh to hold a series of group shows organised around a set of artistic parameters that centred on their gender. Sheikh recalls that though they were offered work and visibility by the art institutional networks in place, they were interested in reframing their work in such a way that questions of a gendered art practice might be foregrounded. She comments that the issue was not about individual opportunities or recognition; rather, it was more a question of investigating the manner in which a grouping as 'women artists' would reposition individual oeuvres in ways that could meaningfully open the field to them.[5] Looking at the extensive work that each of them had done and shown previously, one could wonder at the sense of dissatisfaction that led to the formulation of the shows. Yet it is possible to surmise its use-value in positioning their work in art networks in a manner that worked against the logic of the unmarked, ungendered category of 'artist'.

Staged over several sessions of consultations, their collective decision to work out a set of shows rather than to produce a one-off effort as well as to ensure that each artist would exhibit at least some new works for each show enabled them to build up a body of work. Their decision to use water-colour, a medium that at least one of them had not used till then, and to work on paper rather than canvas, was also significant; more so, because oil and canvas were certainly markers of 'high' art. While these 'material' decisions were partly motivated by the easy movability afforded by small format water-colour work on paper, especially considering that the plan was to have many shows at different places, it was also because the artists wanted the shows to be seen as metaphoric of the marginalised site of gender. Also, opting to show away from major national art exhibition centres in New Delhi and Bombay in places such as Bhopal and Bangalore (then), and in smaller galleries in the major art centres, consolidated the logic of the marginal and the minor in gender relations that was brought into play.[6] The shows, by Sheikh's account, were reasonably successful in market terms, with each of them managing to sell at least two works every exhibition. Nevertheless, despite the conceptual investment in an understanding of gender as it structured the art world, its markets, its modes of display, its imagined histories and its criticism that energised these shows, they did not attract much critical attention.

Crucially, though, these shows positioned the exhibited work as gendered; nevertheless, the catalogue essay by Ashish Rajadhyaksha shies away from attributing feminist intent to the show as also to their step to exhibit only water-colours:

> It would be quite wrong to ascribe feminist intent to this show—as it would be to associate the scale and medium used with 'women' artists. (Rajadhyaksha, 1987: n. p.)

Recognising the necessity of rethinking the conventions that bring together the personal and political, however, he attempts to situate the practices framed in the show in the political climate of the nation:

at a crucial time when, as perhaps never before in recent Indian
history [when] the siege on the 'real', of our circumstances, has
become as much a battlefield of the everyday as of larger issues and
subject-matter. (ibid.)

In an endeavour that locates a distance between the critical edge
of feminist thought and the practices of the women's movement,
he seeks to bypass the 'timeworn feminist slogan'—the personal
is political—and instead reads these works as a site where 'the
intensely personal carves out an area of practice' in the context of
that national moment. Though he is forced to acknowledge the
value of strategies that foreground a gendered (women's) practice of
art, he hesitates to admit its value, seeing it, rather as a condition to
be overcome:

> The sheer willfulness present in each of the artist's work, and in
> the organising of such a show: to point out that the effort here is
> not only one that brings to the fore several issues concerning
> contemporary Indian art, but also a terrain of cultural, and hence
> social, practice that must now be appropriated to support practicing
> artists…. Women artists, painting in the medium of water-colour,
> may get relegated to a certain slot that can only be overcome by
> an alignment of critical means with the effort being made by these
> artists to paint and, now, to exhibit. (ibid.)

It seems quite clear that the artists themselves were engaging with
ideas born of the women's movement; indeed, they were familiar
with Tharu's arguments about women writing particularly through
their association with the Kasauli Art Centre, where she had made
a presentation on the women-writing project. If one takes Sheikh's
work as an example, it is easy enough to locate the impress of the
women's movement on the *Champa* series. It would be possible
to argue that the conceptual visibility of the ubiquitous 'dowry
death' was enabled by the women's movement of the late 1970s
and that *Champa* was shaped precisely by the women's movement's
articulation of the issue. The emotional charge that *Champa* carries
surely draws from the manner it situates a local event and a personal
experience in an overarching conceptual scaffold constructed by the
women's movement. Equally, the *Champa* series formulates strategies

of representation that illustrate the single instance even as it connects that instance with other analogous events that are bound together through the frame 'bride burning.'[7] Rajadhyaksha is clearly able to read the representational strategies involved in *Champa*: '... Nilima's Champa ... had responded to our gaze with a blankness, forcing us to question our involvement with [her] condition' (Rajadhyaksha, 1987: n. p.); yet, at that time, it appears to be difficult to make the connections that link these strategies with the questions raised by the women's movement. Consequently, it was equally difficult to theorise the implications of these new modes of representation for the women's movement, as also, for art practice.

◆◆◆

The 1986 NGMA exhibition of Indian women artists as well as the Festival of India's USSR initiative to showcase contemporary women art practitioners, were also organised at the same time. These events, and the work of several individual practitioners, have had a critical role to play in the context of the emergence of the category 'Indian woman artist'. A few examples are: Anupam Sud, Gogi Saroj Pal and Arpana Caur, based in Delhi, who were working with gendered thematics from at least the 1970s; so also were Arnawaz Vasudevan and Padmini of the Madras School. Navjot Altaf too is an artist who has systematically engaged with feminist thought during this period. In the 1980s, Rekha Rodwittiya, on her return from Royal College of Art, London, consciously positioned herself as a feminist and the sculpture of N. Pushpamala sharply foregrounded issues of female sexuality in a different idiom. However, their shows as well as other parallel government-sponsored initiatives such as the NGMA exhibition were understood, by and large, within a modernist paradigm: for art historical discourse, this helped domesticate a category born out of the critical energies of the women's movement.

One can speculate that this was so at least partly because the theories of the avant-garde that structured the understanding of 'modern' art in India were not framed in a way that allowed a feminist engagement to be read as productive. The process through which art historical/critical frameworks get restructured in a way that permit them to engage with the critical edge of feminist practice is clearly visible in the work of Geeta Kapur. In the significant show that she curated in the 1970s, 'Pictorial Space: A Point of View on

Contemporary Indian Art' (Lalit Kala Akademi, 1977), the work of women artists was framed in and across the language of the modern. For example, she says of Malani: 'Nalini paints alienated, deeply introverted, possibly psychotic persons and the space therefore is a private one, a sealed, dimlit, chamber.' However, by the early 1990s, just a few years after the group shows of 1987–89, she has already been able to draft her enormously influential 'Body as Gesture: Women Artists at Work': of Malani she says

> Nalini Malani began, when still very young, in the early 1970s, to introduce female trauma as the subject of her otherwise conventionally expressionistic painting. Gradually the masochistic injunctions of a body receptive to violence were worked out into an experience of female being as survivor.[8]

Along with this movement that has begun to deal with 'transactions, on gender terms, between private fantasy and public concern' (Kapur, 2000: 3), the chapter, which 'sets up equations between four women artists' (ibid.), effectively fabricates a tradition of women artists that moves backward in time embracing Amrita Sher-Gil and laterally across space to include Frida Kahlo. By 1996, in her catalogue essay for the exhibition 'Inside Out: Women Artists of India', she acknowledges the impress of women's struggles 'to press into service objects coded into cultural significations indifferent or hostile to them'. In fact, she powerfully argues that 'Feminist politics in women's art is at times over and above the intention of the work; it is inherent in the historical context of its production' (Kapur, 1996: Introduction, p. 9).

This arrival of an otherwise innocuous category 'Indian woman artist' should also be placed in relation to a range of other moves in art institutional spaces: the search for lost women artists, the re-valuation of women artists who were dismissed or marginalised, the re-examination of the criteria by which art-works acquired canonicity, and the legitimation and problematisation of gendered themes. These moves, which drew from the feminist thrust of the 1980s, seemed to have had the potential of energising art historical discourse, yet the direction taken has substantially been along the lines of 'loss and recovery' and 'valorisation of the personal' mode in the engagement with the idea of the Indian woman artist.

Such critical practices have tended to naturalise the category and imbue it with an essential presence that defines it away from any historical specificity.

In doing so, they locate the thematic of Indian women artist in the realm of the ahistorical, apolitical feminine. Arguments that erase the historicity of categories, I suggest, obscure the relationship between questions raised by the women's movement and the question of women's art. Consequently, a productive interface, which could enrich the articulation of issues of representation within the women's movement as much as within the art world itself, gets erased.

◆

\# This chapter was first published in 2013 in the *IIC Quarterly*, Vol. 39, Nos. 3 and 4.

NOTES

1. Nilima Sheikh. Presentation and slide show of her work, made at the UGC seminar on 'The Issues of Activism: the Artist and the Historian', Department of Art History and Aesthetics, MS University, Baroda, 6–8 March 2003.
2. See their Curriculum Vitae in Rajadhyaksha (1987).
3. All four artists participated in the path-breaking exhibition 'Pictorial Space' organised by Lalit Kala Akademi and curated by Geeta Kapur in 1977.
4. Gayatri Sinha's edited book (1996) is a key book that systematically invented this tradition. In her 'Introduction' Gayatri Sinha writes 'Against the twin encumbrances of a highly codified representation of the feminine in classical and some contemporary art, the absence of a language to write the body, the nascent women's art of the 1950s attains a renewed significance.'
5. Nilima Sheikh. Personal Communication. 2004.
6. The exhibitions, titled, 'Through the Looking Glass,' were held during 1987–1989 first at Bharat Bhavan, Bhopal, and subsequently at Kala Yatra, Bangalore; Shridharani, New Delhi; Jehangir Art Gallery, Bombay; and Centre for Contemporary Art, New Delhi.
7. See Sheikh in Desai (2001), p. 18.
8. See Geeta Kapur (2000). The first version of the paper was presented in 1993.

REFERENCES

Desai, Vishakha, N. (ed.). 2001. *Conversation with Traditions: Nilima Sheikh and Shahzia Sikander*. New York: Asia Society.

Kapur, Geeta. 1977. 'Pictorial Space: A Point of View on Contemporary Indian Art', in *Place for People*. New Delhi: Lalit Kala Akademi.

Kapur, Geeta. 2000. 'Body as Gesture: Women Artists at Work', in *When Was Modernism: Essays on Contemporary Cultural Practice in India*. New Delhi: Tulika.

Kapur, Geeta *et al.* 1996. 'Introduction', in *Inside Out: Contemporary Women Artists of India.* London: Middlesbrough Art Gallery.

Rajadhyaksha, Ashish. 1987. 'Exhibition of Recent Water Colours: Arpita Singh, Madhvi Parekh, Nalini Malani, Nilima Sheikh.' Catalogue Essay. Bhopal: Bharat Bhavan.

Sheikh, Gulammohammed. 1978. 'New Contemporaries'. Catalogue Essay. *Marg.* Bombay.

Sinha, Gayatri (ed.). 1996. 'Evocations and Expressions: Contemporary Women Artists of India', *Marg.* Mumbai.

Tharu, Susie and K. Lalitha. 1992. *Women Writing in India.* 2 Vols. New Delhi: OUP.

◆◆

Girija Devi
Photo: Avinash Pasricha

16
THE ALPHA SONGBIRDS
Independent and Vibrant

KUMUD DIWAN
JHA#

'*Banawari shyam more, aaj ki rain yahin rahiye*' ('Oh! My lord Krishna, please stay with me tonight'). This is Kishori Amonkar singing the signature *Chota Khayal Bandish* (composition) in Sampoorna Malkauns. '*Ganga reti pe bangle chavaye da more raja aawe lahar Jamune ki*' ('Oh, my beloved, please make a bungalow for me to live in on the sands of the Ganges where the waves of Yamuna come to greet me'). Girija Devi's Banaras *thumri* and *dadras* evoke visions of enchanted lands and timeless traditions. She is quintessentially Banarasi and one of the most celebrated names today.

'Gana Saraswati' may be an embellishment for 'Kishori Tai', as she is fondly called by her admirers, and Vidushi/Thumri Diva for 'Appaji', as Girija Devi is addressed by her growing tribe of fans, but as a musician and their *mureed* (keen admirer) who has grown up in the Hindustani classical tradition, my musical antennae pick up the frequencies of their moods, their music, the force of their personae and performances, and their individuality.

Arguably, they are the 'Alpha songbirds' of Hindustani classical music, who lead by example and epitomise a pioneering spirit in the field of music.

Together with 'Surshree' Kesarbai Kerkar, the renowned Jaipur–Atrauli *gharana khayal* exponent, and Husnabai of Banaras, the legendary thumri performer, these four artistes are the cornerstone of the structure and the elevations of Hindustani classical music. While Kesarbai Kerkar and Husnabai led their genre of music pre-Independence, Girija Devi and Kishori Amonkar have earned their place among the celebrated musicians of today.

As women performers, they are path-breakers. In terms of innovation, they have spawned their own gharanas within the framework of the traditional and historical gharana in which they were trained. Their performances are imbued with a genius' interpretation of the raga and the literary underpinnings of the compositions they sing. Their command over their medium and their ability to transcend its technicalities to rewrite the rudiments of their genre of music has placed them above others in their profession.

They have also inspired later generations of women performers of both the khayal and thumri. Ashwini Bhide, daughter of Manik Bhide, Shruti Sadolikar and Arti Ankalikar are well-known khayal exponents trained by Kishori Amonkar. Girija Devi's biggest contribution to the world of music is her dedicated teaching of Hindustani classical music to young aspirants at the famous ITC Sangeet Research Academy (SRA) in Kolkata for over two decades now.

Although this chapter deals with Hindustani classical music, the rich tradition of Carnatic music must find mention, if only in the work of M.S. Subbulakshmi, the renowned Carnatic vocalist. Her mother was a violinist and came from the *devdasi* tradition. But M.S. Subbulakshmi rose above it to become the only female musician to receive the Bharat Ratna. Her debut, at the prestigious Madras Academy of Music at the age of 13, was her ticket to stardom. The very discerning Academy bent every rule to allow this young girl to regale her audience and critics with *bhajans* and *kritis*. Highly decorated and revered and with a career spanning concerts at Carnegie Hall, Royal Albert Hall, among others, she is the quintessence of women's empowerment through music. Kishori Amonkar called her the eighth *sur* of the seven-note octave!

Hindustani classical music has been largely a male-dominated bastion, but these women have raised the bar, broken traditional moulds, and have become role models for other aspirants and exponents of the genres. Women musicians were referred to as *baiji*, mere entertainers who were looked down upon. The sheer determination of these women empowered them and opened the doors for singers from non-musical families to embrace music as a career.

These portraits are of true leaders in the field of Hindustani classical music. These musicians have contributed significantly to the evolution and acceptance of women as highly sought after and revered artistes. They symbolise an independent spirit in their quest for excellence in their profession. There was a stigma attached to women singing in public, and many singers, like Husna Jan, came from the courtesan tradition, which was taboo. These women have overcome many obstacles along the way to put their music first, ensuring that their names go down in the annals of history as immortal artistes of India.

Vidushi Girija Devi is a living legend from Banaras and a formidable presence in the semi-classical genre of thumri, dadra, *chaiti, kajri* and *tappa*; in fact, she is the torchbearer of the legacy that Banaras is renowned for: thumri and tappa. It is a legacy handed down by immortals such as Siddheshwari Devi, Rasoolan Bai, Jaddan Bai and Badi Moti Bai. Girija Devi is also a khayal maestro.

Thumri was a courtesan art and flourished in Lucknow, Banaras and Gaya, collectively called the *poorab-ang* thumri. Its patrons were the Nawab of Lucknow, Wajid Ali Shah, himself a poet who wrote many thumris under the pen name of 'Akhtar Piya', and the zamindars and royalty, countrywide, who provided the financial support as well as the ambience of their *mehfils* in which the top performers of dhrupad, khayal, thumri and tappa rendered memorable concerts.

Leisure and pleasure defined the lifestyle of the royalty and the landed gentry prior to Independence and the semi-classical genre was the most preferred. The performers of this genre were mainly women who lived in a gossamer world, oblivious of the realities of social oppression or the social changes that swept India between 1857 and 1947.

Girija Devi was born in 1929 to parents who had moved to the heartland of music and culture, Varanasi, and her father, Ramdas Ji, was an avid music lover and played the harmonium (Mishra, 1997). Girija Devi attributes her musical initiation to her father's keen desire to train her in Hindustani classical music with the renowned sarangi player of Banaras, Pt. Sarju Prasad Mishra, who became her guru and mentor. He recognised her sharp mind and her finely defined musical learning. The training was hard and the practice arduous. She became an accomplished and consummate performer at the age of 15 and found many platforms in Banaras to express her khayal, thumri, dadra and tappa renderings. She was groomed in advanced thumri singing by Pt. Shri Chandra Mishra, a musician and a scholar of music.

She has been performing at prestigious concerts since 1950. At one of her concerts, Dr S. Radhakrishnan was so enraptured with her performance that he asked her to continue beyond her two-hour performance (ibid.). She became the darling of the media and the discerning audience of Delhi. Girija Devi is a highly decorated musician and has received the 'Padma Vibhushan' from the Government of India and the 'Tansen Samman' from the Government of Madhya Pradesh, among other awards. She has received critical acclaim for her performances in the UK, USA and many other countries. The SRA–Guru position makes her a leader in male-dominated academies and training institutions.

As an admirer of 'Appaji' from a younger generation, as a musician from the same genre of Banaras thumri, I salute her deep commitment to music and the preservation of our heritage for posterity. Sadly, Hindustani classical music has lost many compositions and styles of performance because many virtuoso performers were not interested in shaping and grooming young minds for a musical career.

I vividly recall my first brush with her as a 10 years old at a concert in Meerut. The seeds of thumri were sown, and I resolved then to be a thumri exponent. Her performance of *Jhoola*, '*Siya sang jhoole bagia me Ram lalna*' ('Lord Rama and Sita are on a swing together in the garden') was unforgettable. Years later, at a *baithak* in Delhi, I requested her to sing that Jhoola and with a smile she did!

I was in conversation with 'Appaji' recently and asked her what her mantra for being 'Girija Devi' was. Her answer touched me with its simplicity.

Man ko hamesha taiyaar rakho, kisi bhi kaam ke liye man ko sada taiyaar rakho beta, ghar me khana banana hai to poore man se banao aur jab gana gana hai to bhi man se gao.

(Keep your mind ready for all the responsibilities that a woman and a musician has to shoulder. As women we are mothers and wives, having obligations at home as well as challenges in our profession. Have the determination and the willingness to manage both worlds so that you can be at peace and be happy).

'*Man razee rakhna ve yaar!*' ('Always keep your heart ready for seeking my beloved!'); strains from the famous *Shori Miyan* tappas that she sings to perfection and which is her holy grail. Her mantra projects femininity as an extension of her personality, and she approaches any dialogue from a graceful feminine platform. There is no need to try and be the number-one man in a man's world, she says, be the number-one woman instead! 'Appaji' leads a full and busy life. She has been a nurturing mother, a doting grandmother, a performer and living legend, and a teacher for those who seek the same path. She places her role of family-head as equally important and believes that women artistes must go about their daily routine with a smile, ready for whatever comes their way.

Her time for focused thinking and reflection are the early morning hours. She rolls the *swars* in her mind and reworks the *kahan* or the way of saying the lyrics, arranging and rearranging it towards perfection. 'Train the mind and the rest will follow', and gratitude for her motherly and affectionate guidance and *margdarshan* are what I took with me after a recent conversation with her.

◆◆◆

Husna Jan or Husnabai was a renowned thumri singer of Banaras at a time when thumri was a courtesan tradition and the affluent royals, zamindars and the *raees* were its chief patrons. Husnabai was a contemporary of Bhartendu Harish Chandra, the famous poet and a leading litterateur of Banaras, who was gaining fame at the time. Husnabai often corresponded with Bhartendu Harish Chandra, and took his advice and opinion on poetic expression. Rai Krishna Das, the famous literary historian and musicologist received many rare photographs of Chandra from Husnabai. Her thumri and other sub-genres of thumri were published as *Madhu Tarang* (Sharma, 2012) Bhartendu Harish Chandra also got her to compose the *Geet Govind* by Jaidev.

The *Kotha* tradition gave livelihood to the singing and dancing divas of yore and their art was a source of entertainment for landed gentry and royalty. Husnabai commanded a lot of respect and popularity even though she was not as famous as the latter-day singers of Banaras, such as Siddheshwari and Rasoolan Bai, who performed all over India. But Husnabai was well known in UP as an expert in khayal, thumri and tappa gayaki. Husnabai was in the

Husnabai
Courtesy: Avinash Pasricha

same league as Vidyadhari and Badi Moti Bai, masters of the art of thumri and tappa. Much is known and written about Gauhar Jan, Siddheshwari Devi and Rasoolan Bai, performers par excellence, but few know that Husnabai was the one who redefined and revolutionised the singing tradition of Banaras in the early 1900s when she came under the influence of Mahatma Gandhi, singing patriotic songs and inspiring other courtesan singers to do the same.

The elite and the royals often sent their scions to these kothas to get a taste and a feel of the *Adab, Tehzeeb* and the *Nafasat* ('the etiquette and the charming social disposition') of which these *Tawaifs*, or courtesans, were the embodiment. The word 'tawaif' is the name given to singing and nautch girls in the Mughal period.

Husnabai was also referred to as 'Sarkar' or chieftain, as she rose to great heights during her career.[1] Trained by Thakur Prasad Mishra and the famous sarangi player Pt. Shambhunath Mishra, her tappa gayaki made her popular with the affluent patrons of Banaras and this she mastered from the legendary Chote Ramdas Ji of Banaras.

The daughters of courtesans became courtesans. They were born into the tradition and were taught by musicians employed by their mothers. Husnabai's family and social circumstances led her to embrace the life of a singing woman or a tawaif and she mastered the art enough to command a name and position in society. But Husnabai was also a leader. When Gandhi came through Kashi (Banaras) and Nainital during the non-cooperation movement, he appealed to the tawaif to jettison the life of prostitution and take on other careers. Husnabai galvanised a movement in which she influenced these women to earn a living by singing bhajans and patriotic songs instead, and be freed from a life of indignity. Many of them joined the *charkha* movement subsequently. While the followers of Gandhi began picketing outside the homes of prostitutes in Amritsar, forcing many to leave, the Kashi courtesans, led by Husnabai, continued their fight for rehabilitation. She redefined the meaning of leadership and formed the 'Tawaif Sabha (courtesan federation of Kashi)' with the twin objective of supporting the national movement and reforming the lives of courtesans. *Varvadhu Vivechan*, the complete text of Husnabai's presidential speech at the inauguration of the Sabha is available in *Varvadhu Vivechan* (Sahitya Sadan, Amritsar, 1929).

Husnabai recited the nationalistic poem:[2]

Mandir me hai chand chamakta, masjid main hai murli ki taan
Makka ho chahe Vrindavan, hote aapas main qurbaan

(The moon shines in the temple and Krishna's flute enchants all in a mosque. Both Mecca and Vrindavan are unified to sacrifice themselves for each other.)

At a time when her only source of livelihood depended on her being a courtesan, Husnabai dared to look at the larger picture, the freedom of her fellow courtesans from a life of indignity, and their collective contribution to the freedom movement. She exhorted fellow courtesans to learn from the life of Joan of Arc and the women of Chittoregarh.[3] Wear iron shackles instead of gold ornaments, she said, but veer away from a life that is not honourable. Together with her courtesan friends, she boycotted foreign goods to embrace *swadeshi*.

She persuaded the courtesans to begin their recitals with a nationalistic/patriotic composition. She advised them to collect these patriotic songs from Vidyadhari Bai, another famous courtesan singer of Banaras. This was Husnabai's masterstroke! These courtesans could not leave their profession without an alternative for financial reasons. This step was a transition to an alternate livelihood, with Husnabai continuing to lobby for the restoration of dignity and respect for these musicians.

Husnabai had a Hindu lover, Husnawale Das. For her, humanity transcended religion, and when he died, she had a *dharmashala* and a *mandir* constructed in his memory. They were called the Radha–Krishna temple and the Krishna dharmashala.

Legend has it that Husnabai once turned down the attentions of a zamindar who arrived at her kotha to hear her sing. His footsteps on the staircase made a thumping sound that offended Husna's refined sensibilities and she refused to sing. If a person did not have basic etiquette, how could he appreciate her music? He turned back with the wads of money he had brought for her. Husnabai died in 1935.

◆◆◆

Padma Vibhushan Kishori Amonkar and 'Surshree' Kesarbai Kerkar are the two ends of the Jaipur–Atrauli Gharana spectrum, arguably the most influential gharana of khayal gayaki along with the Kirana gharana.

Kesarbai inherited the formidable Ustad Alladiya Khan legacy. Her music was not for the masses but for the elite and the affluent kingdoms who were her patrons. Kishori Amonkar has a special place in the hearts of music lovers in the country and around the world with her inimitable style. Kishori Tai, as she is lovingly called, is a living legend and a maestro. Her 'Romantic classicism', as described by Padmashri Gajendra Narayan Singh, renowned music historian and musicologist, sets her apart from her contemporaries and later-day Jaipur–Atrauli performers (Sharma, 1999).

Young Kishori was trained by her illustrious mother Mogubai Kurdikar in the Ustad Alladiya Khan and Ustad Haider Khan tradition of this gharana. Her mother, whom she called 'Maee', Marathi for mother, became her mentor, her axis and her centre of gravity. She learnt the traditional compositions of her gharana and believes in being true to the bandish or the composition; but her approach to a raga and her firm belief that music and its performance is greater than a gharana has taken her to great heights in Khayal Gayaki. For her, '*Gana Gharane se oopar hai*' ('the song is greater than the gharana'), says her disciple Nandini Bedekar. Gharana *parampara* (heritage of the gharana tradition) is the key ingredient, but what makes music memorable is how we relate to it emotionally. This very emotionality imbues Kishori Tai's music with subtlety and lends it an indescribable delicacy. Who can forget her rendition of raga Basanti Kedar, Bageshwari, Jaunpuri, Sampoorna Malkauns and Yaman? In fact, the commonly sung chota khayal bandish in Yaman, '*Ae ri aali piya bina*', when performed by Kishori Amonkar, transcends time and space as she soars into a metaphysical world where the common becomes celestial. Her ability to rise above the ordinary and the mundane gives her an edge and secures her an unbeatable stature in the annals of Hindustani music. Her famous composition in raga Bhoop—'*Sahela re aa mil gayen, sapt suran ke bhed sunayen*'—takes the ordinary and the mundane to the heavenly and metaphysical.

If you thought that khayal is her only forte, think again as you immerse yourself in her Bhairavi thumri '*Koyaliya na bol daar*,

Kishori Amonkar
Photo: Avinash Pasricha

tarsat jiyara hamaar' ('hey Cuckoo, don't sing on the branches of the tree as it makes my heart miss my beloved'). Every note is enveloped in the pathos and the pangs of separation. She manages to live her bandishes.

Kishori Amonkar is often labelled as temperamental, difficult and moody. But this comes from her obsession with being a perfectionist who will not compromise her pursuit of excellence. She is a *sadhak* (one who devotes oneself to practice); she is a *tapaswini* (one who goes into deep meditation). She is the eternal Meera and she sings for her Krishna. Her art is an expression of her meditations of music; her music is an expression of her myriad moods.

Nandini Bedekar reveals how Kishori Amonkar has redefined khayal singing. Once, while practicing raga Bageshwari, she felt a deep sadness when it was over. Perhaps this was the influence of the raga on her mind? This revelation is what led to her singular ability to depict the varying moods that a raga induces. As an intelligent performer she began approaching the raga and deciphering its emotive content. The rest followed. 'Get into the feeling and the *bhav* of that raga', she says to her disciples. 'Go beyond the medium and its technicalities.' She says, 'I can see the raga right in front of me, I can see its shape and dimensions. As I age, I am able to see new nuances in each raga, the bhav of the raga is greater than any gharana or any performer.' Kishori Amonkar's emotional approach to her raga and her rendering of it is her own discovery as an artiste that makes her a true leader who spawned an entire school of the Jaipur–Atrauli vocalists who have inherited her legacy.

◆◆◆

Rabindranath Tagore gave her the title of Surshree (one who is the queen of notes), and the world knows her as the legendary Goa-born Kesarbai Kerkar, the most celebrated khayal singer and perhaps the first woman who commanded a higher price than her male contemporaries like Pt. Onkar Nath Thakur and Pt. Vinayak Buwa Patwardhan, who hailed her as the most accomplished khayal singer ever.

Kesarbai reached this pinnacle through an assiduous and dedicated regimen or *riyaz*. She remained a student of music till she reached the age of 54, continuing to learn from her Ustad and mentor Ustad Alladiya Khan, the great Jaipur gharana exponent, till

सूरश्री केसरबाई केरकर
KESARBAI KERKAR

Courtesy: Gandharv Mahavidyalaya, New Delhi

his death in 1946. She learnt from seven illustrious gurus, including Ustad Alladiya Khan. Such was her desire for perfection that she sang only one raga, '*Miyan ki malhar*', originally invented by Tansen for 10 years till she mastered it with the legendary Senia Gharana's Ustad Barkatullah Khan.

Kesarbai was sought after by the rich, mostly royal patrons, and had amassed a great deal of wealth. Encountering Alladiya Khan was the game-changer. He taught her from the age of 21 and did not let her perform solo on public platforms till he died in 1946, when Kesarbai was already in her fifties. This long tutelage gave her the formidable *taleem* and later the number one position when she started doing public concerts after his death and went on to become the most famous and consummate performer post-Independence.

Padmashri Gajendra Narayan Singh recalls a conversation he had with Kumar Gandharv, the legendary vocalist who used to listen to Kesarbai at the *mehfils* of the royals and the zamindars. Since commoners were not permitted in these mehfils. Kumar Gandharv donned the garb of a waiter, serving tea and snacks and during breaks, sitting quietly in a corner to listen to her sing. Gajendra Narayan Singh recalls a performance in Calcutta in 1962 at which the finest musicians of the country were present, among them Bismillah Khan, V.G. Jog, Nazakat and Salamat Ali Khan. Kesarbai sang raga Lalit at seven in the morning for about three hours. She was 70 then, but graceful and dignified. That same day she announced her retirement from stage, wisely saying that a singer should retire at one's peak rather than continue to sing in a feeble voice. The beauty of her voice was that it had the same 'roundedness'—a pre-requisite of classical music—from the lower to the highest octave and never quivered. Years of learning and dedicated practice made her perfect.

Kesarbai not only etched her music in the hearts of millions but left her great legacy to Dhondu Tai Kulkarni, her disciple and another great singer of the Jaipur gharana. Unlike some gurus who are reluctant to teach their art to students lest they become more famous than they, Kesarbai used to say, 'I will teach only those who have the capability to be one up on me also!'

◆

This chapter was first published in 2013 in the *IIC Quarterly*, Vol. 39, Nos. 3 and 4.

NOTES

1. See 'Sarkar' in Mishra (1997).
2. See 'Nationalistic Poem of Husna Jan', in Sharma (2012).
3. See 'To be Like Joan of Arch', in Sharma (2012).

REFERENCES

Mishra, Kameshwar Nath. 1997. *Kashi ki Sangeet Parampara*. First edition. Lucknow: Bharat Book Centre.

Sharma, A.N. 1999. ' Rasagandha', chapter on Kishori Amonkar by Padmashri Gajendra Narayan Singh. *Swargandha*. First edition. Patna: Hindi Grantha Academy.

Sharma, A.N. 2012. '*Madhu Tarang*' … *Bajanaama. A Study of Early Gramophone Records*. First edition. Lucknow: Kathachitra Prakashan.

◆◆

17
EMPOWERING WOMEN THROUGH EDUCATION
The Story of Indraprastha School*

APARNA BASU*

APARNA BASU*

At the beginning of the 20th century, there were hardly any schools for girls in Delhi. The pioneers in this field all over India were Christian missionaries who were allowed to operate in India in the East India Company's territories after the Charter Act of 1813. Robert May of the London Missionary Society started the first school for girls in Chinsura (Bengal) in 1817. But the pupils in these schools were usually Christians, orphans from lower castes and poor families. 'Respectable' Hindus and Muslims did not send their daughters to mission schools.

In the 19th century, Christian missionaries, British administrators, foreign travellers and scholars all criticised the deplorable condition of Indian women. James Mill, in his influential book, *History of British India,* argued that the position of women could be used as an indicator of society's advancement and, on this count, India occupied a very low position. The Indian urban intelligentsia, newly exposed to Western education, became sensitive to this criticism and turned its attention to the condition of women. Their new-found faith in modern education led them to believe that the education of women was necessary not only to improve the condition and status of women, but also of society. Following the Christian missionaries, social reformers of the Brahmo Samaj in Bengal, the Prarthana Samaj in Maharashtra and Gujarat, the Arya Samaj in North India and the Theosophical Society led the movement for girls' education. John Drinkwater Bethune, Law Member in Lord Dalhousie's Council, started the first secular school for girls in Calcutta in 1849, which was later named after him. In the same year, Alexander Forbes' Gujarat Vernacular Society opened a school for girls in Ahmedabad. The students of Elphinstone College in Bombay started girls' schools. Delhi was far behind the Presidency towns.

In the late 19th and early 20th centuries, north India was one of the most backward areas in the country in terms of women's education. Some of the most enlightened women in public life there such as Rameshwari Nehru, Vijayalaksmi Pandit and Durgabai Vora lacked formal education. Even in an enlightened household such as that of Motilal Nehru, the discrimination against girls' education was marked. One of the early efforts was that of Lala Munshi Ram of the Arya Samaj who started the Arya Kanya Pathashala in Jullunder in 1890 where funds were collected by housewives giving a handful of *atta* every day, and lawyers and merchants standing on the streets begging for money to start a school for girls.

In 1904, Annie Besant wrote a pamphlet entitled 'The Education of Girls', which expressed her concern that Indian women were deprived of education, and sent it to the Theosophical Society in Delhi. The members of the Theosophical Lodge were bankers, lawyers, academics and bureaucrats. They had received Western education and many were alumni of St. Stephen's College, the first college in Delhi, established by the Cambridge Mission in 1882. They were among the first to seriously think about the necessity of educating girls. They faced a difficult task as Delhi society was closed and conservative.

A 100 years ago, getting girls to schools was not easy. Among traditional upper classes and castes, women's lives were confined to the home. Trips outside the home necessitated the use of special modes of transport—the *doli* (palanquin) or the *ekka* (horse carriage). Excursions out of the domestic sphere were limited. Domestic life was focused on the *haveli*—the town house—inhabited by a joint family. There were a few primary schools in Delhi started by missionaries but its students came mainly from poor classes. Affluent middle-class Hindus and Muslims were opposed to sending their girls to schools.

There were deeply rooted prejudices in society against women's education which was regarded not only as unnecessary but also dangerous and unorthodox. There was a superstition that an educated girl would become a widow soon after marriage. Education was supposed to turn docile girls into rebellious harridans who would ruin the peace and tranquility of a family. To grapple with these centuries-old prejudices, not only of men but also of women, was not easy. Reformers, therefore, stressed that education would make women better wives and mothers, that women would not compete with men in the public arena.

The Indraprastha Putri Pathshala, a lower primary school for girls, was started in May 1904 in a rented building in Gali Anar in Kinari Bazar, Chandni Chowk, with seven pupils. Next year, it was named Indraprastha Hindu Kanya Shikshalaya and shifted to its present building behind Jama Masjid in 1907. The school would not have been possible but for the dedicated efforts of about half-a-dozen of Delhi's elite citizens—Lala Jugal Kishore, Rai Balkrishna Das, Lala Sultan Singh, Rai Pearey Lal, Lala Banwari Lal Lohiya, and others.

Along with the founders was Miss Leonora G'meiner, an Australian Theosophist, and the first Principal of the school and later of Indraprastha College, who laid the foundation of both these institutions. Her dedication, zeal and sacrifice were truly amazing. Her primary interest was to educate girls and provide them an opportunity to develop their character and talents. She was also committed to removing the barriers to women's education such as child marriage, purdah and superstitions regarding the fate of an educated woman. A follower of Annie Besant, she also supported the cause of India's political freedom. All these concerns were passed on to her students.

It was with great difficulty that in 1904 the first few girls from traditional upper-middle-class Hindu families were persuaded to join Indraprastha School. The fears and anxieties of parents had to be allayed. Women were sent to fetch the girls and horse carriages with curtains were provided.

The secondary school slowly developed into the first women's college in Delhi, by introducing Intermediate classes with five students in 1924. The shy, nervous young girls who entered the school later showed great enterprise, courage and qualities of leadership. In 1928, for the first time, two former students went abroad to study. Rajeshwari Karki studied medicine in Glasgow, incidentally in the same city where Kadambini Bose Ganguly of Calcutta, India's first woman graduate and female doctor, studied in the late 19th century. Lajjawati Ram Krishan Das went to Paris to do her Ph.D. in pedagogy.

Students of the school and college were politically aware. Many of them joined the Civil Disobedience Movement in the 1930s by taking part in *hartals* (strikes) and picketing and marching in processions. A Girls' Students Union was started in 1930 by a student named Chameli with the support of Aruna Asaf Ali. The Girl Guides Movement, with the purpose of building confidence and the development of personalities, was popular in the school. In 1934, during assembly in the school, the girls demonstrated their spirit by refusing to salute the Union Jack and sing 'God save the King'.

During the Quit India movement in 1942, a group of Indraprastha students, led by Aruna Asaf Ali, was arrested for posting anti-British posters on city walls. On 10 August 1942, Indraprastha students jumped over the college walls and joined a procession of Stephanians and Hinduites to protest against the arrest of Congress leaders. They sang patriotic songs, organised meetings and defied government regulations.

In the post-Independence years, the students continued their social and political activism. They organised a massive rally against the harassment of girls in public buses. The first-ever march and demonstration against dowry was also spearheaded by the Indraprastha Women's College Committee formed in 1978.

Lady Hardinge Medical College had been established in 1916. As women belonging to conservative families did not want to go to male doctors, there was a need for women doctors. Indian families did not oppose girls opting for medicine, which was regarded as a profession suitable for women. Matriculation was the minimum qualification for joining Lady Hardinge Medical College and hence Indraprastha School became a sought-after institution.

Right from the beginning, the founders of Indraprastha School displayed great confidence in the capacity of women. In the latter part of the 19th and early 20th century, there was a debate about what was appropriate for women to study—home-making skills, or all subjects that boys read. Indraprastha School decided that girls must have the same education as boys and made provisions for teaching science, mathematics and English. If male teachers were required for teaching these subjects, suitable arrangements were accordingly made. The school imparted an education of quality to develop the minds and personalities of its students.

The students of Indraprastha have made their mark in various fields—education, medicine, politics, culture and the arts—such as Dr Radha Pant, who started the Department of Biochemistry in Allahabad University; Dr Chandra Kanta Kesavan, an acoustics engineer with All India Radio; Dr Kanchan Lata Sabarwal, Principal of Mahila Mahavidyalaya, Lucknow, who headed the Central Social Welfare Board; Dr Kapila Vatsyayan, an expert on Indian culture, a Member of the Rajya Sabha, who was Academic Director of the Indira Gandhi National Centre for Culture and Arts and is a Life Trustee of the India International Centre; Dr Suvira Gupta, head of the Radiology Department of G.B. Pant Hospital, to mention only a few.

Indraprastha produced the earliest sportswomen in the city. The students excelled in various games and athletics and were runners-up in the 1942 Olympics in Delhi.

Indraprastha was the first school to provide a hostel for girls, the first to provide a library and start science classes with a laboratory, and the first to start a college. Its founders believed that education was not just for imparting factual knowledge, but for changing consciousness. The school and college, therefore, worked hard to pull women out of the four walls of their homes and bring about attitudinal changes, liberating them from the ideologies of oppression and stereotypes of gender roles. It gave girls self-confidence so that they could assume positions of leadership. Indraprastha School and College opened the doors to the world of knowledge and opportunity to generations of Delhi women. It was through education that Indraprastha took its students on the path to emancipation and empowerment.

◆

* This chapter is based on the articles in the book *Indraprastha: The Quest for Women's Education in Delhi*, by Narain Prasad and Subhadra Sen Gupta (eds.), published in the centenary year of Indraprastha School for Indraprastha Society for Education and Welfare, 2012.

This chapter was first published in 2013 in the *IIC Quarterly*, Vol. 39, Nos. 3 and 4.

◆◆

18
GENDER AND GOVERNANCE
From Concern to Indicators

SATISH B.
AGNIHOTRI**#

n his 're-examination' of inequality, Sen (1992) argues that the
space of outcomes is a more appropriate space for examining
inequalities rather than the space of commodities or entitlements.
These outcomes could be social, economic or political, and it is
possible to identify suitable indicators in these to discover how a
group—women in our case—fares compared to the other population
at large. The process of governance has an impact on all these
outcomes that together define the well-being of its citizens.

In judging the well-being of women, the different
components of well-being need to be examined. One can begin with
a very basic outcome, i.e. survival itself, reflected in life expectancy
and in the sex ratio at birth. This can be followed by the quality of
survival; whether life is 'short, nasty and brutish', or otherwise. Then
comes the question of the skills of social reproduction one is able to
acquire and utilise. Is one able to educate oneself? Is the productive
use of a skill impaired? Is the skill remunerated equitably? The
issue of participation in the social sphere comes next. Is one able
to participate in the social sphere? Is the participation equitable?
Where does one stand in the power structure in respect of such
participation? The list can be expanded further.

It is necessary and useful to ask how men and women fare
in respect of each of these outcomes. How does their longevity
compare? Are they equally well-nourished? Are their skill attainments
comparable? Is there a disparity in their wages? How are they
represented in different domains of public life?

If the social processes were equitable, the 'distribution' of men
and women in terms of most of these parameters would be similar.

But, in reality, social processes are not quite equitable and this reflects in different aspects of well-being: the span of life, its quality, access to resources, among other factors. If we draw, at random, a sample of men and women and study any of these characteristics, we will find men and women clustered separately, revealing a gender gap in respect of that characteristic.

These gender gaps may also be sample-specific. Gender is not the only identity a person has. There are many others: regional, religious, caste or class, to name a few. Among these groups, the gender gaps revealed by different indicators of well-being may vary significantly. The gender gap in nutrition may differ by region; sex ratios may differ by class; gaps in educational levels may differ by religion. We need, therefore, two separate levels at which the data are disaggregated by gender: one for different aspects of well-being and the other for different relevant groups to which men and women belong.

The search for useful indicators to assess gender sensitiveness in governance can either precede the efforts to bring greater awareness about gender equity or follow these. In one case, a given indicator, e.g. the sex ratio in a region, can reveal the inequality of survival while in the other, an indicator such as the proportion of women represented in elected bodies can be used for monitoring how society translates its rhetoric into practice.

Finally, gender-based disaggregation of development indicators is necessary to distinguish between 'development' and 'discrimination'. A gender-blind governance may only focus on the overall indicator, e.g. under-five mortality rate, as a measure of development, but overlook the discrimination hidden within it, i.e. the gender gap. A society may have high levels of both development and discrimination, but that is not the desirable goal. Society has to strive for high levels of development combined with a low level of discrimination. The use of gender-disaggregated indicators allows us to monitor if this is happening.

◆◆◆

DIFFERENT ASPECTS OF WELL-BEING
Our concern for gender equity need not stray into the domain of definitions—what constitutes governance? or how perfect is a given definition of well-being? There are accepted indicators of well-being

that are presently used. These should be scrutinised first for gender equity. To begin with, there is no harm in assuming that whatever is good for men, is good for women as well. A 'fine-tuning' of the indicators of well-being can follow later.

SURVIVAL

Mortality rates are a good indicator for levels of development. All other things being equal, lower mortality would usually correspond to higher development. The following indicators can be used for monitoring different aspects of mortality among men and women:

- Crude death rate
- Under-five mortality rates
- Infant mortality rates
- Still-birth rates
- Maternal mortality rates
- Sex ratio at birth

These indicators assume importance in the Indian context, given the high masculinity of its sex ratios and the increasing 'female deficit'. Further, this deficit arises largely on account of excess female mortality under the age of 5 years. Female children are under threat from sex-selective elimination at the foetal stage, infanticide at birth, excess mortality in infancy and in the 1–4 years' age group. Each of these disadvantages is behavioural in nature and not biological.

Increasingly, the masculine sex ratio at birth (SRB) indicates a higher incidence of sex-selective abortion. The extent of excess female mortality in the 1–4 years' age group indicates the extent of gender bias against girl children. Excess female infant mortality indicates its intensification.

Maternal mortality rates (MMR) are an indicator of the extent to which a society cares for mothers. The rates of MMR in India are unusually high and, more important, most of these are avoidable.

QUALITY OF SURVIVAL

Among the women who survive, life expectancy, access to different health facilities and nutritional status become important concerns so that life is less 'short, nasty and brutish'. In this context, the following indicators are relevant:

- Life expectancy at birth
- Immunisation coverage
- Nutritional status
- Age at marriage
- Age at first pregnancy

While life expectancy at birth is a much analysed and monitored indicator, the same cannot be said in respect of immunisation and nutritional status. The asymmetry in nutritional status is either considered to be 'obvious' or not worth bothering about. The age of a woman at marriage/first pregnancy has a bearing on her health status and on the incidence of low birth weight. It is necessary to monitor this indicator closely to locate the emergence of child marriage. It may also become necessary to look at the distribution of age at marriage in different regions/communities to gain a better understanding of the social dynamics of the process.

SKILL ACQUISITION

The next important aspect of well-being relates to acquiring skills for social reproduction. Achievements in literacy and levels of education are appropriate indicators for these. However, there could be a considerable gender gap in these levels, starting with:

- Literacy
- Enrollment
- Dropout at primary level
- Completion of primary education
- Dropout at secondary level
- Completion of secondary and higher education.

Inequality in this sphere is one area where a specific focus by ethnic groups is also needed. Further, women's groups also need to take up female literacy campaigns in small pockets aiming at saturation. Female education up to the primary level has so many spin-offs that a separate focus outside government efforts is called for.

The issue of dropouts needs to be studied at different stages of education. It is quite likely that the tendency to drop out is strong up to a stage and beyond it the level diminishes. Such information is extremely useful for policy.

WORKFORCE PARTICIPATION

Acquisition of skills may still not ensure engagement with the labour market or equitable terms of engagement. Women's workforce participation is a contentious area, and needs serious monitoring. The relevant parameters include:

- Workforce participation ratios
- Patterns of workforce participation
- Wage disparity
- Waged and unwaged work
- Workplace conditions, including safety at workplace
- Patterns of migration
- Women-headed households

The monitoring of these indicators assumes importance given the close correlation between survival and workforce participation. Papanek (1989) has written extensively about the process of withdrawal of women from waged workforce participation for the purpose of 'status production' for the family. Such withdrawal makes it difficult for the woman concerned to get back to work if she needs to. This is particularly so for skilled and white collar jobs. Further, the prosperity of a household may adversely affect the status of female members if their contribution to such prosperity is nil or not recognised (Agnihotri, 2000).

Studying the migration patterns and changing nature and composition of female-headed households assumes importance here. This is especially so in the context of globalisation of the economy and 'feminisation' of poverty.

CONTROL OVER RESOURCES

While high female workforce participation rates definitely improve the status of women, control over resources is a different story altogether. In this context, one needs to study the following:

- Participation in surplus-generating activity
- Control over resources/means of production
- Land ownership
- Property rights

It seems that women are usually allowed to engage in subsistence-level income generation. However, their ability to move to the surplus domain and exercise control over means of production, whether capital or land, gets severely restricted (Ram, 1991; Agarwal, 1994).

PARTICIPATION IN THE PUBLIC SPHERE

Basu (1992) has given a very simple but effective description of the determinants of the status of women. She looks at three factors: exposure to the 'external sphere', participation in it, and the decision-making ability during the participation. It is difficult to evolve indicators for these factors. But to begin with, the sex ratio of voters vis à vis the sex ratio in the population above 18 years of age can be one useful measure of exposure, while the sex ratio in the votes cast can be a useful measure of participation. The stability of the tenure of the elected representatives in local bodies can indicate the degree of freedom in decision-making.

It is not just the ballot-based political process that represents the 'public' sphere. Women's participation in extra-familial groups such as self-help groups (SHGs), trade unions and even political parties needs to be studied in detail.

SECURITY

Women's participation in the public sphere considerably depends upon the security or the law and order environment. Whether a college-going girl feels free to travel by bicycle in the city will depend, to a large extent, on her own perception of safety. It is, therefore, necessary to analyse the incidence of crime against women compared to the general level of crime. It would bear reiteration that a rise in crime will affect the vulnerable sections more, and it should not be surprising that the adverse effect on women will be greater. District-level crime data available from the National Crime Research Bureau (NCRB) will be a useful source in this regard. It is necessary to monitor, in particular, the following:

- Overall incidence of crime against women
- Rape and molestation
- Abduction
- Dowry and marriage-related violence and murder
- Unnatural cases of death below and above 20 years of age

It has been seen that the general crime pattern and the pattern of crime against women differ significantly. Further, different crimes, e.g. dowry-related murders and those related to sexual offences, show different trends. Certain regions contribute disproportionately to these crimes as compared to their share in the population.

◆◆◆

SOME METHODOLOGICAL ISSUES

A question may arise as to what new insights, if any, can such an analysis bring. There are two issues here: one procedural and the other methodological. The procedural issue relates to cataloguing relevant indicators and ensuring that gender disaggregated data on this are collected and made available. The extent to which data collection can be gender-blind can surprise many! Many prestigious 'surveys' are a case in point. One often comes across separate figures by sex—male or female; location—urban or rural; and caste—SC or ST. But more often than not, within the urban or rural break-up, or within the SC or ST category, a break-up by gender is not provided. Is it that the differences are not significant? Hardly anyone will believe that. Yet this omission is apparent in survey after survey.

All these indicators are illustrative, but they capture major aspects of well-being. There is definitely scope and a need to identify further indicators which can fine-tune the 'search'. But that task can take place separately.

The second issue is methodological. Making the data available often becomes an end by itself. Its analysis either does not follow, or follows in a leisurely fashion; and when it does, it is not policy-oriented but oriented to the academic perfection of the 'second decimal point'. However, thanks to developments in IT, many techniques are available today which can provide useful insights at the policy level through the analysis of the available data.

Geographical mapping is one such technique. It can identify regional clusters where particular social patterns are strong or weak (Agnihotri, 1996; 2000). It can identify, for example, contiguous tracts of high girl-child mortality or high female literacy for that matter. Such 'contour mapping' of social variables can have strong synergy with policy formulation exercises.

Another useful technique is to look at the way in which the values of any relevant variable differ by gender compare, and then its deviation from the hypothetical situation where men and women were 'identical' in nature. This technique can be used for longitudinal as well as cross-sectional data. A study of the nature of deviation mentioned above can provide useful insights about the gender bias (Agnihotri, 1999; 2001).

Together, these techniques can reveal the compounding disadvantages among certain groups, e.g. adverse survival chances of scheduled caste girl children in north-western states, or the unusually high male infant mortality in parts of the central tribal belt in the country (Agnihotri, 2000).

◆◆◆

GENDER-SENSITIVE VERSUS GENDER-BLIND GOVERNANCE

The need to develop these indicators is particularly strong in our society where the gender bias against girl children and younger women is well known and adequately documented. India's *de jure* track record about gender equity in governance is quite good. The problem arises in translating this into reality. Where governance is good in preaching gender equity but indifferent about practising it, relentless monitoring of relevant indicators is a must. All the more so when the apparatus of governance is 'manned' by well meaning but gender-blind persons—women included.

Those who might find this description hypothetical, uncharitable or harsh, may consider the following:

- An exhaustive survey of certain artisans provides figures about the family composition of these artisan households in terms of 'adult males', adult females and children. This makes it impossible to calculate the sex ratio, either for the total population or for the child population (useful since it is free of sex-selective migration). The statistician in charge of designing the survey format was a woman. Her remark was that this problem 'never occurred to her'.
- An exhaustive all-India survey on the health of children in a primary school never provided the data by gender. The response of state government officials was that the proforma prescribed by the central government did not 'prescribe' it. The ailments surveyed included anaemia, a problem known to affect girls more than it does boys!
- A well-meaning senior officer had argued that providing a male–female break-up in terms of the nutritional status of children in the Integrated Child Development Services

(ICDS) programme involved 'too much trouble', and that this break up should be dispensed with to make reporting simpler! When this actually happened, there was hardly any protest; academicians did not bother, activists did not even come to know about it.

Does one have to repeat ad nauseum that eternal vigilance is the price for liberty (in this instance even survival)?

◆

* Views expressed by the author are personal and do not reflect the views of his Institution.

This chapter was first published in 2013 in the *IIC Quarterly*, Vol. 39, Nos. 3 and 4.

REFERENCES

Agarwal, B. 1994. *A Field of One's Own: Gender and Land Rights in South Asia.* Cambridge: Cambridge University Press.

Agnihotri, S.B. 1996. 'Juvenile Sex Ratios in India: a Disaggregated Analysis', *Economic and Political Weekly*, 28 December, pp. 3369–82.

Agnihotri, S.B. 1999. 'Inferring Gender Bias from Mortality Data—A Discussion Note', *Journal of Development Studies*, 35(4), pp. 175–200.

Agnihotri, S.B. 2000. *Sex Ratio Patterns in the Indian Population—A Fresh Exploration.* New Delhi: SAGE.

Basu, A.M. 1992. *Culture, the Status of Women and Demographic Behaviour.* Oxford: Clarendon Press.

Papanek, H. 1989. 'Family Status Production Work: Women's Contribution to Social Mobility and Class Differentiation', in M. Krishnaraj and K. Chanana (eds.), *Gender and the Household Domain.* New Delhi: SAGE.

Ram, K. 1991. 'The Ideology of Feminity and Women's Work in a Fishing Community in South India', in H. Afsher and B. Agarwal (eds.), *Women, Poverty and Ideology in Asia.* London: Macmillan.

Sen, A.K. 1992. *Inequality Re-examined.* Oxford: Clarendon Press.

◆◆

19

THE MOVEMENT FOR CHANGE
Implementation of Sexual Assault Laws*

KIRTI SINGH[#]

The incident of the gang rape and murder of the 23-year-old girl in a bus by six men in New Delhi on 16 December 2012 seemed to act as a trigger to release the pent-up anger and frustration of women in India who have suffered various forms of sexual assault and harassment on the streets, in the neighbourhood, or in their homes. Every time they stepped out of their homes, walked on the streets, or boarded public transport, they risked, and continue to risk, being harassed, groped and subjected to unwelcome sexual touching. However, instead of their harassers being targeted, their freedom of movement, their right to dress as they please, and their right to associate with persons of their choice is discussed, curbed and restricted. While raising the slogan of justice for the gang rape victim and other victims of rape and sexual assault, and of severe punishment of the perpetrators of the rape, the protestors highlighted the dismal state of law enforcement in our country. The demand for accountability of the police underscored the fact that the police had not implemented the law and had been guilty of dereliction of duty in cases of sexual assault; and the government had taken very few steps to ensure the safety and security of women in our cities and across the country. By asking for speedy justice and fast-track courts the protestors highlighted the delay and denial of justice by the courts. Some also raised the demand for more stringent laws against rape and sexual assault. Although these protests were started by the constituents of women's organisations and groups, particularly of the Left, they were widely held to have been led by the youth of the country who had supposedly shown the way forward.

The government, which had ignored such demands for decades, suddenly swung into action when it realised the extent of public anger and outrage. 'Nirbhaya', whose gang rape had acted as a catalyst for the protest, was given the best medical treatment. A speedy investigation of the case was carried out in about two weeks, the charge sheet filed, and the case is being heard on a presumably day-to-day basis in the courts. In another quick reaction, a high-level Committee comprising the former Chief Justice of India, Justice Verma, was constituted to suggest 'laws to provide for quicker trials and enhanced punishment for criminals accused of committing sexual assault of extreme nature against women [sic]'. Though the Verma Committee had been set up with these limited terms of reference, the Committee interpreted these terms 'expansively' and, within an extremely short period, suggested several significant recommendations on a wide range of issues. Apart from proposing legal reforms on substantive and procedural laws related to rape and sexual assault, the Committee made various suggestions to strengthen women's rights and the implementation of the laws by the police and the judiciary. The Committee recommended the introduction of a Bill of Rights for women, which detailed the equality and other rights to which women were entitled in different areas. It recommended changes in the Representation of People's Act so that persons against whom a charge sheet had been filed in court for rape would not be allowed to contest elections for Parliament and State Assemblies. The Verma Committee also exhorted the government to implement the laws and pointed out that,

> The most perfect laws also would remain ineffective without the efficiency and 'individual virtuosity' of the human agency for implementing the laws, namely, the law enforcement agencies.

However, although some recommendations of the Verma Committee were new, many of them were recommendations that had already been made to the government over the past several years. The Verma Committee has itself noted that the government had ignored the existence of various Law Commission Reports and Court Judgements by pointing out that:

The Law Commission's 84th Report in 1980 and its 172nd Report of 2000 relating to this subject, the National Police Commission Reports recommending autonomy and seminal improvement in the quality of the police force, which is the principal machinery for the maintenance of law and order, continue to gather dust for decades due to the apathy of all the political dispensations. The Supreme Court's judgment of 2006 in Prakash Singh's case giving certain directions for the autonomy and improving the quality of the police force remains to be implemented by all the governments.

In the meanwhile, it became obvious that instances of rape and sexual assaults continued to accelerate. Successive reports of the National Crime Records Bureau had also shown that while, on the one hand, the registered cases of sexual assaults, including rapes, continued to rise, on the other hand, the conviction rate was dismal.

Even before most of these reports, and as far back as 1993, a Sub-Committee was formed by the National Commission for Women (NCW) after a seminar on Child Sexual Abuse, to examine the laws related to child sexual abuse. This Sub-Committee was constituted of members from women's organisations and groups as well as individual feminists. The Sub-Committee met extensively over six months and submitted a report to the National Commission for Women. The report suggested a complete overhaul of the provisions relating to Sexual Assault in the Indian Penal Code. It noted that the law had become outdated in language and intent as it failed to acknowledge the true nature of the crime of sexual assault. Also highlighted were the definitions of rape and molestation that did not adequately address the various types of sexual assault in terms of women's experience, nor did it recognise the gender-specific nature of such crimes. In addition, the definitions of sexual assault, rules of evidence and procedure did not adequately take into account the serious nature of sexual assault against women and children.

The recommendations of the Sub-Committee were to form the basis for a redrafting of the substantive and procedural rape and sexual assault laws in the coming years. Of the recommendations made, some stated that all the laws relating to sexual violence should be consolidated in one Section as they were all assaults of a sexual nature. It redefined and expanded the definition of rape and included within it penetration into any orifice (vagina, anus and mouth) by the penis, and penetration by an object or a part of the body into the vagina or anus. The Sub-Committee renamed rape as sexual assault to emphasise the violent aspect of the crime and the fact that all these forms of sexual activity constitute a violation of a woman's bodily integrity. The Sub-Committee also recommended changing the definition of molestation which, till recently, was defined as assault or criminal force with intent to 'outrage the modesty' of a woman. The Sub-Committee pointed out that the words 'outraging the modesty' were outdated and reminiscent of Victorian morality with notions of chastity. The Sub-Committee recommended that molestation should be defined as touching for a sexual purpose. Similarly, the Sub-Committee recommended an amendment of Section 509 of the IPC which deals with 'eve teasing'/sexual harassment and punishes words, sounds and gestures 'intending to insult the modesty of any woman'. Past cases had shown how courts had misinterpreted consent to the sexual act if a woman remained passive during a rape and did not raise an alarm.

The Sub-Committee, therefore, suggested that consent should be defined to mean an unequivocal voluntary agreement to engage in the sexual activity in question and suggested other instances in which consent can be vitiated. It also suggested that marital rape should be included in the definition of rape. However, the Sub-Committee suggested a gender-neutral provision for penetrative sexual assault as it recommended the deletion of Section 377 of the Indian Penal Code which targets consensual sex and homosexuality. The gender-neutral provision was meant to apply to same-sex penetrative sexual assault.

As is well known, the first movement to change the laws relating to rape was initiated in the early 1980s after the Mathura rape case was decided by the Supreme Court. The case came into public view when four professors of Delhi University wrote a letter to the Chief Justice pointing out that it was shocking that the Supreme Court refused to believe that a poor village girl had been raped in the police station just because she did not have visible signs of injury and had not screamed and shouted. The women's movement launched a massive protest and demanded changes in the law so that rape in custodial situations was recognised as a more aggravated form of the crime. Finally, in 1983, certain kinds of rape were recognised as aggravated forms of rape. These were rape by a policeman in a police station, rape by a person on the management or staff of a jail or remand home or hospital in these places, rape by a public servant of a woman in his custody, gang rape, and the rape of a girl under 12 years of age. While the minimum punishment prescribed for rape was seven years of imprisonment, these aggravated forms prescribed a minimum of 10 years of imprisonment and a maximum of life. The Evidence Act was also changed to provide that if the fact of sexual intercourse had been proved in a case falling under this Section, and the woman stated that she had not consented to the act, it would be presumed that she did not consent. The 84th Law Commission had also suggested these and other changes in the law of procedure which were also demanded by the women's movement at that time, including the recognition of marital rape.

In 1993, the Sub-Committee suggested a further expansion of the categories of aggravated sexual assault to include sexual assault by a person in the armed forces, and sexual assault on a woman suffering from mental or physical disability. It further suggested that if any person causes grievous bodily harm, maims or disfigures or endangers the life of a woman or child while committing a sexual assault, or if a person commits protracted or repeated sexual assaults on a woman or child, this should also be considered as an aggravated form of the offence. It also recommended that if any person who was in a position of trust, authority, guardianship, or of economic or social dominance, committed a sexual assault on a person under such trust, authority or dominance, this should be considered as an aggravated form of the offence. Amongst the procedural changes that it recommended were some changes that the 84th Law Commission Report had already suggested. The Committee suggested that the statements made by victims of sexual assaults should only be recorded by a woman police officer or by a woman social worker under the directions of the Station House Officer and, further, that a relative or friend of the victim should be present. It also reiterated the recommendation of the 84th Law Commission Report that Section 166A should be added to the IPC to punish a public servant who disobeys any direction of the law with one year of imprisonment. It suggested that, during the investigation, a minor and a woman should be allowed to be accompanied by a relative or friend, and that a police officer who refused to register an FIR should be punished with up to one year of imprisonment. A similar punishment was suggested by the Sub-Committee for a registered medical practitioner who refused to conduct a medical examination of a victim of sexual assault. The Committee recommended a change in the Indian Evidence Act that would put a stop to questions being posed to the victim about her previous sexual history, character and conduct, as this was a normal practice in rape trials; and if a woman had a past sexual history she was seen as someone who would, in all probability, have agreed to the sexual act. Another important recommendation was that a victim of sexual assault who was a minor should not be made to give evidence in the presence of the accused as this would certainly be traumatic for the victim. The Committee suggested that the manner in which such a victim's cross-examination is carried out should not be hostile. It also suggested that the investigation and trial of a sexual offence should be time-bound and not take more than six months. This Report was submitted to the National Commission for Women. However, their expert committee on laws rejected the Report as they considered many of the suggested provisions inappropriate and unnecessary. The Report was also sent to various women's groups for comment and discussion.

In the years that followed, changes and further additions were suggested to the 1993 Sub-Committee draft by national women's organisations, women's groups, feminist lawyers and other individuals working on the issue. One of the members of the Sub-Committee, who was a member of the Centre for Feminist Legal Research, suggested certain changes to delink the clause on sexual harassment from the Section on Sexual Assault, in addition to other amendments. Another member, who was associated with the NGO Sakshi, and had actively pursued a child-abuse case, filed a writ in the Supreme Court for a declaration that all forms of penetration would be included in the term 'sexual intercourse', as contained in the rape section of the Penal Code. However, the Supreme Court directed the Law Commission of India to consider the rape section in a manner that could be interpreted to plug existing loopholes, or otherwise to suggest an amendment to the law. The Law Commission decided to suggest amendments to the law concerning rape and members of Sakshi, IFSHA and the All India Democratic

Women's Association (AIDWA), which had also been members of the Sub-Committee, appeared before the Law Commission as representative organisations. Prior to this, they had submitted the draft of the Sub-Committee to the Law Commission. The Law Commission discussed the proposed amendments with these representative organisations and accepted many of the suggestions made by them, including the conceptual shift from rape to sexual assault. However, the recognition of marital rape and changes in the definition of molestation and sexual harassment were not agreed to by the Law Commission.

Subsequently, AIDWA redrafted some of the proposals in 2002, suggesting the separation of the clause on penetrative sexual assault from the clause on molestation and sexual harassment. It suggested the addition of stalking as a separate crime in the Indian Penal Code and included specific sections to deal with penetrative and non-penetrative sexual assaults on children. After several rounds of discussions with members of various women's groups, AIDWA suggested that the definition of penetrative sexual assault should be gender-specific as far as adults were concerned and should be gender-neutral for children. Thus, it suggested that only a man could be a perpetrator while the complainant would be a woman. This was because there was a real apprehension expressed by all women's groups that, under the earlier draft, men would file cases of sexual assault against women. The AIDWA draft was once more revised in 2005 and later in 2008. An important suggestion made to protect young persons involved in a consensual relationship was that consent should be a valid defence if the girl was between 16 and 18 years of age and the accused was not more than five years older. AIDWA's work with cases of crime and killing in the name of honour had highlighted the fact that many cases of rape are routinely registered by members of the girl's family if she was in a consensual relationship with a boy and, in many of these cases, the family claimed that the girl was a minor.

In 2005, the NCW adopted a draft similar to the one made by AIDWA and, after a series of consultations with several stake-holders, held a national convention in which it invited the minister of home, members of women's groups and government representatives. Although, initially, the home minister agreed with the draft, the government did not change the law or procedure. AIDWA also continued to campaign for changes in the laws and procedures related to sexual assault and made several representations to successive law or home ministers along with other women's organisations. It made representations to Ram Jethmalani, Arun Jaitely, H.R. Bharadwaj, Shivraj Patil, Veerapa Moily and Salman Khurshid. The letter to Veerapa Moily was written by national women's organisations, including AIDWA, AIWC, CWDS, JWP, NFIW and YMCA, after the Ruchika molestation case in which the accused, a high-ranking police official, had only been awarded a sentence of one-and-a-half years as the law on molestation only prescribed a maximum sentence of two years. The letter written by AIDWA pointed out how Ruchika's case had once again highlighted the need to amend the law relating to child sexual abuse. The letter, written in January 2010, also pointed out that both the law relating to child sexual abuse and sexual assault on women needed to be urgently modified.

Finally, in 2010, the government first drafted a bill to address sexual offences against children. This was made into a separate comprehensive law in 2012 and contained many of the suggestions made to the government by women's and child rights' groups. The law, however, defined the child as a person under 18 years of age and kept the age of consent at 18, ignoring the fact that adolescent sexual activity is a reality and should not be criminalised, whether an adult agreed with this or not. This law thus lays down the age of statutory rape as 18 and allows for punishment of young boys or men even in consensual relationships with 10 years or more of imprisonment.

Another bill was also finally proposed in 2010 by the government to deal with adult rape in the Penal Code. The autonomous women's groups and independent scholars and others discussed the provisions of this Bill in April and May 2010 and suggested certain amendments meant to recognise 'the structural and graded nature of sexual violence'. They suggested that all forms of sexual violence against women should be in a comprehensive section, and that sexual violence on persons excepting women should be in a separate Section, 375B. Further, that no woman should be liable under these sections. An important suggestion made by the groups and individuals related to the sexual assault of women as part of sectarian violence. Other suggestions related to the command responsibility of a public servant and doing away with the prior sanction of the government in the case of sexual assault by a public servant. These groups also asked for certain procedures to be followed by the police during the investigation of a sexual assault of a minor, as also for doctors while conducting the medical examination of a child victim of sexual assault. National women's groups also reiterated their demand for the recognition of sexual assault during communal and sectarian conflicts, and sexual assault by members of the armed and paramilitary forces as aggravated forms of sexual assault.

A number of measures to improve the safety and security of women in Delhi had also been suggested to the police by women's organisations following cases of rape, murder and sexual assault in the past. The police was to map the city of Delhi and identify areas where women are most vulnerable to assault. Following this, an increased deployment of police patrolling in these areas was proposed, in addition to the improvement of lighting in streets and in public toilets. It was also decided that buses, taxis and other modes of transport with tinted glasses would not be allowed to ply and the police was supposed to enforce this rule. However, neither had police patrolling substantially improved, even in vulnerable areas, nor had the police enforced the rule against using tinted glasses. The bus in which the gang rape took place had tinted glasses and had passed through several police check points even as the assault was taking place.

In their Memorandum to the Police Commissioner after the gang rape, AIDWA and other national women's organisations had demanded that the police should follow Standard Operating Procedures (SOPs) in all cases of sexual assault. These procedures would mandate the police to immediately register a case and send the complainant for medical examination, collect the evidence, including clothes at the spot, and carry out the investigation in a time-bound manner. The Memorandum also demands that the police should be punished for failure to follow this procedure. The Delhi High Court had in 2007 directed the police to put in place certain SOPs in all cases of sexual assault. In another case in 2007, the Delhi High Court had once more detailed the procedures that the police should follow in cases of sexual assault of minors to ensure that minors are medically examined within 24 hours; that they are treated with compassion and dignity and not called to, or detained in, a police station. Although the Delhi Police had issued certain Standing Orders, including Standing Order No. 303/2010 which lays down guidelines to be followed by the police in cases of rape, they had obviously not followed these.

Apart from this, in 2006, the Supreme Court in Prakash Singh's case had directed the central government to carry out extensive police reforms to prevent political/executive interference in police work and to ensure their independence. The judgement had directed the constitution of a state security commission in every state to ensure that the state government does not exercise influence or apply pressure on the state police. This judgement had laid down rules for the selection of the Director General of Police and the Inspector General of Police and other officers, and a minimum tenure for all of them. It had directed that there should be a separation between the investigating police and the police force which would look after law and order, as this would ensure speedier investigation and better expertise. It had also stated that a police complaint authority, headed by a District Judge, should be set up in every district to look into complaints against police officials up to the rank of DSP, while grievances against police officers of higher rank would be examined by a State-level Complaint Authority, headed by a retired judge of the High Court or the Supreme Court. Both these heads had to be chosen from a panel of names proposed by the Chief Justice of the State or Chief Justice of India, respectively. However, even these directions of the Supreme Court have not been followed by the various states.

The government, meanwhile, introduced the Criminal Law Amendment Bill, 2012, in Parliament which was again both limited and flawed. The Bill broadened the definition of rape to include within it all forms of penetrative sexual assault. It also replaced the word 'rape' with 'sexual assault' on demand by several women's organisations and groups to emphasise that rape is a form of violence against women. The Bill, however, made the offence gender-neutral. As pointed out by AIDWA and others, this seemed to imply that women can commit sexual assaults against men for which there is no empirical evidence at all. It was pointed out that the section would in fact allow men to file false cases of penetrative sexual assault against women. Further, the Bill exempted marital rape from being recognised as an offence and merely increased the period of punishment in Section 354 (Molestation) from two to five years, with a minimum of one year, without changing the language. Women's organisations and groups had also demanded that aggravated forms of non-penetrative sexual assault should be recognised in the law. The Guwahati molestation case, in which a 19-year-old girl was manhandled and groped by a gang of men outside a bar, again highlighted the fact that molestation by a gang is not seen as an aggravated form of the crime in our Penal Code.

After the Verma Committee Recommendations, the government once more brought in the 2013 Ordinance and followed it with an Act to amend the criminal laws relating to sexual assault. This Act, which incorporates many of the suggestions that have been made over the years, however, still does not recognise marital rape or extend the categories of aggravated sexual assault to molestation. It also defines the age of consent as 18 years.

The movement for the change of laws relating to rape and sexual assault involved several actors over a long period of time, acting together and separately. Some initiated the movement and did the work on the ground while others led a relentless campaign to change the laws. Finally, a gruesome incident ignited the passions of the masses which forced a reluctant government to hastily bring about change. However, the one constant actor was the women's movement that still has to struggle to implement the laws.

◆

* This chapter tries to document the various actors who have been part of the campaign for the change of laws related to sexual assault and their implementation. Although one individual or group may get recognition for bringing about a change, any movement for change necessarily involves several people, some of whom may play a more dominant role than others.

This chapter was first published in 2013 in the *IIC Quarterly*, Vol. 39, Nos. 3 and 4.

◆◆

20
CAREGIVERS, CARETAKERS
Dealing with Impunity and Immunity at the Margins

SANJOY
HAZARIKA#

Over the past decades, my colleagues and I have met many people whose lives had been irrevocably changed by the decades of violence that had gripped their states. In Nagaland, parts of Assam, Tripura, Manipur and Mizoram especially, where villagers have borne the brunt of contesting ideas and forces, many families and individuals have stories to tell, of personal loss, of bereavement, of physical and emotional trauma. For many of them, those who campaign for rights, the media or academics and researchers, were often the first interaction with people from another part of India. They came to their villages, sat among them and listened. These are stories that the world does not know of, has not cared to know, contributing to the silencing of voices on the margins. We believe that the telling of these stories works as a form of political intervention and empowerment, building bridges between communities and helping to open up a little-known region and an alienated people.

Analysts say war and conflict are devastating to social and cultural institutions because they impact societies and individuals; every person who has survived conflict is in some way scarred by her/his experience. It takes people and society a long time to come to terms with what happened.

A young woman in Dimapur, who is a member of a women's association which works like an informal, tribal panchayat where social cases relating to women are handled, shared an experience. Her village, she said, was bombed by the Indian Air Force in the 1960s. She was only a baby at the time but her mother, who was running away from the burning village, hid her in the hollow of a tree thinking she'd come back and retrieve her when it was safe. It was three days before she could come back. The child lay inside that hollow—hungry, frightened, alone. We wondered: 'What must she have thought? What sort of impact would this have left on her?' The trauma haunted her, she said, and then as soon as she was old enough she went to join her father, who was a member of the Naga army fighting the Indian State. It was only much later that she came to terms with what had happened to her village, to herself and her father, who was killed in the course of battles with the army. She learnt forgiveness and turned to the Church, which is a very powerful institution in Nagaland and other parts of the North-east.

To say that women have faced violence in situations of conflict is to state the obvious, but what this means in terms of impacts is something that is still being studied. While the most obvious impact is physical or sexual violence, the psychological scarring as a result of prolonged exposure to brutality has an even deeper impact on their well-being. Women find themselves at the receiving end of violence from three fronts: the State, the militants and a corresponding escalation of domestic violence. The effects of violent acts like rape, sexual abuse and assault lead to emotional trauma and what is known as Post Traumatic Stress Disorder (PTSD)—again, this is something that is being understood only now. Facilities such as trauma centres or counselling centres for such cases are few and totally inadequate to deal with the complexity and scale of the problem.

According to the psychiatrist Dr P. Ngully from Nagaland—who was associated with a study I had helped conduct (*Bearing Witness, the Impact of Conflict on Women in Nagaland and Assam*, 2011, in collaboration with the Heinrich Boll Foundation) and is among the very few specialists to have looked at PTSD in his state which has faced confrontation and violence both from the State and non-State groups for over 50 years—the sight of a uniformed person evokes fear and terror in villagers in Nagaland. 'They have rarely seen any other face of India barring the army and the paramilitary, which they associate with harassment and violent behaviour,' according to Dr Ngully.

In fact, the respondents to the survey and interviews set out therein were posited on a set of questions developed by the National Institute of Health (US) which are internationally accepted as indicative of whether a person has suffered/suffers from PTSD. This questionnaire was discussed at the initial workshop with the two research teams at Shillong in November 2008, and it was made a prerequisite to the identification of the 'victims' to be interviewed under this project. This was done on the advice of two prominent psychiatrists.[1] These were the hinges which opened the doors to an unprecedented and moving outpouring of experiences, narrations and stories from victims. The questions were the following:

> In your life have you ever had any experience that was so frightening, horrible or upsetting that, in the past month, you:
> - Have had nightmares about it or thought about it when you did not want to?
> - Tried hard not to think about it or went out of your way to avoid situations that reminded you of it?
> - Were constantly on guard, watchful or easily startled?
> - Felt numb or detached from others, from activities or your own surroundings?

This approach has helped in the process of enabling women to share their experiences of coping with the realities of daily life, experiences which they perhaps would not have felt confident enough to share were it not for the fact that the research teams in both states chosen for the study were 'local' and that contacts with those interviewed were made with extensive help from friends, neighbours, civil society groups, local women's groups, local interpreters and guides.

Women, after all, are responsible in these situations as mothers of children, wives of the wounded; they are innocent victims of wars and conflicts not of their making (Gill, 2006). They suffer as civilians with greater restrictions placed on them. They are assaulted, raped, humiliated, beaten and murdered during conflicts. They are displaced, turned out of their homes, disinherited, widowed and orphaned; they lose their children to bullets and beatings. Many just disappear without a trace. Others are trafficked across state and national borders and face a nightmarish lifetime of sexual abuse and disease.

The loss that they face is not just emotional or physical but transfers into the economic and social spheres as well. Most women face a decline in social legitimacy and find themselves relegated to the fringes of society with no one to care for them or to speak on their behalf.

Since they form the bulk of the unemployed and the uneducated, they find themselves unable and ill-equipped to take on the burden of the household and as a result become completely poverty stricken. Young widows are forced to head households, even though in a patriarchal feudal setup they have little or no access to land and property. In tribal societies the economic burden is generally considered a primary responsibility of women and, for this reason perhaps, women get very little help from men or from the State in the aftermath of violence when the work of reconstruction begins. In Nagaland, for example, the women do extensive fieldwork as in so many hill communities. In addition, they carry on with 'normal' life and do 'normal' chores to sustain their households—cooking, washing, fetching water, bringing up and nurturing children.

Other impacts of conflict include loss of livelihoods and food scarcity as a result of the destruction of fields and farmlands, the destruction of basic infrastructure such as roads and bridges, hospitals, shelters and schools. The women are forced to take on the role of food providers and caretakers of the old and the infirm, the wounded and the young. In times of war, women's access to public spaces becomes even more restricted and their mobility further hampered by the presence of security forces and armed militias. All too often their bodies become the site of battle with both sides treating them as the spoils of war. Women who lose their 'honour' find it extremely difficult to lead normal lives and to live down the stigma. There is a total breakdown of structures, of the norms of behaviour, of what is socially sanctioned behaviour, and the results are the atrocities and human rights abuses that are reported by the print, visual and audio media.

When there is a complete turning on its head of the known circumstances, the known life and exchanging it for the unknown, the uncertain, the insecure and the dangerous, how do people, especially women, who are the most vulnerable sections of society, cope? What happens when they are forced to flee, to leave the familiar environments of their villages and towns, and find themselves cut off from their tribes and cultural moorings? What dangers confront them in their new environments? These are difficult and challenging issues and troubling questions.

Continued violence, especially in the rural areas, has resulted in the large-scale migration of young women and men to urban centres. Without any effective support system, they become extremely vulnerable to exploitation, violence and trafficking. The incidence of HIV/AIDS, drug abuse, alcohol and substance abuse increases substantially in such situations. The feminisation of the AIDS epidemic is becoming all too apparent and the increased vulnerability of women to HIV/AIDS in situations of conflict is an area of growing concern to social and health activists. The presence of armed forces in large numbers also increases the demand for sex-workers and young women are sucked into this and become pawns in a larger brutal network that thrives on human misery and conflict: human and drug-trafficking proliferate with women and children being sent to other parts of the country. This is also as a result of the loss of other economic options and increased poverty as a result of long-standing conflict situations and their aftermath.

The state of women's health is another picture of neglect and apathy in areas of conflict. There is a lack of infrastructure, of adequate facilities, of health personnel and most of the Centre's much-hyped health schemes remain just on paper, with few being able to access these. Travels to the remote hinterland of both Nagaland and Assam showed us how the most marginalised segments of its population hardly figure in the 'Incredible India' promoted by large corporations and governments, marching, the public is informed, towards 'development' and 'health for all'.[2]

Another point important to flag here is what is happening to the young people, 'the children of the conflict', who are increasingly leaving their violent homelands for education and jobs elsewhere in the country. There are large numbers of students who flock to Delhi University every year. A Manipuri professor in Delhi says that there is a Manipuri student in every house in a colony behind the capital's Patel Chest Hospital. There has been a social impact of this out-migration: even vegetable-sellers there have picked up the Meitei language. While this is significant, we must also look at the other side of the social dimensions of this migration: what does the movement of a large amount of human resource capital mean for a small conflict-ridden state? Do these youth ever go back and, if so, to what?

Conducting interviews, travelling with research teams into remote villages and sitting in on conversations with victims of conflicts, we have come across many striking stories and experiences. The reason for telling these stories is to underline two points: first, to buttress their contribution to the sustenance of their communities is crucial; and, second, to appreciate the near-trauma when asked to speak on camera, or even be recorded and photographed, while victims were willing to recount their painful experiences orally to research teams.

◆◆◆

It was April in Nagaland, the rains were abundant and the villages were beautiful. We went to the village of Benreu, set high amongst the hills in Peren district. It was not easy to get there. It took us six hours from Kohima through beautiful high hills and valleys, slushy mud and a landslide on the narrow winding hill road. It was cold and we sat in front of a huge, open fireplace where a warming fire glowed and we talked to the villagers gathered there. They told us that the army came to the village after a brief mortar attack, which killed a young mother and her child. All the villagers fled to the jungles, the granaries were destroyed and so were the homes of the people. When they finally returned, the villagers faced beatings and harassment each time the forces came looking for insurgents and their contacts. There was one saving grace—the village was not burnt as so many had been in those days. This was because of a young army officer who did not permit it. That was in 1958 and the villagers still remember 'Captain Dorairaj'.

The things which struck us were how one person in power, sensitive to local fears and insecurities, local customs and traditions, can make a difference to the way a conflict is fought, the way an 'invading force' is perceived, the way local populations are dealt with. The other was that we were among the few independent groups of people from mainstream India to have visited Benrue in half a century.

The study on the impact of conflict on women in Assam and Nagaland needs to be seen in the larger context of the challenges of nation-building, regional growth, and the broader issues of just laws, the use of State power and the rights of citizens, especially women. The project was built around the assumption that women have been particularly and severely affected by on-going civil conflicts in these two states as indeed in much of the North-east region of India. Women are known to be vulnerable during times of armed conflict in ways that are different to men.

The definition and measurement of conflict can be also accessed by materials given in the Uppsala Conflict Data Programme (UCDP) and the International Peace Research Institute, Oslo (PRIO), which is widely regarded as a primary source for armed conflict data.[3]

Apart from the obvious impacts such as physical and sexual abuse, beatings and torture, there are other insidious ways in which their safety and well-being is threatened. As a result, the foundations of a community are under attack. There are greater restrictions placed on their mobility, and their access to health, education, means of livelihood and employment. Very little by way of documentation exists, especially of issues such as Post Traumatic Stress Disorder, the links between trafficking, drug and substance abuse, HIV/AIDS and conflict, or the escalation of domestic violence and sexual abuse in areas affected by armed conflict.

The core of the project is the field survey in the two states with specific and detailed questionnaires that were administered to households. The research team felt it was important to look at individual cases as well as collective fears and tensions that had accumulated in the collective psyche of communities faced with years of armed conflict and insecurity. The subtext of denial, defiance and trauma needed to be especially noted.

The project began with the interviews and selection of the teams in the respective states in September–October 2009 with extensive discussions with a range of scholars and health professionals as well as those in the policy framework in New Delhi, Assam and Nagaland. Primary and secondary research and extensive field travel was done in the two states from December 2009 right up to August 2010 in an effort to take a detailed look at the impact of violence and insecurity in Assam and Nagaland. The project has assessed the people's need for security from physical violence and threat, the need for health and treatment and also the protection of human rights. It has also looked at the challenges posed by some of the direct and indirect social impacts of conflict and specifically instances of domestic violence and substance abuse, HIV/AIDS, trafficking, migration as well as the attitudes/use/abuse of women by armed groups, a reality that has not been adequately reported or researched.

It must be emphasised, however, that the reports from the two states are quite different, although the basic issues of rights and dignity remain the same. The Report documents and recounts these differences because the background and other details of conflict, confrontation and social ethos are very different in either state. While the Naga conflict is among the oldest of contemporary ethnic conflicts in the world and was the first to challenge the idea of India and to insist on independence and a separate homeland, the problems in Assam began much later—in the late 1980s, in fact. Each situation grew, ebbed and flowed with very different trajectories and there is a complex range of issues associated with movements in both states. Thus, unlike other contemporary political movements such as the Maoists who seek a change of government structures, the insurgent groups in Nagaland have sought political independence, while groups like the United Liberation Front of Asom (ULFA) in Assam have been agitating on numerous other issues (foreigner, Bangladeshi, Bengali settlers, migrant labour), and the Bodos and Dimasas, among others, have been demanding greater autonomy and representation in the existing political structure. To further illustrate the points of difference, here is an example.

In the district of Dhemaji, Assam, the team found evidence which reflects specific challenges to the rights of the displaced and migrant communities. This is an aspect of the crucial migration issue in Assam which has not been as well researched in earlier projects but which the present one focuses on especially through detailed, extensive interviews (recorded and transcribed). The Assam report looks at the impact of a large agitation on smaller ethnic groups and the victimisation, deliberate or otherwise, of these groups. It is important, for it is concerned with a period in Assam's contemporary history that is regarded as crucial to political formation to the entire North-eastern region and the responses of the Indian State, post the 1980s. In Dhemaji, the combatants were not security forces and organised fighters from one militant group or another, but ethnic groups which saw threats from 'the other' to their identity and control of land. The specific incidents revolve around the tragedies of 1983, a time when Assam was in turmoil caused by opposition to State and Parliamentary elections; agitators said that illegal migrants from Bangladesh were being allowed to settle and vote, threatening the identity and rights of local residents and the indigenous. The victims, predominantly Bengali-speaking Hindus and members of the Hajong (also Hazong) tribe, were reluctant to speak, as in Nagaland, saying they did not want a re-visitation of the nightmare of the past. In Dhemaji, the research looked specifically at this aspect as well as the better-known and documented attacks and incidents involving ULFA and the army.

There have been studies of conflicts earlier and, even in the context of the two states, that is the focus here. What is perhaps significant here is that there has been very little work on how women have been impacted by conflict. This was a gap that needed documentation—to see how women were coping with situations in which they found themselves and, through this, to understand the resilience and coping mechanisms built up in communities to 'handle' situations of great stress.

Almost all the rural women we spoke to under the aegis of this study in Nagaland and Assam were illiterate. Moreover, it was apparent that they had no professional, or any other kind, of assistance and they had to cope with their situation and that of their families on their own. Indeed, in many respects, this study is the first of its kind.

The stories of these women interviewed, like women elsewhere, need to be told since their contribution to the sustenance of their communities is crucial. A common difficulty was that while victims were willing to recount their painful experiences to the research teams, a number were reluctant to speak on camera or even be recorded and photographed for the documentary film (*A Measure of Impunity*) made alongside the research and report. Some of those who spoke to the research teams insisted for various reasons, including security, that they not be identified by name. In a few cases, they were not willing to have their villages named: this shows the extent of fear and trauma that continues.

BEARING WITNESS, DOCUMENTING MARGINALISED HISTORIES
To bear witness has been a challenging and disturbing experience; listening to and reading the testimonies of the victims has been

particularly painful and saddening—especially as we are deeply aware that virtually none of the victims have had access either to compensation or justice by getting the legal system or even the administrative system to take care of the harm they have suffered. To some, the nightmare persists because they remained unhealed, unreached and uncounselled; for others the nightmare is renewed when they see the killers of their relatives walking around free and unfettered. We have been privileged to have been included in some of the most personal and difficult situations those women and other individuals have faced. Of course, suffering is not confined to women alone. Indeed, while they have suffered acutely, other members of society also have been harmed, across the gender divide.

Reports of these kinds are often repetitive, in terms of experiences shared and stories told, of the nature of the relationships between victim and oppressor, as much as between the State and non-State actors (the armed groups), and the ordinary people who are preyed upon and find themselves caught in an unwitting and relentless cycle of hatred, violence, grief and unmitigated injustice. But it is the nature of such inflicted harm, no matter where we are in the world, to be repetitive for, as stated earlier, women's bodies have become the battleground for ideas and contesting fighters, in and out of uniform. It is the latter, as much as any other issue, that we seek to address and call the attention of readers of this report. These unaddressed injustices as well as physical and mental harm and trauma need to be faced by State, non-State and civil society groups, as well as the international forums and discourses on human rights. The lack of justice has bred a sense of impunity among both State and non-State as well as the rent-seekers and quasi-State, which are patronised by the State, such as those responsible for the 'secret killings' in Assam.

It would also be important here to reflect on the quality of resilience shown by the victims and their families. Astier Almedom, a scholar from Tufts University speaks of this quality thus:

> How people cope depends on their own resources, sense of coherence, ability to find meaning in their situation—not what humanitarian agencies do for them. If you lose your home during a disaster, you have to go somewhere else. You risk losing your identity.

In the course of her own work in Eritrea she found that, despite the disruption, certain mechanisms of social support alleviated some of the people's emotional pain and difficulties. The help that she was referring to in that particular context included warning of imminent raids from the neighbouring country; vehicles for people to travel safely; the government trying to keep communities together; providing material support and aid.

Similar survival and coping mechanisms are apparent in the case of Nagaland and Assam in the context of the present study as well. We would like to flag these here as something that is crucial to the way people manage their lives after traumatic events, especially conflict and war.

The women attribute their ability to cope to several factors, including faith in their gods. Religion often plays a huge role in providing help and support to communities and the simple act of being able to talk to the priest helps women to share their pain and to find peace. In the absence of help from the State and the lack of medical and counselling services, prayer was frequently their only strength. Often due to displacements, community help and help from the Church was difficult to access.

Since most of the women interviewed were illiterate they did not know the mechanisms of the State and whom to approach for help, whom to lodge complaints with, and they had no idea of the State's role of protector of their interests. They were unable to understand the random violence, torture and killings, and even after so many years had passed, speaking to the research teams recreated the sense of pain, fear and trauma they had suffered.

The women also felt that what helped them to cope was the knowledge that they were not alone, that their suffering and trauma was part of a larger community/tribe trauma. This, too, came out very strongly in the statements that the women made to the interviewers.

It is our view that efforts at this should energise the setting up of counselling centres for trauma victims, women, men and children, in places of internal conflict so that the nightmares are not repeatedly visited on them or others who suffer.

The violence institutionalised in law by the Armed Forces Special Powers Act (AFSPA) as well as the Disturbed Areas Act and other security legislation that continues to harm and humiliate ordinary men, women and children, 55 years after they were passed by Parliament, must be repealed. These laws, which enshrine Immunity and Impunity in the armed forces, have a direct connection to the decades of suffering and prejudice those communities and individuals have faced. The law often has been abused, not used, and protects those in the employ of the government and not the victims. The Disturbed Areas Act is the enabling legislation which gives the army legitimacy to implement the AFSPA, a bare six-clause law which empowers soldiers to detain, conduct searches, destroy property, and shoot and kill. This could be part of the process of healing and peace—an experience that we believe has come to many of those who shared their stories for the first time with us, some, at the close of their lives.

Many researchers are asked by victims: 'We have been interviewed by researchers so many times but nothing has come of it, so what is the point of giving so much time and reliving our trauma?' This stresses the need to share the findings of these reports in an open forum, and with the stakeholders, so that those who have suffered may speak clearly to those in authority and non-State groups, as well as the general public to seek not just justice, but compensation for harm inflicted for no fault of their own. In addition, what is required is the empowerment of individuals and tackling issues like insurgency through an inclusive approach rather than a bulldozer effect, where it assumes that it knows the answers because of the political leadership which has been 'elected', and the administrative and security strength which are 'existent' in the system.

Many stories remain untold, many tragedies undocumented, many voices unheard.

As long as that remains undone, our work will remain incomplete. The democratic deficit is too extensive not to map and too dangerous not to address and remedy.

It is difficult to finalise the conclusions without an overlap of the states, for some of the recommendations and findings are of a general nature and apply to not just the two states but to conflict-hit areas of the North-eastern Region (NER), of other parts of India and South Asia, as well as different regions of the world.

It has been humbling to be listeners and tellers of those stories, to see their courage and resilience and to understand the depth of their tragedy, inflicted at times by those whom they trusted or those who are assigned to protect them from harm.

Such research affects those who listen and narrate the stories. For example, Dr Buno Liegese, of Nagaland University, felt that the most significant part of the study was the change in the people conducting this study of human tragedy, even if the study touched only the 'tip of the iceberg'. The process of study was often tedious, stressful, and emotionally and physically draining. Women in their late sixties and seventies weeping uncontrollably could not but affect the interviewer/researcher. Dr Liegese later said that she often wondered how victims of horrific experiences could remain sane. Sometimes, she said, she just sat at her computer table and wept.

Charles Chasie, the well-known independent researcher and writer, says how de-sensitisation, even unconsciously, can happen to a person living in a prolonged conflict situation, bombarded by daily incidents of killings. He said he often was angered by the continuing presence of undemocratic legislation which allowed the conduct of atrocities with impunity and built the foundations for inequality. The state of such lawlessness also encouraged criminal elements to further vitiate law and order in society.

One gripping aspect of the years of conflict is that many did not know they had access to justice or to rights. In the study we speak of here, a majority of women interviewed in Nagaland never complained or thought of claiming compensation or relief. When asked why, they said they had no hope that any action would be taken. Some said this was because of poverty and total ignorance about such mechanisms. A few had actually refused help. One woman said that when the army came to enquire about her husband's death (allegedly killed on suspicion by one faction) and offered to help with the children's education, she turned down the offer.

Almost all the women respondents were unaware of the extra-judicial legislation such as the AFSPA and Nagaland Security Regulations Act or the Disturbed Areas Act.

Building on this experience and many years of field work and conversations across the region, I drafted a note that sought to tackle issues of PTSS and develop it into a policy that could be used by victims of internal conflict to access rights and regain dignity. This was for the Planning Commission's National Steering Committee on

Health in 2012; I wrote that while medical courses on PTSS should be encouraged, extensively funded and specially designed and developed, the Government of India, in association with the states, should frame policies to fund, develop and expand a network of Counselling Centres, manned by trained psychiatrists and counsellors round the clock, to help victims of conflict and other stress.

1. These would be located in all conflict-affected states.
2. These would work at two levels: at the district level, where they could be located in a new wing of the existing District Civil Hospital, and would be connected to a State Centre. The State Centre would, in turn, be linked to the National Institute of Mental Health and Neuro-Sciences (NIMHANS) in Bangalore with e-medicine facilities.
3. Regular training and refresher courses for faculty.
4. In addition, the State Commissions for Women, along with the National Commission for Women, must be pro-active in addressing issues of legal access and redressal. This appears to be a huge gap as people were just not aware of their rights. Special video capsules highlighting these entitlements need to be extensively broadcast and distributed. A large proportion of women in the cited study did not complain to authorities about their grievances. It may be repeated that during the 1950s and early 1960s, there was no proper authority or administration in the area which comprises the state of Nagaland. There were village leaders and other figures of authority, but 'everyone was going through a difficult time'.
5. The Security Forces also need counselling as they work in very stressful conditions; they regard themselves as 'misunderstood' and unfairly 'targeted' by civil society groups and the media, but need sensitising to local conditions and concerns. Specialists should do this in their system, but with the help of local counsellors familiar with field conditions.

It is significant that this was part of the Approach Paper to the 12th Five-Year Plan of the Planning Commission, enabling concepts to be built into policy and processes, and providing not just an opportunity for democratic principles to be strengthened, but for basic care to reach the most vulnerable, those who have suffered in the past from the violence of State and non-State actors. This is a step forward for transparency and conciliation; it is only through funding for counselling in internal conflict areas that some of the wounds can be healed. For no nation can allow such nightmares to continue.

◆

This chapter was first published in 2013 in the *IIC Quarterly*, Vol. 39, Nos. 3 and 4.

NOTES

1. Dr Sandi Syiem, who runs the San-Ker Centre in Shillong, Meghalaya, and Dr Ngully.
2. See Preeti Gill (2006).
3. North Eastern Vision 2020, Ministry for the Development of the North Eastern Region, 2008.
   http:www.pcr.uu.se/research/udcp/database

REFERENCE

Gill, Preeti. 2006. 'Women in the Time of Conflict: The Case of Nagaland', in Geeti Sen (ed.), *Where the Sun Rises, When Shadows Fall: the North-east*. New Delhi: India International Centre/OUP.

◆◆

ABOUT THE EDITOR AND CONTRIBUTORS

EDITOR

OMITA GOYAL is presently Chief Editor of the *IIC Quarterly*, the Journal of the India International Centre. She started her career in the voluntary sector with the Indian Social Institute, New Delhi. Shortly thereafter she moved into academic publishing where she has spent over 27 years. She worked at SAGE Publications India Pvt Limited for 20 years, leaving as General Manager. Omita took time off to work as a freelance editor for SAGE and other institutions such as The World Bank, UNICEF, UNDP, Voluntary Health Association of India, Centre for Women's Development Studies, WHO, Institute of Social Studies, The Hague and TERI. In 2005, she was invited by Taylor and Francis to start a social science programme under their social science and humanities imprint, Routledge, as Publishing Director.

CONTRIBUTORS

DEEPTHA ACHAR is Associate Professor at the Department of English, M.S. University of Baroda. She has co-edited *Towards a New Art History: Studies in Indian Art; Discourse, Democracy and Difference: Perspectives on Community, Politics and Culture*; and *Articulating Resistance: Art and Activism*. Her research interests include childhood studies and visual culture.

SATISH B. AGNIHOTRI, of the Indian Administrative Service, is currently DG (Defence Acquisition) in the Ministry of Defence. His doctoral research and further work on the problem of declining sex ratios in India has been acknowledged. He has worked as Secretary in the Women and Child Development in Odisha and with UNICEF, Kolkata, as Consultant on Child Nutrition and Health. His book, *Sex Ratio Patterns in the Indian Population,* has been published by SAGE.

APARNA BASU, a Ph.D. from Cambridge, was Professor of History, University of Delhi. She has written extensively on the history of education in India. She was President and is currently Patron, All India Women's Conference.

DEEPSHIKA BATHEJA is an economist and researcher with a special interest in Women's Studies.

RADHA CHAKRAVARTY has co-edited *The Essential Tagore*, nominated Book of the Year 2011 by Martha Nussbaum. She is the author of *Novelist Tagore: Gender and Modernity in Selected Texts*; and *Feminism and Contemporary Women Writers*. Her translations of Tagore include *Chokher Bali; Gora; Boyhood Day; Farewell Song: Shesher Kabita*, among others. She has edited *Bodymaps: Stories by South Asian Women;* and co-edited *Writing Feminism: South Asian Voices* and *Writing Freedom: South Asian Voices*. She teaches English Literature in Gargi College, University of Delhi.

UMA CHAKRAVARTI is a feminist historian who taught formally at Miranda House, Delhi University till 1998. She is now an independent scholar who lives and works from Delhi. She has been associated with the women's movement and the movement for democratic rights since the late 1970s and writes on gender, caste and labour.

KARUNA CHANANA is a former Professor and Chair, Zakir Husain Centre for Educational Studies, Jawaharlal Nehru University, New Delhi. She is the Editor of *Socialisation, Education and Women: Explorations in Gender Identity*; author of *Interrogating Women's Education: Bounded Visions, Expanding Horizons*; and joint author of *Inclusion and Exclusion: A Study of Women and Men in Delhi Police*.

J. DEVIKA teaches and researches at the Centre for Development Studies, Thiruvananthapuram, Kerala. She has a doctoral degree in history but does interdisciplinary research focused on Kerala on the intertwined themes of gender, development, politics and culture. She also translates extensively between Malayalam and English and offers commentary on contemporary Kerala on www.kafila.org.

GOPAL GURU teaches at the Centre for Political Studies, Jawaharlal Nehru University, New Delhi. His interest lies in making elevated sense of the Dalit question. He has published on social justice and social movements for social justice. He has edited *Humiliation: Calims and Context* and co-authored *Cracked Mirror: An India Debate on Theory and Experience.*

DEVAKI JAIN is a feminist economist and a pioneer in the field of women's studies in India. She was awarded the Padma Bhushan by the President of India in the Honours list of 2006, and is the author of many books, essays and articles broadly on the theme of women and economic development.

KUMUD DIWAN JHA is an established exponent of Banaras Gharana Gayaki. She is currently under the mentorship of Padmabhushan Pt. Chhannulal Mishra of Banaras. She has been an avid researcher and has written extensively on the *Thumri* genre. She has performed both nationally and internationally, and has been awarded the Women's International Award for excellence in music in 2011 and the Indira Gandhi Priyadarshini Award in 2010. Diwan also has a doctorate in Business Studies.

SANJOY HAZARIKA is Director, Centre for North-east Studies and Policy Research, Jamia Millia Islamia, New Delhi, and founded C-nes in 2000 in Assam. Hazarika is a prolific writer, renowned author, columnist and documentary film-maker. He has been a member of various official committees of the Planning Commission, Chairman of the Task Force NER Vision 2020; and on boards such as the Commonwealth Human Rights Initiative, and the Committee to Review the Armed Forces Special Powers Act, among others.

RENANA JHABVALA is best known for her long association with the Self-Employed Women's Association (SEWA), India, and for her writings on issues of women in the informal economy. She has been active in many government committees and task forces which have formulated policies, and is at present Member, Prime Minister's National Skill Development Council as well as Member, Steering Committee on Urbanisation, Indian Planning Commission. Jhabvala was awarded the Padma Shri in 1990.

MALAVIKA KARLEKAR is Co-editor, *Indian Journal of Gender Studies*. She is the Curator of *Re-presenting Indian Women, 1875–1947: A Visual Documentary* based on over 300 archival photographs for the Centre for Women's Development Studies. Her interests lie in memoirs and in archival photographs, and recent publications include *Re-visioning the Past—Early Photography in Bengal, 1875–1915* and *Visual Histories—The Photograph in the Popular Imagination*.

ASHISH MOHAN KHOKAR is an internationally reputed dance critic and historian, with over 40 published books and thousands of articles to his credit. A simple net search shows his outreach and work. He wrote for 20 years for *The Times of India* in Delhi, then Bangalore, as its dance critic; contributed culture columns to *India Today*, *FirtsCity* and *Life Positive*. He edits and publishes India's only yearbook on dance—*attendance*—in its 16th year now. An authority on Indian dance history and heritage, he has made films, educational programmes and discourses on dance that are internationally popular. He served the Indian government in several cultural posts and projects and is on many councils and committees. He is also the inheritor-curator of India's largest dance archives (www.dancearchivesofindia.com). He is India's only dance biography publisher (Ekah). He mentors many young talents and helps mount special academic dance DISCourses. He chairs the Dance History Society, which has instituted annual awards in memory of dance greats.

SARAH RAHMAN NIAZI is a Ph.D. scholar at the School of Arts and Aesthetics, Jawaharlal Nehru University, New Delhi. Her research project focuses on the revival and recuperation from the debris of archives the absence of the cultural history of women performers in modern India and attempts to understand the role of cinema as an agent of transformation and reinvention. Currently, she is working as a Research Fellow at the Indira Gandhi National Centre for the Arts, New Delhi.

SUDHA PAI is Professor at the Centre for Political Studies and Rector of Jawaharlal Nehru University, New Delhi. She was Senior Fellow, Nehru Memorial Museum and Library, Teen Murti, New Delhi, from 2006 to 2009. Her areas of interest, on which she has published extensively, include State politics in India, Dalit politics, globalisation and governance.

RITU SETHI is Chairperson of the Craft Revival Trust and Editor of the principal online encyclopaedia on the intangible cultural heritage of the arts, crafts, textiles and its practitioners in South Asia. She has chaired the UNESCO Consultative Body examining nominations to the Intangible Cultural Heritage of the World list; was on the Steering Committee for the 12th Five-Year-Plan, Planning Commission; and is Board Member, Indira Gandhi Rashtriya Manav Sangrahalaya Samiti, Bhopal.

KIRTI SINGH is a lawyer and activist working on women's issues, and is based in Delhi. She is Legal Convener of AIDWA, and was a part-time member of the 18th Law Commission of India.

PUSHPA SUNDAR is the author of five books, including *Foreign Aid for Indian NGOs: Problem or Solution?* and the most recent, *Business and Community: The Story of Corporate Social Responsibility in India*. She has over 30 years of experience in the developmental field, and is, and has been, closely associated with several non-profit organisations.

PADMINI SWAMINATHAN is Professor in the Tata Institute of Social Sciences (TISS), Hyderabad. Swaminathan also teaches courses in M. Phil. in Women's Studies, and in M.A. in Rural Development and Governance. She was formerly Director of the Madras Institute of Development Studies and Chair in Regional Economics of the Reserve Bank of India. Swaminathan has researched and published extensively in the fields of industrial organisation, labour studies, occupational health—all from a gender perspective.

◆